ROUTLEDGE LIBRARY EDITIONS: AGING

Volume 6

AGEING

AGEING

Recent Advances and Creative Responses

Edited by
ALAN BUTLER

Routledge
Taylor & Francis Group

LONDON AND NEW YORK

First published in 1985 by Croom Helm Ltd

This edition first published in 2024
by Routledge
4 Park Square, Milton Park, Abingdon, Oxon OX14 4RN

and by Routledge
605 Third Avenue, New York, NY 10158

Routledge is an imprint of the Taylor & Francis Group, an informa business

British Library Cataloguing in Publication Data
A catalogue record for this book is available from the British Library

ISBN: 978-1-032-67433-9 (Set)
ISBN: 978-1-032-71007-5 (Volume 6) (hbk)
ISBN: 978-1-032-71011-2 (Volume 6) (pbk)
ISBN: 978-1-032-71010-5 (Volume 6) (ebk)

DOI: 10.4324/9781032710105

Publisher's Note
The publisher has gone to great lengths to ensure the quality of this reprint but points out that some imperfections in the original copies may be apparent.

Disclaimer
The publisher has made every effort to trace copyright holders and would welcome correspondence from those they have been unable to trace.

AGEING

RECENT ADVANCES & CREATIVE RESPONSES

edited by
ALAN BUTLER

PUBLISHED IN ASSOCIATION WITH
THE BRITISH SOCIETY OF
GERONTOLOGY

CROOM HELM
London • Sydney • Dover, New Hampshire
In association with the British Society of Gerontology

1985 British Society of Gerontology
Croom Helm Ltd, Provident House, Burrell Row,
Beckenham, Kent BR3 1AT
Croom Helm Australia Pty Ltd, Suite 4, 6th Floor,
64-76 Kippax Street, Surry Hills, NSW 2010, Australia

British Library Cataloguing in Publication Data

Ageing: recent advances and creative responses.
    1. Aged
    I. Butler, Alan   II. British Society of
    Gerontology
    305.2'6   HQ1061
    ISBN 0-7099-3927-2

Croom Helm, 51 Washington Street, Dover,
New Hampshire 03820, USA

Library of Congress Cataloging in Publication data applied for.
L.C. 85-17481

Printed and bound in Great Britain by Mackays of Chatham Ltd, Kent

CONTENTS

Preface

PART THREE : ASPECTS OF SOCIAL WELFARE

PART FOUR : DEVELOPMENTS IN PSYCHOLOGY

PREFACE

This volume contains a selection of the contributions to the Annual Conference of the British Society of Gerontology held at the University of Leeds from 21st to the 24th of September 1984. As such it is a successor to two earlier books published Croom Helm Ageing in Modern Society edited by Dorothy Jerrome who collated the 1982 conference papers, and Gerontology: Social and Behavioural Perspectives edited by Professor D. Bromley who undertook the same task for the 1983 conference.

As in previous years the job of the editor has been made difficult by having to make some hard choices about which papers to include and which to exclude. Many excellent contributions submitted for publication have had to be omitted because of the pressure for space. I have confined my editorial work to the clarification of the odd obscurity of meaning and attempting to impose some consistency on format and layout.

I should like to take this opportunity of thanking all those people - contributors, administrators, secretarial and technical staff - whose efforts made the Leeds conference the great success that it was. In particular I owe a great debt to Susan Walker, from the Department of Psychiatry at the University of Leeds, for her word processing and organisational skills in preparing this book for publication.

Alan Butler,
University of Leeds.

Chapter One

INTRODUCTION

Alan Butler

The chapters in this book are based upon a
selection of the contributions made to the
1984 British Society of Gerontology conference held
at the University of Leeds. The theme of the
conference was Ageing: a creative response.
The British Society of Gerontology is an
organisation which is dedicated to the study of the
social and behavioural aspects of human ageing and
later life. One of its principal aims has been the
promotion of a dialogue between on the one hand
academics and researchers, and on the other policy
makers and practitioners. Another aim has been to
disseminate multi-discipliniary studies of later
life from around the world to a wide audience. The
1984 conference was an accurate reflection of these
aspirations featuring contributions from as far
afield as Canada, Israel, Western Europe and Japan.
In terms of interdisciplinary work papers were
presented by professional groups as disparate as
psychologists, social administrators, geographers,
architects, medical staff, adult educators and
service providers.
It is now becoming possible to distinguish a
distinctive social science contribution to the study
and understanding of old age. A number of forces,
historic, political and social, have made this more
salient. First, we have the frequently noted
increase in the numbers of older people, and a
consequent shift in the balance of dependency away
from young children to the very old. Secondly,
throughout the 20th century, we have witnessed the
increasing formalisation of retirement, with the
result that this now represents a significant life
stage and a reification of the divide between young
and old. Compulsory retirement has proved a
doubled-edged sword. On one side it has liberated

1

many people from the rigours of labour, and made time available in which to develop new skills and enjoy leisure activities. On the other side it has reduced many people in later life to poverty and dependency, and for some induced feelings of marginality and futility. Retirement policies are used by governments in order to regulate the labour market. Older people are encouraged to leave the work force in times of unemployment, or invited to return when the need for more manpower occurs.

Finally, it is possible to see among older people a change in their attitudes. The growth of self-help groups and political lobbying, notably in the U.S.A., has meant that attempts are being made to reclaim areas of life both for and by the elderly. The battle is being raised around issues such as choice in later life, autonomy, legal and welfare rights and more generally the right to be heard. None of us who were in Hamburg for the 1982 XII International Congress of Gerontology could fail to remember the impressive march, in favour of rights for older people, mounted by the German branch of the Grey Panthers.

Many of the chapters in this book resonate with these themes.

Raymond Illsley has recently noted the way many of our policies and services for the elderly are based upon the narrow sterotype of old age; "lonely; socially isolated and frequently perceived as a burden by her immediate social network" (Illsley, 1983). He suggests that one of the future tasks for social scientists is to concentrate upon studying "normal ageing" so that this monolithic view of the elderly may be "disaggregated". A number of the papers in the book begin to take on this task, and challenge the commonly held stereotypes. For example friendship patterns and associative links are examined. Other papers are concerned with how retired people use their time, and how useful and creative leisure activities may best be promoted and located.

The contributions may be taken as a reflection of the current interests being pursued by social gerontologists. As such it is possible to identify a number of themes which seem to be of present concern. For psychologists there is an interest in the refinement of assessment techniques, and the benefits that earlier detection, and possibly intervention may hold. With the squeeze

upon health and welfare finance, which is being felt
in many parts of the world, come attempts to fund
projects for the elderly in innovative ways. Two of
the papers, those by Osborn and Ferlie et al., take
a critical look at some of these alternative sources
of funding, and raise important issues for current
and future service provision.

Attempts have been made in the last decade to
shift the focus of social gerontology away from what
some believe to be a potentially distorting concern
with the pathology and miseries of later life. It
has been pointed out that only a minority of older
people require help and assistance in their later
years, yet because they are identified and known to
the helping services, they cast a long shadow over
our view of ageing. Increasingly we are being
encouraged to study "normal" ageing, to look at
coping mechanisims, friendship patterns, and leisure
interests. This paradigmatic shift is reflected in
a number of the chapters which examine friendship
patterns in later life, the division of domestic
tasks, leisure activity, both formal and informal,
and patterns of association.

Some commentators have suggested that the
attention paid to older people's special needs has
deflected attention from some of the basic human
requirements which they share with other sections of
the community: for example, the right to an adquate
income, and the availability of suitable housing.
It must be remembered that the elderly constitutute
20 per cent of those in poverty and live in some of
our poorest housing stock.

Victor usefully explores the issues of income
and the apparent failure, on the part of many
retired people, to take up their full welfare
benefit entitlement. Poor housing appears to be a
major contributor to many of the handicaps and
disabilities evidenced by older people. An
unsympathetic housing environment, lacking basic
amenities or difficult to heat or maintain, may
create or bring forward the need for hospital or
other institutional care. Chapters by Fennell,
Phillipson and Strang, and Eley and Middleton, each,
in their different ways, examine some of these
issues.

Finally both Tinker and Midwinter reflect upon
some of the broader social and political issues as
they affect older citizens. They question the roles
older people are forced to play in our society, and

suggest various ways in which older people could be more involved, and seize greater autonomy. Midwinter queries the stance adopted by welfare professionals towards older people, and throws down a challenge to all who seek to create, provide, or administer services for older citizens. He begins by identifying the need for information, arguing that informed choice lies at the heart of democracy. Secondly, he urges greater consultation between providers of health and welfare services and the consumers. Next, he calls for greater negotiation between old and young so that purported ills may be examined and righted. Finally, he calls for representation, and implicitly suggests that we should cease to "provide for older people" and begin to provide services with them and foster "popular control".

The book will be of value to all academics, policy makers and practitioners with an interest in human ageing and later life; the health and social difficulties encountered by this age group; and the positive responses that can be made by both the providers of services and the elderly themselves.

References

Illsley, R. (1983) The contribution of research to the development of practice and policy in: Elderly people in the community: their service needs, D.H.S.S., H.M.S.O.

PART ONE: THE OVERVIEW

Chapter Two

AGEING - WHOSE CREATIVE RESPONSE?

Anthea Tinker

Introduction

By choosing the theme of 'Ageing - a creative response' the organisers of this conference are to be congratulated on concentrating on a previously neglected aspect of ageing. The involvement of elderly people themselves is also often a missing dimension on many occasions.

But the theme is not as straightforward as would appear and can be used to demonstrate some of the current dilemmas for society in general and for policy makers in particular. What I would like to do is first to ask what we mean by a creative response, second to suggest reasons for the increased attention to the creative response of ageing and third to ask whose creative response is involved. Is it elderly people? Is it professionals or is it society?

First we must get to grips with what we mean by a creative response. Is it an emphasis on the positive, good, happy, cheerful aspects of growing older and a recognition that there are other dimensions apart from problems? This of course is the theme of the past week in Leeds and is similar to a recent issue of New Age where the heading about an item was "Six days of sailing, canoeing, archery and pony treking for people who dreamt about doing it but never dared". (New Age, Winter 1984). Among the photographs there is "seventy year old Flo, safe in her harness, braves the aerial runway, some 45 ft high above a 150 ft stretch of open water". (New Age, Winter 1984). Is it a view that for many elderly people becoming old is not necessarily depressing or traumatic? The view for example in brochures for private sheltered housing. "Spread your wings at 60 in a community of people like you."

7

Is it a sense that when problems do arise something positive can be done about them? Such as the recent advertisement about hypertension in a medical journal of an elderly person in a technicolour field of poppies headed "a bright outlook". Or does it mean that the creativity of elderly people should be brought to the fore perhaps in ways they have not formerly experienced? (witness the endless television programmes on this subject).

Different people will interpret the phrase in different equally valid ways and I suggest that these demonstrate a change in the way ageing is looked at. I would like to suggest some of the reasons why growing attention is being given to the creative aspects of ageing and then to pose questions about whose creative response is involved and examine some of the implications.

Reasons for the increased attention to a creative response

One would like to think that one of the reasons is the result of informed writing, particularly by doctors, during the last few years. (Hodkinson, 1975, Keddie, 1978). For geriatricians and psychiatrists have been foremost in stressing the positive aspects of ageing. For example Keddie argues that "Positive thinking is needed here. Unfortunately many of the public still feel that little can be done for an elderly man or woman who is ill - it is assumed that the old person's condition is simply due to his age. In fact, most old people, who are unwell, are suffering from a treatable disease of one sort or other". (Keddie 1978, p.64). Alex Comfort's views too (that people cease to be people, cease to be the same people or become people of a distinct and inferior kind, by virtue of having lived a specified number of years) and his argument that the concept of ageism is part of the prejudice against elderly people must surely have played some role (Comfort 1965, Comfort 1977). Social scientists have also been quick to take up the banner on behalf of groups they feel have been the subject of discriminatory practices in the past such as women, ethnic minorities and now eldery people.

Perhaps too the constantly reiterated view by many that elderly people are as different as other age groups has finally got through so that they are

not all seen as "old dears" or worse "poor old
dears".

Nor can the influence of pressure groups be
ignored. Foremost among these in this context must
be Age Concern with its growing involvement in
sponsoring, encouraging and writing about the
positive aspects of ageing and especially of the
many activities elderly people are involved with.

Another strand I would suggest is a purely
pragmatic one. If the very old are now seen as the
major problem group in the future who better to
suggest as helpers than the young elderly. The two
fit together almost too neatly. How likely this
marriage is I will discuss later. There is also the
cynical view that by directing attention away from
problems increased expenditure can be avoided.

Finally, among the many other possible reasons,
I would suggest is the simple swing of the pendulum
of fashion in social policy. For a good many years
elderly people have been studied as a problem group.
Their housing conditions, the effect of their
disabilities, the special problems particular to
some of them and special services such as meals on
wheels have been the subject, quite rightly, of
endless studies. I would argue that this is
necessary and that there is constant need to update
such knowledge. But others do not. For example it
has been said that we probably know enough about the
housing conditions and problems of older people
(Goldberg, 1983). I would not accept this although
I sympathise with the sense of déjà vu. What has
all too often been ignored have been those who live
out their lives with little state intervention and
why and how they cope. Also very largely ignored,
apart from a few studies, has been any charting of
the contribution of elderly people to society.

So the scene has been set for some time for
more attention to the creative and positive aspects
of ageing.

Some questions about whose creative response is involved

So we come to the issue of whose creative
response is involved. Is it from elderly people
themselves? From professionals? Or from society?

Ageing - Whose Creative Response?

Elderly people

What are some of the factors which will have an
influence on elderly people and what sort of
creative response is to be expected? Always
remembering that generalisations are dangerous about
any age group.

On the one had there are the negative factors.
There is a growing body of evidence that points to
the diminution of physical and mental abilities in
very old age. This has to be recognised for it is,
as is well known, this group which will increase in
numbers so dramatically in the next few years. The
distinction between the under and over 75s is one
which is increasingly being made. National studies
such as the 1980 General Household Survey (OPCS,
1982) and that by Hunt (OPCS, 1978) show clearly
that the over 75s have a higher rate of illness,
spend more time in hospital, fall more and are more
likely to be mentally confused. All these findings
are similar to those of our recent Department of the
Environment (DOE) survey for DOE and Department of
Health and Social Security (DHSS) of 1,310 elderly
people living in the community and receiving
innovatory schemes (Tinker, 1984 a). For example 26
per cent of the over 75s were housebound permanently
compared with 9 per cent of the under 75s, 48 per
cent were in the top dependency group compared with
27 per cent of the under 75s and nearly twice as
many were unable to perform certain domestic tasks
such as catering or personal tasks such as bathing
or going out unaided.

There is also the effect of early retirement
often accompanied by loss of income, status and
esteem which could lead to a feeling of uselessness
in the face of ageing.

But these negative factors have to be balanced
by the positive ones. For example there may be a
re-thinking about the whole concept of retirement.
If a large proportion of people are going to spend
long periods not in paid employment either because
they are unemployed or have retired, then what they
do in an unpaid capacity may be recognised in some
more positive way. Parker in Work and Retirement
(Parker, 1982) claims that an incentive to live
actively and positively is what some of the present
generation of elderly people see retirement for. He
thinks that we should talk about retirement to and
not retirement from. For a minority (politicians,

10

artists, writers) there is often a continuity of paid employment and notable contributions to society. Another positive factor is on the income side where there are encouraging initiatives to increase income, for example by cashing in the value of an owned home by reverse mortgages.

Nor must one discount the effects of pre-retirement education. Although few people go to courses labelled as such many more watch programmes on television which stress the value of positive action - whether it is exercise to keep fit, mental activities or ways of making a voluntary contribution to society. Whether the status and satisfaction of such activities will ever equal those of paid employment is, I suggest, a moot point. Less quantifiable but not to be disregarded is the pure enjoyment some people get from creative activities such as gardening and the likelihood that more free time will bring an increase in these activities.

Another factor is the growing militancy of certain groups of elderly people themselves. At one extreme are banner waving elderly people on demonstrations while on the other are the growing number of television programmes, books and articles by elderly people. And surely the next generation of elderly people, many of us here, who have been brought up to question and to argue are going to be very positive in our response to ageing.

But what will this positive response be? For some it will undoubtedly be a disinclination to let younger people ride rough shod over them. This will especially be the case for people brought up to know their rights either through Claimants Groups at one end or years of reading Which at the other. The insistence on rights and services by a growing number of articulate people may be hard to resist (although the ultimate pressure of a strike or withdrawing labour is never a possibility). For others the positive response will be to say "hands off - this is my life and I shall run it the way I want it." For others it may be what the majority probably believe a positive response means - i.e. being involved, helping, refusing to be passive.

And it is this last reponse which I would like to reflect on for a few moments.

It is difficult to tell whether there is more or less participation by elderly people now in various activities because comparative information

is difficult to get. What is certain is that it is
increasingly being measured. For example the 1981
General Household Survey included evidence about
voluntary work. (OPCS, 1983). Nearly a quarter of
all respondents (23 per cent) had participated in
voluntary work the year before. For those aged 65-
74 it was 21 per cent and for the 75s 11 per cent.
As I have pointed out elsewhere it is interesting
that the recently retired participated less than any
group except those under 24 and the over 75s.
(Tinker, 1984b). Although one explanation is that
help to families and friends is not included, and
this is an area where it is known that elderly
people do give a great deal of help (especially to
grand-children), we do have to be wary of expecting
too much from this age group. To return to my
earlier point how realistic is the idea that the
young elderly will help the old elderly? Does there
have to be positive encouragement?

If we are to encourage a greater positive
response in the way of voluntary help and to use the
skills of the newly retired then some of the
constraints must be recognised. Lack of confidence,
lack of money and practical difficulties such as the
absence of telephones need to be overcome. Perhaps
one of the most encouraging initiatives is the
'lifeskills' programme of community involvement by
Age Concern. With financial help from the Carnegie
UK Trust schemes are being set up in conjunction
with other organisations. Some of the most
successful seem to be very modest ones. For example
retired people are being used as volunteers in
Surrey to help with other elderly people's gardens
and, near Preston, to give emergency help with
plumbing, electrical repairs etc. In each case a
younger person goes too to help and to be shown the
necessary skills. Another interesting development
has been along self help lines and the University of
the Third Age is one of the outstanding examples.

In an overview of research on older people as
volunteers Goldberg and Connelly found that
voluntary work was seen as enhancing self-esteem and
life satisfaction. (Goldberg and Connelly, 1982).
Most of it was concerned with meeting and supporting
one another rather than taking up issues with
outside bodies on general problems. Nor must we
ignore the many informal ways in which elderly
people make a contribution to society. For example
in our recent study of elderly people in the

community many elderly people were able to give help to others (Tinker, 1984a). Often this was over shopping, knitting and sewing but also such tasks as babysitting and taking in the post. There were people among the most dependent in every scheme we looked at who were able to do something for others. And this, of course, only includes activities that can be physically measured. Emotional and other help is another dimension. The stability in life that a parent and grandparent can give is I suggest incalculable. One great advantage that elderly people often have is time. Time to listen and time to be an audience.

The great question to my mind is how far elderly people will change their activities as they age. If they have never been involved in voluntary or self help how can they be motivated to do so? And how far should there be positive intervention to encourage this?

The cut off point in society has been much more acute than in the past. The point at which a person retires from paid employment has become a watershed. How much less acute is the position of people where this does not arise - and in some jobs people go on for a very long time. Those of us who spend our holidays in French villages can fantasise that here too there seems no abrupt cut off point. Making a living out of the land and tending crops from cradle to the grave give a continuity and ensures a positive contribution in a way that modern society does not.

Professionals

So what of the creative response to ageing by professionals. Despite much good work by many involved in teaching groups such as medical students and future social workers it is unfortunate that the response to ageing is often still not a positive one. An obvious reason is that professionals like doctors and social workers tend to see the problems rather than the norm and for them the picture may not be an attractive one.

If there is agreement that the response of professionals must not be ageist how else is it to be positive? Too often it seems to be a well meant encouraging elderly people to join in group activities. This is nowhere more obvious than in sheltered housing where wardens are sometimes assessed by the number of activities going on in the common room. Some people obviously do like socials, bingo and wearing party hats. While it is right to encourage people to use their hands or minds isn't there a hint of the Protestant work ethic here or the attitude of the parent to the child - always wanting the person to be busy and occupied. And there is also lack of imagination by professionals about what elderly people might want to do.

Another way for professionals to encourage older people to be positive and active themselves is to draw in more help (for example by arranging adaptions/improvements to the home) for the frail and disabled of whatever age but particularly to aid the vastly increased number of very elderly people. This alone is a cogent argument for trying in an organised way, as Age Concern have done, to capitalise on the time and talents of the retired. Whether this will come naturally to the newly retired is difficult to say. It may have to be organised.

But the most acute dilemma for professionals it seems to me is how far they can take a robust positive attitude to the rights and risks of old people. If older people are to be encouraged to help and not to be over-protected then risks have to be taken. Nowhere is this better illustrated than in the recent research by DOE and DHSS referred to earlier (Tinker, 1984,a). One of the findings was the extent of the dependence of some elderly people living, successfully according to them, in their own homes. The majority lived alone. This is what they wanted (with a few exceptions) and even the most disabled were loath to give up their independence. What does this mean to professionals? It is sometimes much easier to take people into care or encourage them to go into sheltered housing than to leave them at home and risk them being found dead or wandering. I would suggest that a positive response to ageing means that these risks often have to be taken and that society must be educated to support professionals if things go wrong.

Another dilemma follows on from this and focuses on the question I have posed about whose response. When it comes to decisions about the lives of elderly people whose views are to prevail? I can illustrate this dilemma again by referring to the DOE/DHSS research where there was a conflict between the views of most elderly people who wished to remain in their own homes - whatever their disabilities and whatever the condition of their home (though some would have liked more help) and some of the paid carers who thought some of them would have been better off elsewhere. That 'elsewhere' was usually Part III accomodation.

May I quote from the two groups of people involved. Here first are typical comments of some of the elderly people concerned in answer to a question on how they would manage if they did not have the innovatory service:

"Well, I'd just fall and hurt myself and burn myself. When you have the blood pressure you do get a little giddy specially in the morning - I'm sure I'd hurt myself - well you'd be pushed in the geriatric ward and I don't want that. I don't like being in these homes since you have to share the toilet"

"Well I'd have to wait and see and what would come along - they'd chuck me into a home or something/horrible/they told me down at the hospital as I wasn't getting on and the doctor said to me I'd have to go into a home if I didn't improve and my God! that did it for me".

"God knows. I would have to go into a home but I wouldn't go. I stay here till I die, I've been here 27 years and they can't get me out, they've tried to get me out. They've polished the steps and I've slipped and hurt myself. I can't go anyway because of Polly the parrot".

"I would have to go somewhere like a home or the flats and I just wouldn't like that, I will be able to stay in my own home with this telephone here".

Now here are typical comments of the paid carers in answer to the question:

"Despite your help would the person you visit be better off in your opinion in some form of care? If yes then: Why do you think he/she would be better off in some other form of care?"

"They worry us to death .... they're at risk and are not safe to be on their own".

"The three or four who don't have a full social life they get very lonely and would be better off with company"

"Well some of them are very reluctant to accept help from other services for instance meals on wheels - nursing from the bathing point of view - some of them don't feed themselves".

"Some of them sign themselves out of hospital and are sent home - they say they want to die naturally at home".

My own view is that we have failed to listen to the views of consumers in too many areas of social policy and that no opportunity should be lost to take serious account of what they say. We did this recently in DOE in a study of families in flats when even quite young children gave their views. (Littlewood and Tinker, 1981). In the current study of elderly people we were careful to question elderly people directly. Despite warnings about their age and disability only two per cent were too ill to give an interview. I have misgivings about studies that rely solely on professionals such as wardens of sheltered housing.

But professionals must also balance the needs and wishes of relatives of elderly people and this is another dimension we need to bear in mind constantly.

Society

What of the response of society? On a pessimistic note society is still dominated by a youth culture and many ageist attitudes remain.

However, if one of the features which differentiates elderly people from the rest of society is the lack of paid employment then this is shared by many more people both young and middle aged who may perhaps be more tolerant of lack of earning power. Hopefully there will be a reassessing of attitudes so that what people contribute to life will be of more or equal value to paid employment. In addition more part-time jobs would be a creative response so that individuals ease themselves out of employment gradually. Another factor which is only just beginning to be realised is that elderly people have become a

growing proportion of society. Nowhere is this more obvious than in the political field. In the United States elderly people are becoming greatly involved in lobbying and it will be interesting to see their effect on political programmes (Abrams and O'Brien, 1981). In this country there is recent evidence that elderly people were as likely as younger people to have been involved in a political campaign, to have stood for public office, to have voted and to be a member of a political party. (Oriel in Hobman, 1981a). Yet they have been slow to develop as a pressure group. Perhaps this is to come although Abrams and O'Brien suggest some reasons why this may not necessarily happen. (Abrams and O'Brien, 1981).
Among these are differences between elderly people (eg, car owners may oppose free public transport on buses which incidentally have proved to be a great step to mobility), dislike of being labelled old and an awareness of lack of power (eg being unable to withdraw their labour). The sheer number of elderly people who could be involved in politics may have an effect on the way they are regarded.
I have mentioned some of the points that society will have to take into account in the previous section, most importantly the implications of allowing elderly people to take risks. There is one other aspect which should be mentioned. That is whether society should in fact recognise that people as they age may need positive discrimination in policies. While it is fashionable to argue that if elderly people are to be treated as first class citizens there should be no form of discrimination surely it is only right to exercise positive discrimination on occasions. David Hobman has given examples from commerce, travel, education and health care to show how options open to elderly people can be increasd if there is positive discrimination (Hobman, 1981,b). By helping them to travel, to keep fit and to function new experiences and achievements become possible. The new experience and achievements may, as Mary Stott has argued benefit the whole of society. When she wrote about the bracing approach of the American National Council of Senior Citizens, in their campaigns for the whole of society and not just senior citizens she commended their watchword: "Although many of us are retired from our jobs we are not retired from citizenship" (Stott, 1981).
In conclusion I would argue that a creative

response to ageing has a nice liberal tone to it but it is not clear exactly what this means. If it means that we concentrate on the contribution of elderly people and the positive aspects of ageing it is to be welcomed. The previous undue emphasis on problems and negative aspects of ageing has been counter productive and reduces the image of elderly people to a dependent minority. But it would be as foolish now to ignore these problems and to suggest that incontinence, confusion, poor housing conditions and lack of professional help are minor issues. The concern now must be to balance the positive aspects of ageing with the need to activate society's conscience about the needs of eldely people and how they may be met.

References

Abrams, M. and O'Brien, J. (1981) Political Attitudes and Ageing in Britain, Age Concern.

Comfort, A. (1965) The Process of Ageing, Weidenfeld and Nicholson

Comfort, A (1977) A Good Age, Mitchell Beazley

Goldberg, E.M. Some current implications and future issues in the social care of elderly people in DHSS Elderly people in the community: their service needs, HMSO, 1983

Goldberg, E.M. and Connelly, N. (1982) The Effectiveness of Social Care for the Elderly Heinemann

Hobman, D. (1981) Community Care 19 February

Hodkinson, H.M. (1975) An Outline of Geriatrics, Academic Press

Hunt, A. (1978) The Elderly at Home, OPCS, HMSO

Keddie, K.M.G. (1978) Action with the Elderly, Pergamon

Littlewood, J. and Tinker, A. (1981) Families in Flats, HMSO

OPCS, (1982) General Household Survey, 1980, HMSO

OPCS, (1983) General Household Survey, 1981, HMSO

Oriel, W. In Hobman, D. (ed); (1981) The Impact of Ageing, Croom Helm

Parker, S. (1982) Work and Retirement, Allen and Unwin

Stott, M. (1981) Ageing for Beginners, Blackwell

Tinker, A. (1984,a) Staying at home: helping elderly people, HMSO

Tinker, A. (1984, b) The Elderly in Modern Society, Longman, Second Edition Chapters 11 and 14.

Chapter Three

THE AGEING CLASS: VANGUARD OF THE REVOLUTION

Eric Midwinter

The 'self-evident' truths of the American
Constitution, and the heart-cry of 'liberty,
equality, fraternity' from the French Revolution,
have informed modern progressive thought for 200
years. They voiced the disgust of people sickened
by corrupt, greedy government and oppressed by a
regressive economy. It is fashionable now, stepping
beyond the mere 'looking after' of older people and
sustaining them at a bare minimum of existence, to
speak boldly of guaranteeing their dignity and their
self-respect, offering them life-enhancing
opportunities and a life of autonomy and
independence. These good and optimistic terms run
the hazard of becoming among the battered ornaments
of the language we used to discuss the issue of
ageing in our society, and it could be of use to
examine them more closely in the light of their
political derivation and implementation, for, in the
main, these principles of self-determination for
elderly citizens derive, in their modern idiom, from
that late 18th century tradition.
What, then, should we mean, exactly and
politically, by self-determination? There is a
curious and double parallel about the ostensibly
varied political thought that evolved from that era
of revulsion against burdensome government and the
initial horrors of industrialism. All political
theorists were critical of the State, and saw it as
the grand evil. All of them argued towards removing
that yoke, that men might enjoy that very self-
determination we now rather hazily feel should be
the lot of elderly people. In essence, the ideal,
across the board of apparently competitive
philosophies, was anocracy: government, that is,
without a state apparatus, external to the will of
men. From France, Rousseau issued his famous dictum

that man, born free, was everywhere enchained in the
shackles of political and economic slavery. During
the 19th century, the socialist thinkers jostled and
elbowed angrily for intellectual dominion, and, of
course, Marx and Engels, the self-styled Scientific
Socialists, contemptuously rough-rode over the
claims of what they called the Utopian Socialists,
the likes of Saint-Simon, Fourier, Wilhelm
Weiibling, and our own Robert Owen, all of them
making much play of communitarian and associationist
principles and methods. Yet all of them had in
common the ultimate hope of a state-free society,
for the state, according to Marx, was the instrument
of one class mastering another. In Engel's popular
phrase, "come the revolution", and the state would
'wither away' ... 'the administration of things
would flow more abundantly'. This was no less
attractive, indeed, no less moralistic, cataclysmic
and non-scientific, than the views of Owen and
Fourier and their confreres that men and women might
live more equitably and, a favourite word of the
genre, in harmony, were they to find themselves in
associations or communities, or what the Russians
eventually came to call, but not for long, soviets.
    In the United States of America, from quite a
different stance, Thomas Jefferson and many of the
Founding Fathers, argued for frugal government: that
style of agrarian democracy, which, in Jefferson's
picturesque phrase, was based on no man living so
close to his neighbour that he could hear his dog
bark. The determination of local communities in the
United States, most importantly, the individual
states themselves, to retain their independence and
a wide measure of political control, stems, in a
degree, from that firmly held notion that the
federal state was a dangerous threat.
    In the United Kingdom, and there were echoes
throughout Europe, political scientists who, like
Thomas Jefferson, would have looked askance on
scabrous, socialist wild men, criticised the state
strongly. Jeremy Bentham, arch-exponent of the
Utilitarian principle, was convinced that general
happiness was most likely where men were free to
follow their self-interests, and that the sum of
these ego-centric individualities would offer
optimal contentment. An unwieldly and over-
complicated state contructed insurmountable
obstacles, and, until they were demolished, such a
pleasing outcome was impossible.

The Ageing Class: Vanguard of the Revolution

Thus, the assumed opposing pole of 19th century laissez-faire and communistic yearnings pointed, rather unexpectedly, in the same direction; towards a distinctive, non-state paradise, and that word is used advisedly, for, somewhere under the dustcovers of all their mental furniture lay a vague metaphysical and apocalyptic vision drawn from the Christian/Jewish tradition, of another Eden, to enjoy here on earth.

But there then followed the second of those parallels, and that, emphatically, was a more mundane one. Inexorably, all those pieces of political thought led towards degrees of corporate statehood unprecedented in human history. The thought of Rousseau and the French 'philosophes' very shortly became the classic lines of the neat and rational Napoleonic state, first, perhaps, of the tight, unified, bourgeois states of the modern dispensation. In the United States, the contesting views of Andrew Jackson - the federal state as champion of the people - and Alexander Hamilton - the federal state as protector of big business - both led toward the strong American state of today. In the crucial test of the American Civil War, which was, of course, not so much about slavery as about the rights of secession, the 'indivisibility' of the Union was insisted upon, and the 20th century super-state was in the offing. In the United Kingdom, the device of what S. E. Finer called the 'tutelle' - the determination of Victorial social engineers like Edwin Chadwick to procure an artificial harmony of interests by direct state activity - helped lead remorselessly, if paradoxically, to a present where the central state intervenes decisively at every point in our daily lives; so much so that over the last 120 years a succession of governments of varying party labels has gradually erected the heavily centralised collectivist state of today.

Most paradoxical of all, however, the anocratic vision of Marx has led in the U.S.S.R., and elsewhere in European and other countries of a purportedly Marxist persuasion, to a form of all-powerful, monolithic statehood, unknown hitherto in human history, and there is no sadder sight in the development of political science than that chasm between communist idealism and supposedly communist reality.

What, naturally enough, is apparent is that the political thought of itself had not too much to do with the structuration of all these omnicompetent states, but that great economic and social forces were at work, rationalising, merging and collectivising, until the massive dead-weight of bureaucracy was and is a global phenomenon. An appropriate example would be the official institutionalisation of old age. Although there were some mild precedents, the year 1859, when the British Civil Service finally decided that, for administrative convenience, civil servants should retire on a certain birthday, is the annus miserabilis. Like football, railways, penicillin, television and other British pioneering inventions, the idea of formal and official old age was exported so that, across the developed world, whether pseudo-communist or neo-liberal, retirement is institutionalised at 60 or 65 or thereabouts. That strangely neglected 1940s study, James Burnham's, 'The Managerial Revolution', charted the manner in which the Tweedle-Dum and Tweedle-Dee of the world's political manifestations had assumed massive control over the individual by the contruction of an enormous officialdom.

What price, therefore, the liberty, equality and fraternity of revolutionary thought? Liberty has had some play, although, as Aristotle warned, there are too often those ready to label a privilege as a freedom and speciously defend it on those terms. Some service has been paid to equality, although we have tended to accept the rather half-baked, half-way house solution of equality of opportunity, which, on examination, is found to be no more than uniformity of opportunity. Fraternity has scarcely had even a mention. If liberty has had some exercise and equality has enjoyed an occasional trot, that third steed of the radical troika has scarcely made the stableyard. Indeed, a glance at the present British political scene might suggest that freedom (liberty) and egalitarianism (equality) are securely established as the opposite and only poles. The arguments seem to be between the privatisers and the nationalisers: BUPA vs NHS; Eton against St. Pancras Comprehensive; and should your dustman be an entrepreneur or a bureaucrat? Most people uneasily search for compromise locations somewhere in between, with, for example, efforts to rediscover R. H. Tawney in rather more temperate zones than he might himself have chosen. Yet it was Tawney who argued that the opposite of private enterprise was not necessarily centralism, and that there was - and is - a strong case to be urged for de-centralised public ownership. It was the French utopian socialist, Etienne Cabet, who wrote: "If we are asked: what is your science?, we reply, Fraternity. What is your principle? Fraternity. What is your theory? Fraternity. What is your system? Fraternity. Yes, we maintain that Fraternity is everything."

The effects of corporate statehood, and the absence of a reasonable chance to express fraternally, either individual or group concerns, are cumulative, apropros the dispossessed and disadvantaged sections of the population, such as the unemployed, children, and, of course, older people. The alienation, economic and political, of older people, has its roots in our over-institutionalised and over-burdened centralism, which gives little or no thought to that civic co-operation and popular democracy which fraternalists would recognise.

It is clear that the economic alienation of older people, with regard both to cause and consequence, is linked to their political alienation, for it is those technical and economic forms of private, multi-national and state capitalism which, across the world, have created that despairing inequality which leaves many older people in many lands, if not destitute, at least unable to involve themselves in the everyday life of our present society, let alone be materially resourced and equipped to participate in a more progressive political and democratic arena. And here I would pay tribute to the British scholars, among whome I would especially mention Chris Phillipson and Alan Walker, who have eloquently drawn attention to the political and economic reality of older people's place in our society.

All of this is a major reason why the Centre for Policy on Ageing will publish in 1985 a broad-based philosophic study of the optimal level of income maintenance for older people, stressing the need for a move from a subsistence/welfare axis to a social inclusion/civic axis as a means for calculating a decent social wage for the post-workforce. Certainly, a sensible income is a prerequisite of the self-determined life; otherwise, available choices are not legitimate ones, and the freedom to dine at the Ritz persists.

Conversely, the argument must also be pressed on the political front, if the capacity of older people to join in making decisions about their lifestyle is to be increased. At a human level, one can only be appalled at the wealth of knowledge and stock of experience which is lost with the abandonment of elderly people. Like the medieval traveller seeking anxiously for the candle-light of the monastery in the bleak darkness, we seize on the very occasional examples of older people successful in self-help moulds, these exceptions that prove the rule that we do not utilise them, but we should.

There are the various pensioner action groups, the over-sixties employment bureaux, the repair-and-maintenace workshop exchanges, the interesting schemes backed by Pensioner-Link and Age Concern groups, and a modicum of resident committees in old people's homes. The educational and leisure field has also provided scope for fraternal co-operation, as the splendid initiatives in terms of leisure associations in Stoke, Huddersfield and elsewhere illustrate. The first ever annual conference of the University of the Third Age, in September 1985, demonstrates the possibility quite plainly. There are now over 50 groups, or sub-groups, amounting in total to something approaching 5,000 members, each autonomously and democratically run, each self-programming its own activities on a voluntary basis, and with many providing not only the organisers but the tutorial lead from within their own ranks. While small, even puny in sum, these pilot endeavours bear witness to the potential.

And yet, through the centralised largesse of the state or its municipal agents, willing or unwilling, services are provided for older people, as for everyone, with hardly any show of allowing the recipient any degree of control or influence, save for the vague and generalised 'X' on the episodic ballot-paper. There is an endless list of libraries, transport services, housing and environmental facilities, leisure and educational amenities, health provision and the like, over which the paying customer has no authority, although, in rates, taxes or fees, he is the paymaster. That is apart from the services more directly targeted on older people like day-centres, meals-on-wheels, residential care or home helps. How many local authorities have handed day-to-day control of homes to the residents? How many local authorities monitor the meals-on-wheels service by regular and independent interview of the consumer? How many local authorities have a client on the panel when interviewing for home help appointments?

There is little evidence of a new approach which looks upon the client as consumer rather than product, as the centre of consideration, as Hamlet rather than his father's ghost. There is not much testimony of services being provided intelligibly and civilly at the customer's convenience, recognising that the public services, technically, belong to the people and that this should be consummated in practice. This calls for the prior professional obligation to the systematic informing and stewardship of the laity, so that it might more independently and fruitfully engage in a professional-lay dialogue. It does not expect that the older layman or laywoman would know all the answers: it would hope that they would at least know or be informed of all the questions. At the fount of this is perhaps the axiom of the 'right to know', that access to information without which choices and decisions are blind. It is not just the issue of that confidentiality so highly secret and prized that information must be kept private even from the clients, nor it is a question only of explaining the 'big words' used so myseriously by professionals, as they zealously converse in codes as arcane as priestly Latin. It is more often quite straightforward stuff about simple organisational matters and procedures, with professionals guaranteeing to explain and justify their actions and judgements to their immediate public individually and collectively. And further, that they should do this in a manner understandable to and familiar to their - and the word is used with great correctness - masters.

And yet, today, many of these professional organisers of activities talk glibly, gaily and garruously about autonomy and self-reliance. it is the new dogma, but it is often a self-defeating one. During CPA's surveys for the publication 'Bricks and Mortals: design and management in residential care homes', and through other contacts with such agencies, its officers constantly find (despite the genuine efforts of a minority who actually understand the political implications of the novel catch-phrases) professionals fiercely insisting on the resident or day-care members being independent and autonomous, whether they like it or not. When there is no freedom to choose, there is no self-autonomy: the game is lost before the kick-off. To take a homely example, one might find ladies who had worked hard all their lives somewhat reluctant to wash-up or even make their own beds, tasks set them as a token of their independence and need to remain self-reliant. Having paid good money for a residential place, they might feel cheated at having to follow the domestic rather than the hotel model. It's all very well making a residential home as much like your own home as possible, but what if you didn't like your own home, especially the washing-up and bed-making bits of it?

'Home life', the DHSS-sponsored code of practice for residential care, produced by a working party convened by CPA, is an admirable account of how to preserve dignity and self-respect in that institutional setting; a 'Rights of Residential Man' of which Tom Paine himself might have been proud. This and similar documents are aimed at the professionals in the field, because it is the professionals who exert an enormous influence. When one argues that life is over-bureaucratised and over-institutionalised, one infers that it is over-professionalised. There is little doubt that, on this interpretation, the professional cadres are the Old Guard of the Napoleonic state. They are the props of the corporate state, on both sides of the Iron Curtain. Theirs is an ambivalent role; on the one hand, no one could discount the enormous benefits they have often-times wrought. On the other hand, they are the dead-hand of the body politic, firmly squashing most hopes of lay liveliness.

In the United Kingdom, the parlimentary democracy we now enjoy and suffer in about equal parts was an 18th century resolution, a modifiction of absolutist sovereignty in terms of that national sovereignty legally embodied in some loosely representational vehicle. During the 19th and 20th centuries, the state has recruited, centrally and locally, public professional regiments to enforce its will, and offered opportunities for private, professional batallions to enlist in the professional army as well. There are very many of them. It is a lengthy list, for it includes not only doctors, child psychologists, other medical workers, social workers and teachers, but prison and

probation officers, policemen, public health
officials, social security and supplementary
benefits officers, housing managers, and a dozen
more. One sometimes begins to believe that life is
made up of a series of mortal combats between
professionals and the laity. They may not all enjoy
being thus lumped together, but social history, like
diplomacy, makes for strange bedfellows. These are
the agents of interventionist policies, and, as
such, they are placed in an extensive series of
professional-lay relationships. In popular
folklore, these are not always engaging figures -
the authoritrian teacher, the disciplinarian nurse,
the over-clinical doctor, the condescending social
worker, the abrasive social security officer, and so
on. However tiny the sparks of fire which give
rise to such billowing clouds of smoke, they are
still part of the nation's gut-reaction to its
public servants. It is often their seeming refusal
to be human, and this fear of being human, being
one's true self, within the professional pale, which
helps sustain the gap between them and clients beset
by difficulties and thus at their most vulnerable,
as is frequently the case with older people in
receipt of social services. They find themselves
faced by complicated and incomprehensible
procedures, negotiated by varying species of techno-
bureaucrats. It is sometimes said that
professionals have replaced the priests. That is
unfair to the priesthood. It may, like the new
surrogate social priesthood, have had rituals, but
at least it had a more finely tuned ear for show-
biz. Whether your tastes tempted you to the
awesome beauties of the Mass, the reassuring
sing-song of the Anglican church, the stirring
tub-thumping of the Methodist lay-preacher, or the
rousing um-paw-paw of the Salvation Army, there
was life and colour. There is little of such
entertaining vividness in our public care services.
For the mass of the population, perhaps particularly
the older population, their treatment by such
services is, at worst, undignified and humiliating,
and, at best, very tedious and dull. What the Webbs
called the 'prescribed qualification', grew to be
the norm for every specific role in the providing of
services, on the respectable ground that the user
should be properly protected from inefficiency.
But, almost without exception, most of the
professions have slavishly adhered to the historic

fate mapped out for professions. They have become bureaucratised, defensive about manning and function, haunted by fears of dilution, jittery about evaluation and open accountability, jargon-plagued, status-conscious, and sheltering, in a pother of insecurity, behind a barricade of mystiques.

How fascinated we are to learn of laymen who have managed to hoodwink the professionals! In recent years there has been a biology teacher who set up in St. Anne's as a gynaecologist, and a Manx avid reader of textbooks who rose to be a senior anaesthestist in St. Alban's on the back of a mock Australian medical qualification. At the time of the Great Train Robbery, what bothered British Rail management and labour was that someone had managed to move one of their trains without having first undergone many, many years of apprenticeship, and how relieved they were to find it was a suborned retired driver who was guilty! And how professions always hate their training, bitterly complaining, often rightly, that it was a waste of time, impractical, over-theoretical, outdated, and irrelevant - but woe betide anyone who attempts to practice whatever obscure art-form it is, without benefit of this useless mess of instructional pottage.

There is, thankfully, a new role for professionals. It consists in practising what many now preach by way of self-determination. It calls upon them to be the servants, not the masters, of the consumer, to enter into dialogue with them, within whatever borders are laid down by financial and physical constraints, to lead them actively and constructively into the fraternal world of popular democracy. The going will be slow and tough. Professionals will argue, as they always have done, that consumers will not want to become involved, just as, in the debates before every Parliamentary Reform Act, it was argued that people would not want, or were not able to exercise the franchise. Professionals will argue that lay people will make mistakes. We should remember Ghandi's dictum, that these would be, at least, our own mistakes, native mistakes and not imperial ones.

Four criteria, offered in logical progression, might be useful in assessing, service by service, how far the users or customers have been or should be drawn into the pale of decision-making by professionals or managers.

Firstly, as to Information. Fraternal or popular democracy is about informed choice. Professionals often say that the consumers cannot decide because they do not understand the situation or appreciate the difficulties. Thus, the first obligation on the provider is to ensure that the recipient or potential recipient is fully acquainted and updated, clearly and simply, with the requisite knowledge of what the service consists of and what it promises.

Secondly, as to Consultation. Fraternal and popular democracy is about tapping opinion. If changes are to be made, or when decisions have to be taken, the second obligation on the provider is to guarantee optimal modes of consultation with the consumer or, as is sometimes the case, the surrogate consumer, such as the relative of a dependent older person, that the weight of their views might be appropriately measured.

Thirdly, as to Negotiation. Fraternal and popular democracy is about righting wrongs. The professional and managerial monitoring of any service should include some device for hearing of complaints. The third obligation on the provider should be the establishment of some mechanics for the independent resolution of purported ills or departures from agreed contracts, so as to permit of the means of advocacy by the complainants or their proxies.

Fourthly, as to Representation. Fraternal and popular democracy is about localised control. Eventually, the users of the field service, within whatever parameters must be laid down by the upper tier of democratic management, should have oversight of that which so closely concerns them. The fourth obligation on the provider is to arrange, as non-formally and practicably as possible, some forum in which this popular control might begin to develop.

It has been said that Marx turned Hegel on his head. I would not presume to such boldness, but rather, more tentatively, content myself with turning Marx on his side. Let us assume that, taking the United Kingdom as an example, the older population of retired people and those finished with major social responsibility, a number, perhaps approaching 14 or 15 millions, are the have-nots, in the sense of being 'haves not work'. Work is so indicative, in our toil-conscious society, of status and identity, as well as income. How irritated one becomes at the newspaper that describes Mr. Bloggs as an ex-engine-driver; or what of all those Mastermind competitors, who should by that token know better, who in answer to the opening question 'occupation?' say, 'retired secretary' rather than say 'pass'? And how interesting it is that those are the only two questions asked of competitors: their name and occupation: those dog-tags of the work-orientated society. Needless to say, the range of income for these have-nots is vast, although it must be stressed that all of them are having to live at a level lower than that to which they had become accustomed, and many of them are living in situations of relative penury as over against the mainstream of society.

Nonetheless, it is status as well as income that flops with retirement at the given age, except for those, such as actors or politicians, whose peculiar circumstances allow them to retain status and the self-respect that goes with it. Otherwise, older people are, to employ the Marxian word, the expropriated: They have been robbed of their personal 'property', their career, their profession, their trade or other mark of social identity, as well as their mainline income.

Could they, under the leadership of re-professionalised professionals, become the vanguard of the new-style revolution? Could they be the neo-proletariat of the post-industrial class war? In contradictory fashion, time is on their side: on the one hand, because they have, day by day, untold leisure to go about this revolutionary business; and, on the other hand, because they have, year by year, very little time, and, to quote (if I may dive headfirst into the trap I've dug for myself) an ex-bus driver at the Transport and General Workers Union Retired Association for Branch Officers' Conference: 'we need to move quickly, because we're in a bloody hurry'.

What I foresee, or rather phantasise over, is an uprising of the dispossessed, resentful of and frustrated by the yawning emptiness of 25 and 30 year retirements; a kind of pensioners' peasants' revolt; a determination to assume control over their own lives and to work at the invention of their destiny.

In CPA's study of education and older people, Age is opportunity, we risked a paraphrase of Jane

Austen and suggested that it is a truth universally acknowledged that a voluntary enterprise in search of continual success must be in want of professional guidance, and we advocated, for the educational co-operatives we had in mind, the use of tutors as animateurs rather than didacts. Naturally enough, the notion is tranferrable to professional activities of this kind across the social frame, with officers energising and sustaining networks of elderly people about the business of retaining dignity and self-determining their lifestyle. It was suggested that the professional in question must be a barker, a broker and a booster. He or she should be a strenuous barker for building up a vigorous set of public relations mechanics, as socially legitimate and suitable for the clientele in question. He or she must be a broker, adept in the relating of people to people in a deft free-wheeling exercise, building up a para-professioal system of modules of social mutuality. He or she must be a booster, above all, gifted in the inculcation of self-assurance and confidence into the putative revolutionaries. These make up the essential qualifications of the new professional, novel in the unusual sense of experts willing to convey some of their expertise to the laity that they might prosper socially and politically. This new professional would be the convenor or steward of the activities of elderly people, rather than the purveyor of services to them.

It could be the sacred lot of these professionals to be the bolsheviks of the revolution, the spearhead of the vanguard of the alten-proletariat. It would not be the police stations or the power stations that would be the prior objectives. It would be the day centres, the residential care homes, the meals-on-wheels amenity and the home help service that might first be seized in bloodless coup after bloodless coup. Who knows? If we can occasion and persuade older people to invent their own destiny and determine their own salvation, the notion might catch on, and the revolution might, as Trotsky hoped of his own in the 1920s, prove infectious and spread to the rest of the population, led in turn and as appropriate by their resurrected professionals.

Aneurin Bevan spoke of the 'opposite poles' in society, of what he thought of as the dog and cat tendency, with first one and then the other dominant. What Gilbert and Sullivan might have called the 'cat-like tread', is the egotistical one, the selfish self-contained harbouring of one's resource, and the refusal to share and enter joyously into helpful and outwardly profitable activity in the unremitting pursuit of the good of self. The canine trend is, conversely, towards a loyal determination to join in and co-operate with a generous and affectionate zeal, in collective endeavour for the good of all.

One does not need to stray too far from the zoological path of political impartiality to suggest that since about 1950, we have been gravitating fairly definitely towards the feline pole. Alternately, this vision I attempt to conjure up of a pensioner-led reformation, a septuagenarian soviet, or a senior syndicate is defiantly dog-like. For, in promoting the notion of fraternity among the third age, one looks, ever more ambitiously, beyond that objective to a society within which, for all ages and conditions of men and women, that self-programming ethic might prevail.

The ideal would be the absorption of professional intolaity, the melting of institutionalism into the popular culture, and the disestablishment of the great public social and welfare churches. We must, argued Schumacher, 'learn to think in terms of an articulated structure that can cope with a multiplicity of small-scale units'. That, in my opinion, applies no less to social and political than to economic organisations, and, as we endeavour to survive the next quarter century, the criterion for the public service professionals may of necessity become their ability to find this human scale and human face for their efforts, as their vital part in meeting the appallingly vigorous challenge of the corporate state; in particular as it presses ever more depressingly upon older people in our society, those very people who hold such immense reserves of knowledge and skill to place at the disposal of us all.

PART TWO: LEISURE, FRIENDSHIP AND ASSOCIATION

Chapter Four

LISTENING TO THE VOICES OF OLDER WOMEN:
CREATIVITY AND SOCIAL WORK RESPONSES

Alison Froggatt

Abstract

     This paper discusses ways to work with older
women in broad references to social work, with three
objectives in mind. Firstly it is important to
acknowledge that old age and being female present
two structural disadvantages, and where these are
combined social workers may need to rethink their
response to older women, whether being cared for,
living independently, or as a carer for another in
old age. The second objective is to tap into the
hidden world of old people, particularly that of old
women, and release their creativity, for their own
satisfaction, and to gain more insight into their
experience. Thirdly it is hoped to suggest a
variety of more creative paths for social workers
and others to take in their interaction with older
women. Latterly, literature and research into
gerontological social work in this country has
tended to be service oriented, tied into the
functions of welfare agencies. New emphases in
research from social gerontologists and feminists
suggest that an interpretive and interactionist
approach needs to be developed if we are to
understand the ageing experience of older women.

Introduction

Being Old and Being Female
     To focus on older women does not reflect any
sexist bias, but rather firstly, a recognition that
there are many more old women than old men in the
population over sixty-five, and proportionately more
as their years advance. (Jefferys 1983). One of
the lesser griefs of widowhood can be the
recognition that one is moving into a predominantly

35

female society. Secondly there seems to be a
difference in the way society treats old men and old
women. Social gerontologists are now more ready to
accept the structural disadvantages which seem to be
built in for old women in relation to old men, such
things as a smaller pension, and the increased
likelihood of living alone or in institutional care.
(Fennell, Phillipson and Wenger 1983).
Sontag (1979) describes the double standard,
the humiliation for women of an ageing body.
Harrison (1983) outlines in the Australian context
the struggle for identity of elderly women coping
with the double disadvantage of being old and being
female, and Newton gives the insider's view from a
nursing home. Additionally there are writers who
question the basis of gerontology, the assumption
and the knowledge base behind the research
questionnaires which have the normative patriarchal
model of society in mind. (Obler 1983).
Recognising that women and elderly people share the
same 'marginal social skin' (Ritcey 1983) has called
for a more interpretive approach and has
demonstrated with a small scale research study how
five 'deviant' old women in a nursing home held on
to their sense of self, refused to accept society's
devaluation of them, and retained some measure of
control. So they held on to a capacity to act
dynamically, to interact, in circumstances where to
submit passively was the expected norm.
The approach of this paper is to suggest means
to strengthen that sense of self, by stimulating the
creativity of older women so that they reconsider
and re-evaluate their place in the scheme of things,
to recognise their worth, and the value of their
contribution to society; by giving others insight
into the experience of being an ageing woman, such
women may be able to accord themselves and be
accorded, status, using the interpretive model, with
its emphasis on the validity of the individual life
story, the unique 'voice'. This approach needs to
be incorporated or re-emphasised in developing
gerontological social work, as will be shown later.
An example of the normative approach came to
light in the course of a recent research project in
an area office, where in studying a series of
referrals, seven out of eight married couples
involved turned out to consist of elderly husbands
caring for sick and disabled wives. My inference
was that there was a tendency for older women

simply to be expected to cope with disabled husbands. Men coping domestically as the principal carer were seen to need earlier relief and more support. (Froggatt 1983). Another normative illustration is shown by Evers (1981) in her paper making a vivid point of how much more devalued women are in institutions. The 'dethroned carer' is easily despied, whereas it seems natural and right for women as paid carers to look after frail old men. This diminution of status comes later in life than any post-retirement trauma, which in any case has up to now been more common for males. (Yarrow et al 1981).

It is not possible to think for long about the lives of old women without becoming aware of those who care for them, principally older women, and while a detailed consideration of the meaning of being an adult child falls outside the scope of the paper, some acknowledgement must be given to the ambivalent position of carers. Ambivalence is a keynote of the experience of caring. The sometimes suffocating societal expectations of carers, mainly women, are explored fully by Walker et al (1982). I want here to emphasise again the personal experience of both confronting with sometimes horrid clarity the degenerations of bodily, mental and emotional changes, as a foreshadowing of what happens to each of us, and simultaneously striving to retain the very old person as a family member, in tune as far as possible with recent events. Time and again much of this work falls to a woman, even for a man's relatives. As Graham (1983) describes:
"Caring is 'given' to women; it becomes the defining characteristic of their self-identity and their life's work."
Distance therefore makes little difference. The patience to contain depressed or disorganised phone calls, to talk someone through the winter, comes from within a woman to woman network of solidarity, an extension of the solidarity which sustains at earlier stages through pregnancy sickness, post-natal 'blues', broken nights and childhood traumas. Finch and Groves have elaborated on the structural position of carers (1983), and within their compilation Graham (1983) distinguishes between the labour and the love of caring; Ungerson's analysis of caring for as distinct from caring about someone confirms that the work of caring for old people can be immediate and daily

caring for them, or at a distance emotional support caring about, or a mixture of the two. What is undoubtedly true is that care in old age, in both senses is often costly, not time limited, and having a profound effect on both carer and cared for. The revaluation, exploration, and recognition of the self-hood of the oldest women is, it is suggested, also of value for the older woman as carer.

So, as indicated earlier, one of the aims of this paper is to suggest ways in which older women can retain and indeed enhance their self-esteem, right through into extreme old age. This kind of approach could be helpful to the wide range of voluntary, residential and field workers who are involved with older people and particularly with old women. It is intended to balance the way social work with old people is at present much influenced by recent research collated by Goldberg and Connally (1982) which has a service oriented, task-based approach.

The descriptive demographic gloom, if not panic which seems to have reached the highest levels in government, has not only been elegantly deflated by Jefferys (1983), but also needs combatting within social work. Social workers need to rethink their approach to older women, whether living independently, acting as carers, or living as cared for old women. To recognise and come to terms with the double structural disadvantages of being old and female is the first stage; the second stage would seem to be a development of the capacity to get the insider's view by one of the means to be suggested, namely reminiscence, narrative, written material and letters or poetry. There seems every reason, indeed the Barclay Report offers encouragement (1982), to bring social work with older people into line with current social work thinking, which stresses a mixed methods approach, involving work with individual families, groups, and in the community. In particular, learning to communicate on many levels with children is something social workers are encouraged to do. The theme of this paper is to suggest ways of doing similar work with older women.

The emphasis on reminiscence, recall, and the life story approach needs to be carried further in an interpretive model of understanding ageing. Recent developments in counselling, psychotherapy, family therapy and group work with older people are also beginning here to be valid means of facilitating change, development and self-enhancement. No-one has more hard emotional work to do than older women newly admitted to residential/institutional care, grieving over loss of spouse, or loss of young hopes, loss of home, role and health. If older people were as incapable of change as the stereotypes suggest, there might be psychological immobilisation, instead of resilience and humour and great adaptability in many situations.

Tapping the World of Old Age - The Insider's View

This paper incorporates a collection of writings made over the past eighteen months. The voices of older women, their perceptions of themselves, whether spoken or written, and the narrative flow of their life stories became of interest. Many sources have been tapped in this compilation: newspaper interviews, informal interviews in a day centre, participant observation in a nursing home over a period of time, written autobiographical fragments from kind older friends, collections of letters, poems written by older women, fragments of conversation of exteme old age collected and written down. The focus in this work has been on women because much less of their self-perception is known. Blyth's 'View in Winter' considers mostly men. (1981). Feminist literature is contributing much more understanding of the women's perspective. Conrad (1983) is culling diaries written over the past two hundred years by Canadian women, for example.

Again there is not just a woman's point of view; culture, class, and education are of importance in what people can achieve, retain, and create in old age; however the interesting feature of reminiscence is that it crosses these barriers. Someone with a good memory, an eye for detail, who is a natural story teller can be found anywhere in society; such a woman (or man) is usually well known to her neighbours, the gift is recognised. In making this collection, what I have been searching for and indeed finding, is confirmation of what I have known intuitively since being a child with a close loving grandmother who lived to be a great-grandmother, who said "I feel just the same inside as when I was young. It's as though I'm imprisoned in someone else's body". (Bosanquet 1964). The mind and spirit mostly last out, and remain themselves; it is just the body that betrays. We can only increase our understanding of old age by listening to the voices of those who are experiencing it at that time. There are few retrospective accounts of old age. With more insight into how people feel as they age, it may be possible to encourage others to re-evaluate themselves as one of the activities of ageing which bodily infirmity need not cripple.

Very old famous women are sometimes interviewed by journalists, as a phenomenon, for being articulate and alive in their eighties or nineties. (Defying the sterotype!) Amabel Williams Ellis (Daily Telegraph 17.3.83) interviewed on the publication of her autobiography described her reason for writing it as a 'kind of case-book, to see exactly what had stuck in my memory, for I found I had to relive many of the events, painful ones included, in order to describe them properly.' She described herself as pondering 'sphinx questions', the vast life and death issues that have beset humanity through history.

Rebecca West, in a ninetieth birthday article (1983) wrote of the "ever recurring difficulty that really vexes the old who for some reason feel this passionate concern for the future of our kind ..." She analysed a feature of reminiscence "one of the curious things about being ninety is that the power of memory is so strong that it often makes one feel as one were several ages at the same time."

Katherine Moore's first novel was published for her eighty-fifth birthday, based around a description of life for residents in a private old age home. "Their lives are a series of tiny but seriously undertaken battles to retain small comforts." Interviewed to mark the occasion Mrs Moore described herself as "having had the enormous privilege of having children, grandchildren and a job - of course I'd have liked more time to devote to every thing, and to have more children, but there you are; I'm just greedy." (Perrick 1983).

Fry gives confirmation (1955) of the feeling she gained from her contemporaries, "I believe to many old people their age hardly seems to belong to them at all." And as a way of coping with ageing, "As the limits of self-determination grow narrower the ageing person clings more anxiously to what remains ... choice is a precious prerogative .. the external stigmata of old age must not be allowed

to obscure the lasting divergencies of character;
individuality must be respected." She reminds us
"the ebb and flow of strength must be learned and
accepted by those who suffer, but also has to be
constantly remembered by those who are making plans
for using elderly activities to useful purpose." A
useful warning here for any too ambitious plans for
working exhaustively with older people.

Pincus (1981) has drawn on her life experience
as an octogenarian, and psychotherapist to describe
her own life, and those of friends and colleagues.
She shows how both unresolved family differences,
and life's experience shape up people's perceptions
of themselves into old age.

Drawing on letters and writings by women in
older age gives us the opportunity to add to our
understanding. As probably more literary works of
men are published giving them the chance to reflect
on experience, this section has been expanded by
asking some older women to write their views of
ageing as it strikes them.

First someone of young old age, writing aged
seventy-three:

"Since retiring from teaching adult classes
twelve months ago, I have often stared through
the windows of the Old People's Day Centre and
looked at the women sitting, apparently
speechless, side by side and I don't feel that
I belong among them - yet. Rather I identify
in imagination with the men and women I see
wandering around the Job Centre studying the
vacancies hopefully, hopelessly. I, too, have
days when I long for the busy rush of earlier
years. But on other days I welcome the time I
now have to educate myself a bit further.
There is so much still to learn.

"Of course, lumbering up towards my seventy-
fourth birthday, I have travelled quite a bit
of the way beyond the biblical tally of life-
expectation. But remembering that the life
spans of my mother and grandmother and my aunt
have averaged 94 years, perhaps I must be
prepared for <u>four</u> score years and ten. Should
I consider myself then, still in middle life?
Maybe, until I look in the mirror at a face
wrinkled like a dried fig - an old woman's
face.

"Is mine an old woman's body too? The body
that in childhood and middle age was prone to

endless accidents, diseases and operations, is
magnificently resistant to the common cold and
finding occasional rheumatic twinges are just
an excuse for longer walks and more comical
physical exercises. Only increasing deafness
is an irritation to myself and my family.
"And my mind? The memory that sixty years ago
failed to hold tightly to Latin declensions,
today has an awkward habit of mislaying proper
names or nouns instantly wanted in
conversation. The remoter past is more vivid
than the middle years.
"H and I are survivors. Where now are my
school friends, college contemporaries,
working colleagues? Dead, almost all of them,
in youth or in their fifties or sixties.
After H's illness last year and my sister's
continuing health problems, I realise that the
ice we walk on is brittle.
"But how fortunate H and I have been in our
forty-six years together. Fortunate in our
work, fortunate in our children and fortunate
now to be living in a small urban oasis where
everybody - young and old, black and white -
stops to pass the time of day when we meet on
the street. No - I can't send you yet a real
autobiography of ageing - try me in ten years
time!" (Hardman 1983).
        Then someone aged seventy-seven who defines
herself:
"I am on the brink of being old and had thought
it couldn't happen to me. But at sixty-nine I
developed glaucoma and hip arthritis; now I
have two 'new' hips, but no pain, some hearing
difficulty and severe sight handicap. This
means drastic physical slowing down in
everything I do.
"I've accepted that I must never be in a hurry,
to avoid a fall - THE great dread. I've also
accepted the fact that my memory for names,
even of intimates, is faulty as is my
rememberance of details in the immediate past,
both of which lapses are embarrassing. But
all the vital things - personal relationships,
cleanliness, 'godliness' - are still primary
and clear. Women have the advantage of
feeling needed (domestically anyhow) and also
of being creative with their hands if they can
knit or embroider. If they can laugh about

the disabilities of getting old, they are
safe. And if they can record their vivid
memories so that the key ones are 'distilled'
they break through the bonds of disability to
a   true   victory,   'consciousness',
individuation', call it what you will."
(B Schieffelin Bosanquet 1983).
    In the eighties, a comment comes from a letter
to a daughter:
  "When the thought of what next is presented to you
  in the eighties it has a way of obtruding itself
  in the quiet lonely hours." (Bosanquet)
    Grappling with the problem presented by the
difference in perception on old age de Beauvoir
(1972) writes: "The unrealizable is my being seen
from without which bounds all my choices and which
constitutes their reverse aspect - old age is
something beyond my life, outside it, something of
which I cannot have any full inward experience."
This passage tries to come to grips with the lack of
fit between the outward appearance and the inward
reality.
    To conclude the section of personal glimpses
from writings, a very old lady of ninety-eight, who
had been raised as a Quaker, reverted to living
silently 'in the Spirit', when age, poor eyesight,
and severe deafness, were combined. Occasionally
she spoke, and her significant sayings were noted.
Amongst these were:
  "May I see this time as an honour, and not as a
  ludicrous mistake."
  "I feel I am dead and only an unimportant
  little bit of me remains. I would like to
  hurry away. I don't know who I am."
  "I must let go everything." (Jones 1972)

Poetry

    Poetry offers a way of distilling, of reaching
and communicating a wider audience. Some poets
continue to write, explore and express themselves
into old age.
  Perhaps I have ended doing, effective doing,
  "Si vieillesse pouvait", the bitter screed
  runs to rust,
  Limbs stiffen, energy is not in excess
  Of need that must be met. Perhaps I have done
  The best of my work, and must work clumsily
  now -

But there's one word that rings with curious
comfort,
I can watch and indeed I think I see exquisite
things
That never before gave me such haunting joy,
Such pangs of sharp edged pleasure, such surprise
If I am confined to a mile or two of country
I shall never be starved:
  ...
Old age is flooded with unexpected delights -
Sprung from the brimming cup of eternity
                                        (Cropper 1983)
    But it does not have to be poetry of great
literary merit to give satisfaction. Nursery
rhymes, folk songs, pop songs; old age has its fun
too.
    The song of the Eighties written by one
octogenarian to another
  v.2   Oh isn't it fun to be eighty
        Your wit seems unquestioned in age
        Your lightest pronouncement is weighty
        Your nonsense confirms you a sage
        The chestnuts that yesterday slighted
        Are rare marrons glacee today
        The youngsters applaud them delighted
        Oh yes! Being eighty is gay. (E S Bosanquet)
    Another short poem is circulating from one
octogenarian to another, from as far afield as
Canada and South Africa. It is called I'm Fine by
W A Bradley:
        It's better to say "I'm fine" with a grin
        Than to let folks know the shape we're in
        How do I know my youth is all spent
        Well my "get up and go" has "got up and went"
                                (many more verses)
    This one is now circulating on linen tea
towels!
    This leads one on to consider the possibility
of running poetry groups, encouraging older people
either to write poetry for themselves, or to read
and discuss other people's poems. (Getzel 1980)

Social Work with Old People: Alternative Approaches
to Intervention

    The ways used in the previous section to
compile additional material giving insight into how
old women feel about their ageing are all applicable
to social workers and voluntary helpers, in the

neighbourhood or in residential care. the use of letters, writings, shared poems (The ubiquitous use of the poem 'Katie'), narratives, collected projects could all be explored in a variety of settings, whether with individuals, their families, in small groups, or in larger clubs.

So far much of what has been said could refer to older people, older women, in any kind of companionate relationship, and social work has not been in the forefront of the discussion. But any social worker can use and learn from these methods. One way in social work education, to help student social workers tune in to older people, could be by project work on reminiscence. Social workers too experience societal stereotypes of ageing (DHSS 1978), and need to unlearn, to be sensitized, before they can begin to give attention to the person before them, as a prelude to planned activity. The pity is that at present with current pressures, social work must give precedence to social service delivery; an old person becomes a client whose need must be classified according to available resources and often 'felt wants' must in those terms be redefined as 'not needs', in other words, as not something a social service manager believes merits priority. The research study carried out in 1981 (Froggatt 1982) which focussed on following through some forty referrals to a social service department seemed to indicate that taking enough time to visit newly bereaved clients was something social workers really needed a mandate from a line manager to undertake. It was not easily seen as a high enough priority in its own right.

Feminists are beginning to write about older women and old age. Social workers who adopt a feminist perspective in their other work should see this area of work too as one which needs positive discrimination of time and effort to help older women cope with their experience of being doubly disadvantaged by sex and age, and to change their perception of themselves. (Hale 1983). One way might be to acknowledge with them in recall, narrative or writings, the roles they have sustained throughout life, the child rearing, kin-keeping roles. (Rosenthal 1983). These have been followed by roles sustaining friends, relatives and peers. (de Graves 1983).

Acknowledgement may be helpful too of how life for them has often been determined by their relationship to the most dominant male in their intimate circle, a dominance sometimes mediated by a humorous dismissive resistance. 'Him and his ways'. I believe those who are old today sometimes have a strong sense of opportunity having passed them by, in terms of the changing role and status of women in society. While they maybe dutifully gave a high and inevitable priority to caring for their elderly relatives, any shortfall on the part of carers of this generation can be seen as part of the changing expectations of women, and possibly experienced with a certain jealousy, of opportunities not so readily offered or grasped then. All of this complex agenda of the changing position and status of women, and of the continuing victimisation of women, especially older women, could be discussed as appropriate with older women who are interpreting their lives in society. This point is elaborated clearly by Nett (1983).

Social workers can continue to use a broad range of methods, and could be more optimistic and adventurous. Family relationships do not disappear, in fact, they are of fresh significance, when adult children have to take responsibility for ageing parents. So there are descriptions in recent literature of family therapy (Quinn and Keller 1981), psychotherapy (Goodstein 1982), task-centred work (Furtune and Rathbone McCuan 1981), crisis intervention, and group work (Brandler 1977). The involvement of old men in this work and in mixed sex groups must also be seen as important for them and for their female contemporaries.

The evaluative research of Goldberg points to positive ways of helping with the inevitable practical problems of declining years, and in a dialogue on cost effectiveness clearly questions the value of case work. (Goldberg 1981). By contrast Rees and Wallace (1982) have evidence of the recognition of the value of intangible help to older people. Pincus considers ways of helping individuals (1981) and Sher (1983) describes recent psychotherapy in this country with an older woman. Howie (1983) gives an account of group work with elderly people using bibliotherapy to write poetry and share readings and experience.

As already suggested, working with the oldest women almost inevitably involves contact with the older women who care for them. Just as child care involves two generations, so does old-care, the work

with the person, and the work with the carer.
Practical reliefs, services provided, and needs met
are essential, but so also is the recognition of the
impact of being a cared for person, and of needing
to be a carer, needing to be a parent to one's
parent, a child to one's child. These role
reversals are painful matters, and mostly ignored.
Talking through feelings produces no dramatic
results, no measurable research, yet guilt and
bitterness eased, thankfulness and acknowledgement
expressed, can all help the oldest people, the
oldest women on their road which Margery Fry (1954)
describes as "the inevitable end which each must
face, whether in the bright light of faith or the
dimmer equanimity of reason." Working with the
older and oldest women must acknowledge the reality
of imminent or eventual dying, and because the time
is so uncertain, the longer people live the more
immortal they seem to be and so the more difficult
it can become. It is important that any attempt to
re-evaluate experience with the person is not just
going through the motions of paying attention.
Listening to repetitive stories can be helpful if
the pattern is picked up and understood. Pincus
(1970) contributed a full understanding of the uses
of reminiscence. To allow someone to ramble on
without direction can be using oneself as an anodyne
listener, helpful up to a point, but could it be
quietly controlling? An experience of collective
reminiscence in a day centre focussing on the First
World War showed how a group could pool memories to
explore themselves. (Froggatt 1984).

Conclusion

Remaining One's Self
     This qualitative reflection on the experience
of being old has drawn together threads from a
disparate range of resources to add to our
understanding of ageing. Is it not the hope of all
of us that whatever the vagaries of vicissitudes of
life we may remain ourselves? And are not the
indications from the contributors of this
compilation that this is indeed so? Old people (old
men must surely be included), do remain themselves,
minding about the hurts of earlier years, keeping
secrets that have long been kept, rejoicing in the
happinesses across the years - 'We were very happy
as children'. We who observe old age rather than as

yet participating must marvel at the way a person can flit back and forth across time and say which now feels the most important period. Learning to pay close attention to where the person is in memory, as well as in physical and mental health may be the extra dimension we have to add in the composite of knowledge that makes up social gerontology. And gerontological social work could raise its head and lose its self-denigrating status if the richness of understanding in coming to terms with, for example, seventy years of sibling rivalry were seen for what it is, or the strengths of a marriage understood in terms of the depth of commitment necessary to care for a declining spouse. All the knowledge, skill and feeling which is needed for social work in the earlier stages of life comes to the fore in social work with old people and their carers. What is also needed are the imaginative leaps necessary to visualise that which has not yet been much described from the inside: the hidden world of old women and old men. The fact that society would prefer not to acknowledge the painful reality of that hidden world, that society ignores the double stigma of old women makes it all the more important for social workers and voluntary workers to speak out. Within all the constraints we have to find a way of creating and realising meaning for the very last years, especially for those women who are experiencing it right now, in a state of structural disadvantage, of powerlessness, and often in invisibility. This struggle to add meaning is after all ultimately for ourselves.

References

Abrams, M. (1978) Beyond Three Score Years and Ten, Age Concern

Baker, Winer M. and Taggart, White M. (1982) 'Depression as the Search for the Lost Self', Psychotherapy, Theory Research and Practice, 19, (4)

de Beauvoir, S. (1972) Old Age, Andrew Deutsch, Weidenfeld and Nicholson

Blyth, L. (1981) View in Winter, Penguin

Bosanquet, E.S. (1964) Private Communication

Bosanquet, E.S. (1983) Private Communication

Conrad, M. (1983) 'No discharge in this war' in Women as Elders: Resources for Feminist Research,

11, (2)

Cropper, M. (1983) Poems, W G Print, Kendal

DHSS (1978) Social Services: The Practitioner's View, HMSO

Evers, H. (1981) 'Care or Custody' in Hutter and Williams Controlling Women: The Normal and the Deviant, Croom Helm

Evers, H. (1983) 'Elderly Women and Disadvantage' in D. Jerrome (ed.) Ageing in Modern Society, Croom Helm

Fennel, Phillipson and Wenger (1983) 'The Process of Ageing: Social Aspects' in DHSS Elderly People in the Community: their Service Needs, HMSO

Froggatt, A. (1982) 'The Initial Assessment of Frail Elderly People Within Social Services' unpublished paper delivered at IASSW Congress Research Seminar, Brighton

Froggatt, A. (1983) 'In Sickness and in Health', Community Care, No. 484

Froggatt, A. (1984) 'Keeping the Home Fires Burning' New Age, No. 75

Fry, M. (1955) 'Old Age Looks at Itself', National Old People's Welfare Council pamphlet

Getzel, G. (1980) 'Old People, Poetry and Groups', J. of Gerontological Social Work, 3, (1)

Glampson, A. and Goldberg, E.M. (1976) 'Post-Seebohm Services - The Consumers' View, Social Work Today, 8, (6)

Gibson, F. (1984) 'Ulster Remembers', unpublished paper to accompany slides, New University of Ulster

Goldberg, E.M. (1981) 'So what about Social Work?' in E.M. Goldberg and S. Hatch (eds.) A New Look at the Personal Social Services, PSI Discussion Paper No. 4

Goldberg, E.M. and Connelly, N. (1982) The Effectiveness of Social Care of the Elderly, Policy Studies Institute

de Graves, D. (1983) 'Women Caring for Women' in Women as Elders: Resources for Feminist Research, 11, (2)

Hardman, D. (1983) Private Communication

Howie, M. (1983) 'Bibliotherapy in Social Work', Brit.Journal of Social Work, 13 (3)

Jeffery, M. (1983) 'The Over Eighties in Britain: The Social Constrictions of Panic', Journal of Public Health Policy, 4, (3)

Jones, L.G. (1982) Private Communication

Kuypers, J.A. and Trute, B. (1978) 'The older family

as the focus of crisis intervention', The Family
Co-ordinator, 27, (4), 405-412

McLaren, A. (1983) 'The Myth of Dependency' in Women
as Elders: Resources for Feminist Research, 11,
(2)

Marshall, M. (1983) Social Work with Old People,
MacMillan

Moore, K. (1983) Summer at the Haven, Allison and
Busby

Neth, E.M. 'A call for feminist correctives to
Research on Elders' in Women as Elders: Resources
for Feminist Research, 11, (2)

Newton, Ellen (1980) This Bed my Centre, Virago

Obler, L.K. 'Sex Differences in Ageing' in Women as
Elders: Resources for Feminist Research, 11, (2)

Perrick, P. (1983) 'Home is Where the Life Force
is', The Times, 27.4.83

Pincus, A. (1970) 'Reminiscence in Ageing and its
Implication for Social Work Practice', Social
Work, July 47-53

Pincus, L. (1981) Challenge of a Long Life, Faber
and Faber

Rees, R. and Wallace, A. (1982) Verdicts on Social
Work, E. Arnold

Ritcey, S. 'Substituting an Interactionist for a
Normative model in Gerontological Research' in
Women as Elders: Resources for Feminist Research,
11, (2)

Rosenthal, C. 'Family Responsibilities and Concern'
in Women as Elders: Resources for Feminist
Research, 11, (2)

Sher, M. (1983) 'Psychodynamic Work with Clients in
the Latter Half of Life', Journal of Social Work
Practice, 1, (1)

Sontag, S. (1979) 'The Double Standard of Ageing' in
V. Carver and P. Liddiard The Ageing Population,
Hodder and Stoughton

Scott, M. (1981) Ageing for Beginners, Blackwell

West, R. (1983) 'The Memory of All That', Sunday
Telegraph, 19.12.83

Williams, Ellis A. (1983) All Stracheys are Cousins,
Weidenfeld and Nicholson

Yarrow et al (1981) 'Marriage and the Elderly',
Canadian J. of Social Work, 7, (2)

Walker, A. (ed.) (1982) Community Care, Paul
Blackwell and Martin Robertson

Chapter Five

VOLUNTARY ASSOCIATION AND THE SOCIAL CONSTRUCTION OF OLD AGE

Dorothy Jerrome

Introduction

Voluntary association in old age - i.e. social relationships with individuals or groups entered into by choice - has aroused sporadic interest in American and British gerontology in recent decades. Enquiries into patterns of voluntary association have normally rested on the assumption that it has implications for social integration, or the lack of it. The focus has been levels of participation, measured in terms of number and frequency of contacts with associates, and attendance rates at meetings.

More recently enquiries have been conducted with different theoretical perspectives into the social characteristics of participants and the social processes involved in the formation and conduct of voluntary, informal relationships. Attention has been paid to the content and quality of interaction, its meaning for the social actors and implications for identity. This more phenomenological approach guides the current discussion of social participation in old age.

In this paper I examine the age composition of particular social networks. Beginning with those which are age-homogeneous I attempt to account for the choice of peers in terms of the reduced status and the need for security in some elderly people. I go on to discuss the experience of older people in age-mixed settings and, with reference to the social organisation of a church community, speculate about their effect on the ageing experience. I start with the most intimate level of interaction: the primary group.

Voluntary Association and the Social Construction of Old Age

Peer Grouping in Old Age

Primary groups are traditionally defined in terms of continual face-to-face contact, small size, long-term commitment, affectivity, and diffuse and non-instrumental role relations. But Dono and others (1979), following Litwak and Szelenyi (1969), argue that primary groups have different structures and functions. Thus the primary group consisting of kin is characterised by permanence and long-term commitment but often lacks propinquity. A primary group based in a neighbourhood tends to lack permanence and long-term commitment: it is propinquity which underlies the primary-type exchanges which go on. A primary group consisting of friends may lack both permanence and propinquity. Based on free choice and mutal attraction, it is characterised by affectivity and matching of status, age and interests in its members.

In terms of permanence, propinquity and affectivity, then, primary group structures vary. They also perform different functions in an individual's life. Broadly speaking, tasks involving long-term commitment are undertaken by kin and tasks involving immediate and short-term commitment are taken on by neighbours. The provision of companionship, advice and other exchanges requiring positive affect and shared life experiences lies with friends.

Dono and his colleagues go on to speculate about the effect of age on primary group structures and functions. The changes associated with age - physical frailty, income loss, increased leisure, ageism - are likely to affect both primary group structure and function. Increasing frailty, for instance, is likely to increase reliance upon primary networks which are mixed in terms of age - kin and neighbours. Loss of income and an increase in leisure, on the other hand, is likely to promote primary group ties with peers, with similar life experiences, expectations, tastes and needs for companionship and moral support at a time of status loss and role change. The suggestion is that primary group ties involving peers might assume greater importance in the early years of retirment, giving way to kinship ties with the onset of physical frailty in old age.

The task-specific model of primary groups adopted by Dono and his colleagues is shown to be

Voluntary Association and the Social Construction of Old Age

theoretically and empirically more reliable than those of other writers. A limitation of their approach, however, is the tendency to ignore class and gender as variables in primary group formation. In their model age is the only variable. But we know that peer grouping takes different forms among men and women with different social backgrounds, some (e.g. middle-class women) relying on informal friendship networks, others (e.g. working-class women) finding peer group support in formal settings such as old people's clubs.

Chris Harris (1983) is also concerned with peer grouping, and shares the view of Dono et al that it is a phenomenon of old age. One would expect peer grouping to occur "when the life experiences of successive age cohorts are radically different, leading to the creation of distinctive age-related cultural styles ... It is also found at points in the life course characterised by transition between statuses and by normative confusion." Peer grouping is a mechanism whereby deprived people associate with others similarly deprived, hence reducing the sense of deprivation and avoiding exposure to people who might reinforce it.

Harris is primarily interested in voluntary associations and not primary groups though he explains increased participation in the former by elderly working-class women in terms of their inadequate primary group ties. Like peer grouping, associational activity is likely to occur at certain points in the life cycle, namely when various activities and relationships are lost: One would expect both associational participation and peer grouping to increase in old age; the former to make up for losses in activity and relationships, the latter to reduce the sense of deprivation arising from lack of status. For some old people with a history of active participation in associations it may be possible to find peers within these associations. Middle-class people are likely to be able to do this. For others, joining clubs may be a novel experience which meets the need for both companionship and activity and for solidarity with similarly placed individuals.

Old people's clubs (OPCs), which are age-homogeneous and (claims Harris, though this is questionable) established by old people themselves, can be understood in this light. Their main participants are elderly working-class women who

objectively are the most deprived and who, with the
lowest rates of associational participation in
earlier life, are the least able to find a
supportive peer group within their existing
networks. Thus Harris establishes the tendency for
voluntary grouping to occur in old age, through
informal arrangements in the case of middle-class
men and women and to an extent working-class men,
and for the working-class women through formal
organisations. The organisations favoured by
middle-class elderly tend to be age mixed, except
for those founded by and for themselves for
political purposes (such as the University of the
Third Age; see also Rose 1960). Supporting evidence
of the predominance of working-class women in clubs
for the elderly is found in Abrams (1980), Unruh
(1983) and Wenger (1984).

Drawing together the work on primary groups and
voluntary associations, we might conclude that
elderly people's needs for status and security can
be - and are often - met within the peer group.
(For another discussion of peer grouping in old age,
see Keith, 1982).

Two other studies of old people who choose to
associate with their peers makes this clear. There
are parallels between the role of OPCs and the
Jewish day centre described by Hazan (1974, 1981,
1983). In his essay (1983), "Discontinuity and
identity', Hazan is interested not so much in peer
grouping or the existence of primary-type activities
as in the issues of continuity through the life
span. It is almost taken for granted that the
social vacuum created by retirement and ageing will
be filled with contents and meanings drawn from the
individual's past. But this need not be the case.
For some populations discontinuity of ties and past
involvements serves as a resource in the
construction of new identities. One such population
is the group of poor Jewish immigrants in East
London who together have achieved a new, viable
social reality based on the loss of kinship ties,
disintegration of community life and increasing
dependence on charity. All mention of real family -
the sons and daughters who have let them down - is
banned, and a structure of egalitarian fraternity
has been substituted for the breakdown of family
relationships. This disintegrated community has
been replaced by a system of care and help among

members. The stigma of the association with the
Jewish Welfare Board has been obliterated through
the creation of autonomy and the stress on self-
reliance within the centre. Surprisingly, then, the
creation of a social vacuum, far from producing
personal disintegration, is a necessary precondition
and invaluable resource for social integration in
old age. "The relinquishing of irrelevant,
meaningless bonds enabled people to reform and
reconstitute   their   social   world, transforming
themselves from being a scattered category of
stigmatised persons into a defined and viable
group."

The absence of social continuity is a critical
difference between the Jewish day centre and other
old-age segregated environments such as the
retirement community described by Jennie Keith
(1977). One-hundred and twenty seven people live at
Les Floralies, a glass and concrete building made up
of one-bedroom apartments in a working-class suburb
of Paris. Les Floralies is a community in a sense
of being a territorial unit with its own highly
developed social organisation and a strong sense of
we-feeling, "We old people ..." "We working people
... "We people who lived through the wars ..." and
"We residents." This is a product of shared social
backgrounds and prospects. Friendships, sexual
ties, pseudo-kinship; distinctive norms about sex
and death; internally focused conflicts; resistance
to outside status ranking; reciprocity of goods and
services; support for ill or handicapped; autonomous
definition of roles and formal activities: all these
make Les Floralies a community.

Keith's main interest in her article "Old Age
and Community Creation" (1980) is the extent to
which age-homogeneous units do or do not form
communities as she defines the term. Her analysis
of the eight other ethnographic studies which have
been conducted by American Gerontologists in
retirement communities is useful in identifying the
factors which promote or inhibit community
formation. Negative factors include the absence of
communal facilities such as dining room, and
directors who refuse to allow participation in
decision-making. Positive factors include social
homogeneity, an absence of perceived alternatives,
high investment in the situation and a move which is
irreversible.

Keith concludes from the evidence that peer

relationships can meet important needs for old
people. Because of this we need to know more about
their friendships, groups and communities. It is,
claims Keith, essential to extend ethnographic and
anthropological research on ageing to the vast
majority of old people who do not live in separate
residential settings. The data we have so far are
predominantly quantitative: how many and what kinds
of contacts old people have with what categories of
individuals. We need to know the significance to
old people of different types of ties to peers and
others.

In the light of the evidence offered by Harris,
Hazan and Keith it seems clear that peer grouping is
an important principle about which we need to know
more, particularly at the level of meaning, the
significance such arrangements have for
participants, the identities and roles they manage
to negotiate among themselves. In view of the
obvious benefits of membership of a peer group, it
might be even more interesting to ask about the
experience of older people in age-mixed settings.
What do we know about old people in age-
heterogeneous settings? Is the experience
personally damaging? Do age-mixed clubs and
associations provide arenas for the acting out of
conventional age roles, and confirmation of negative
stereotypes?

Age-mixed groupings

We do not know much about age-relations in
voluntary associations. Some writers suggest that
age-mixing of this sort is relatively rare. The
anthologist Christine Fry notes that formal and
informal associations where an individual exercises
choice in deciding whether or not to participate are
likely to be homogeneous. Friendship cliques and
most voluntary associations are noted for the
commonalities in interests and other features,
including age (Fry 1980). But using the variables
of class and gender as well as age, Chris Harris has
argued that this preference for age-homogeneous
settings is class-specific. Middle-class people
have a distinct preference for the opposite: age-
mixed settings (unless the homogeneous grouping is
one that they have organised themselves and can be
seen as demonstrating skill and ingenuity). The
argument that middle-class people wish to avoid

identification with older people and do so by
continuing to operate in the heterogeneous clubs and
associations of earlier adulthood is convincing.
But we do not know enough about the interpersonal
processes of such associations to pronounce on their
significance for ageing.

A detailed account of social participation in
later life which goes some way towards supplying
this information, is David Unruh's Invisible Lives
(1983). Unruh uses the concept of the social world
to show how elderly people are integrated into
society. Their participation may be hard to
measure, for social worlds - of stamp collecting, TV
viewing, square-dancing, for example - are marked by
fluidity, informality and an absence of bureaucratic
roles and territorial boundaries. Participants can
move freely in and out of social worlds, their
involvement varying in intensity and possibly
unacknowledged by other participants. In terms of
age, Unruh identifies worlds which are youthful,
age-mixed and older. His interest is in the quality
of involvement in a social world rather than simply
frequency of attendance of named associations, and
this enables him to clarify the roles played by
elderly people and their personal significance.

Old people do not occupy strategic positions in
youthful worlds. Participants of all ages are
involved in the worlds of bicycling and auto racing,
but the largest proportion of people in roles of
leadership, importance and high visibility are
youthful. Even in age-mixed worlds, such as the art
world, old people do not occupy central positions.
They are there but invisible, in nooks and crannies,
seeking prominence when their ages or age-related
disabilities can be disguised, as in the case of the
disabled artist who exhibited her work anonymously.
Many choose to remain marginally integrated through
the media. It is only in older worlds that old
people hold positions of leadership and power.

In short, older people who are integrated into
younger worlds tend to engage in activities that
situate them near the periphery of social world
involvement - consuming and perhaps collecting,
rather than creating, evaluating, marketing, or
organising. Those engaged in central activities are
considered exceptional. In Unruh's descriptions we
come closer to an answer to the question posed
earlier: What is the experience of older people in
age-mixed settings? How significant are other age

groups in the ageing process?

In the age-mixed worlds of square dancing and cycling, cultural stereotypes are reaffirmed through a process of inverted ageism. Jack's return to the world of square dancing with a heart condition and other signs of physical ageing made him an object of admiration. Never mind that Jack occasionally slowed the pace of the entire group because of his diminished capacities, what mattered was his involvement. Fred, similarly, stood out among fellow cyclists on account of his age. He felt obliged to continue not only for himself and his friends but for old people everywhere. He had come to view himself as a symbol of what the aged are capable of doing if they have his courage, stamina and resources. To his fellow participants he was a wonderful man, perhaps the exception that proves the rule of failing powers with age.

Even in older worlds, younger people sometimes occupy strategic positions, and negative stereotypes are confirmed. Unruh describes a senior citizen's centre whose middle-aged director refuses to allow activities unsuitable for the stereotypical "old person" in spite of pressure from members.

A social world not mentioned in Unruh's study (because it did not, presumably, feature in the lives of his middle-class Californian informants) is the age-mixed world of Bingo. Bingo is very popular among considerable numbers of elderly working-class women in Britain (Dixey & Talbot 1982). Half of the bingo playing population are over 55, a quarter over 66. In 1982, people in their late 70s and older amounted to 20 per cent of all bingo players. If they play at all, they play regularly, making more visits per week than any other age group. Of these very old people, 12 per cent played every day, 42 per cent three times a week or more, 32 per cent twice a week and 11 per cent only once a week. Only 5 per cent played less frequently. The public leisure life of elderly working-class women, it seems, revolves around bingo halls and social clubs (where bingo is also played).

Older people are said by younger people (and the researchers) to participate largely for the company, as a response to loneliness. The club is often their only point of contact with other people: the only alternative is the pub. One might speculate that they are accepted on other people's terms consistent with popular stereotypes, as lonely

old people in search of company. Alternatively,
perhaps in the world of bingo, a game of chance with
big prizes, age matters little and the elderly
winner acquires a status unobtainable in the world
outside. The researchers were not primarily
interested in age-relations and in their discussion
of elderly players appear to be influenced by
popular stereotypes. One would need to approach the
game differently to see how, through social
interaction, age categories are constructed.

From these brief references to age-
heterogeneous settings it can be argued that old age
is socially constructed in formal and informal
groupings through the interaction of members.
Without more detailed evidence of social processes
the way in which this happens is a matter for
speculation. But the anthropological accounts of
homogeneous groups such as the Jewish day centre
indicate the sort of questions we might be asking
about heterogeneous ones. Through the principle of
caring for each other, elderly Jews assert
themselves against the management, professional
caretakers and neglectful children. Are there
status preserving mechanisms in other old people's
clubs with ageist directors? or in Bingo clubs?

Age-mixed settings are not necessarily inimical
to elderly people's age interests. There are some,
such as churches, in which conventional age
relations are modified by occasional role reversals,
and the value system enables elderly people to
confront some of the dilemmas of ageing in a youth-
oriented society.

It may be significant that membership of
churches and church based groups is a popular form
of social participation in retirement. (See Table
1). Religious observance and membership of
religious organisations is even higher in rural
areas such as rural Wales, where almost half of the
population of retired men and women attend church or
chapel monthly or more (Wenger 1984). For many
people, participation in church and church-based
activities is a novel experience. Abrams (1980)
found that for 2/3 of the middle-class (AB) members
of church-based groups association dated from
childhood and early adult life. Nearly half the
working-class members, however, had joined after
passing their 60th birthday.

TABLE 1

Leisure of the Elderly and Social Class, by age, sex and household

Percentage in each group who belong to named organisations
and attend its meetings at least once a month

	clubs for elderly	sports clubs	social clubs	church groups	church attend.	polit. parties	T.U.S.	other clubs
WOMEN, 65-74								
Middle class living alone	11	11	7	18	35	2	2	8
not living alone	5	4	13	9	36	1	0	15
Working class living alone	19	0	8	13	30	0	0	12
not living alone	8	1	10	8	20	0	0	4
MEN, 65-74								
Middle class	3	12	17	12	27	1	0	9
Working class	5	5	10	5	12	2	1	9

(M.Abrams, B.S.G. Annual Conference, Aberdeen 1980)

Voluntary Association and the Social Construction of Old Age

The Church: a case study

The last part of this paper consists of some preliminary observations of age relations in a church community with which I am slightly acquainted. My comments are based on participant observation in half a dozen church services and some related church activities, involvement in one of the youth movements of the church and a content analysis of a dozen of its newsletters.

Florence Road Baptist Church is in a socially mixed residential area in central Brighton. Its 120 members - 50 men and 70 women - tend to be middle-aged and elderly though it has thriving companies of boys' and girls' brigades and a fairly large Sunday school. The average Sunday morning service attracts about 60 people, two-thirds of them over 50 and two-thirds women, a handful of widowed men and about 25 single people divided between older women and young people of both sexes. In social class terms there is little spread: the church is uniformly lower-middle and upper working-class. In terms of doctrine and practice is is non-evangelical, a church rather than a sect (Wilson 1959).

In one of my earliest encounters I was made aware of the importance of age as a social category. At the end of a Sunday morning service an elderly woman invited me warmly to come to the women's meeting the next day. "Of course, they're nearly all elderly, not like you, you're young to us. But our visiting speaker, she's younger ... but older than you! Do come ..." Younger people operate with similar categories. A woman in her thirties had difficulty in identifying her mother - a member of the Ladies' singing group - to me. "She's the one with the glasses and a grey dress" - shamefaced laugh - "They all look like that, don't they?" Her comment relegated her mother to the uniform, category of 'old person', the existence of which she acknowledged with an embarrassed laugh.

A third case of age consciousness occurred at a morning service, held to commemorate the Sunday School Anniversary. The visiting speaker, himself an ex-Sunday School superintendent, was in his 70s but looked 25 years younger. In the space of a few minutes he showed a preoccupation with age, his own in particular through two jokes:
"I was afraid he (the former pupil, now grownup, who introduced him) was going to

say 'my old Sunday School superintendent!'"
"Way back in the 1930s - you didn't hear
that, did you?" and a comment: "Now, if I
were to ask people's ages they'd be very
offended ..."
The address was carefully composed to suit the large
youthful element in the congregation. But at the
same time it could be interpreted as dealing with
problems of age and time. There were readings from
The Book of Genesis, references to the problems of
beginning and to the importance of planting ideas in
the minds of new generations who grow up and take
over. It would be said that in this message the
speaker was confronting the dilemma faced by older
people in our society: of not wanting to age but of
having to acknowledge the existence of rising
generations. In some organisations there are no
social mechanisms for resolving this dilemma. In a
WEA branch committee with which I am acquainted, the
more youthful members, defined as rebels by the
elderly executive offers, are discredited and
disqualified from competition. The incumbents
operate in a timeless world which denies the reality
of ageing. In the church, religious beliefs help
the aged to be reconciled to their situation, and
public proclamations from the pulpit on behalf of
the congregation minimise the loss of face involved
in this. Indeed, the older generation are given an
important role in socialising the young and a
lifespan perspective is advanced which gives place
to both age groups.
All the services that I have attended make some
reference to time, and the ephemeral quality of
human life. The following verse is typical,
reassuring with its message of continuity.
Frail as summer's flower we flourish;
Blows the wind - and it is gone.
But while mortals rise and perish,
God endures unchanging on.
H.F. Lyte (Baptist Hymn Book No. 23)
The Sunday School Anniversary goes beyond ordinary
acts of worship in providing an occasion for
conscious acknowledgement of problems of age and
time. Easter services, again emphasise in an
obvious way the principle of regeneration, and the
cyclical nature of time.
Mother's Day services, too, can be seen to
confront and resolve certain dilemmas. Mothering
Sunday, taking place the day after the Spring Tea

party, provides the older women of the church with
their opportunity to plan the services and take part
in running them. At the morning service flowers are
handed to every woman in the congregation, whether
technically deserving or not, and the importance of
kinship - real and fictive - is thereby underlined.
Filial piety on the occasion of my visit -
especially towards one's mother - was stressed in a
fierce address delivered by an elderly woman who on
weekdays sells bread in a local bakery. Motherhood
demanded sacrifice and children - both young and
adult - should be eternally thankful. Her remarks
were put into perspective afterwards when it
transpired that several of her closest friends were
caring for frail old parents, one at least with
great difficulty. Possibly for the woman who gave
the address, the occasion provided an outlet for
negative feelings and a chance to come to terms
with the strain and sacrifice involved in the caring
role. One could see how in the context of the
church old age might be converted from a personal
burden into an opportunity for service and thence
become a route to salvation. This conversion might
lessen the sense of obligation on one side and
exploitation on the other.
     Kinship networks are fairly extensive in the
church community. The intermarriage of succeeding
generations of church families has produced a close-
knit core of people with multifaceted ties. The
Brigade, the Sunday School, the running of the
church (by a group of Deacons), the Women's
Fellowship and liaison with other Baptist Churches
in the district, all provide the opportunity for
involvement and interaction with others in the
community. Different facets of church life draw
commitment at different stages of the life cycle.
For the women in particular there are opportunities
for social contact. There are three women's
meetings during the week, though nothing exists
exclusively for the men. In the words of the
minister, "There used to be a men's Cosy Corner Club
but it folded. Men are good at coming together to
do something but not just to be together."
     Indeed, the heavy presence of elderly women
gives an impression of power and influence not
available to elderly women in society at large. But
elderly women do not, in fact, achieve office in
proportion to their number in the congregation.
They "have their day," it is true, in the

organisation and conduct of the Mothers' Day services and the Spring Tea Party. They also have their 3 week-day meetings, while there are no equivalents for men. But perhaps these events, which give the impression that the church is a matriarchy, simply confirm the women in their conventional service-giving roles? Certainly, in terms of address and other aspects of organisation, the style is conventionally sexist.

However, it might still be the case that participation in church-based activities provides the social status, solidarity and sense of personal significance not available to old people in the wider community. This possibility brings to mind a phenomenon identified by students of minority racial and religious groups: the use of religious and other symbolic systems to articulate their political and economic interests (Cohen 1969a), 1969b), Yinger 1946, Sundkler 1961, Jerrome 1974, Hazan 1981, 1984). Can we say that religious institutions are attractive to older people because they are among the few age-mixed institutions in our society where age is not a handicap in the attainment of high status?

Clearly, many interesting issues remain to be explored. We need to establish the salience of age in the social organisation of the church, to identify the pattern of age-relations, the age roles and the expectations governing the behaviour of church members in the context of church activities and outside them. In anthropological terms, the object should be to trace the extent of age differentiation - the extent to which age is a social boundary (Keith 1982). Age differentiation has several dimensions: the categories people use (cognitive dimension); beliefs about appropriate behaviour (normative/ideological dimension); the pattern of social ties (interactional dimension); and membership of formal groups (corporate dimension). More specifically this might involve asking who, in the context of the church, is allowed to do what, and why? Who seeks whose company for support, companionship, advice etc? Who is allowed to be intimate with whom? How much peer grouping takes place, for what purposes and with what consequences? Do members interact differently with associates who are not church members?

Voluntary Association and the Social Construction of
Old Age

CONCLUSION

In this paper I have considered social
groupings at three levels of organisation: the
primary group, the formal organisation and the
social world. I have suggested that social
participation in old age is an interesting and
under-investigated area. The choices, and
restrictions on choice, revealed through voluntary
association are insufficiently understood. My
reading of the literature suggests that the age
distribution of participants might be crucial and
that age-heterogeneous and homogeneous settings have
different implications for age roles and
identities.

Some writers, such as Dono et al and Harris,
have established theoretically and empirically that
particular groupings are popular with certain
categories of old person. I suggest that we need an
anthropological approach or, in sociological terms,
an interactionist perspective which enables us to
understand the significance of these groupings for
the ageing process.

References

Abrams, M. (1980) Beyond Three Score and Ten, 1st
    Report London: Age Concern Research Dept.
Abrams, M. (1980) Beyond Three Score and Ten, 2nd
    Report London: Age Concern Research Dept.
Cohen, A. (1969a) Customs and Politics in urban
    Africa, Routledge & Kegan Paul, London
Cohen, A. (1969b) 'Political Anthropology: the
    analysis of the symbolism of power relations:
    Man, Vol. 4. No. 2, 215-235
Dixey, R. & Talbot, M. (1982) Women, Leisure and
    Bingo, Trinity and All Saints' College, U.K.
Dono, J. et al (1979) 'Primary Groups in Old Age',
    Research on Aging, Vol. 1.4, 403-433
Fry, C. ed. (1980) Aging in Culture & Society,
    Praeger, New York
Harris, C. (1983) 'Associational Participation in
    Old Age' in D. Jerrome, ed. Ageing in Modern
    Society, Croom Helm, London
Hazan, H. (1980) The Limbo People, Routledge & Kegan
    Paul, London
Hazan, H. (1981) 'Totality as an adaptive Strategy',
    Social Anaysis, No. 9, 63-76

Voluntary Association and the Social Construction of
Old Age

Hazan, H. (1983) 'Discontinuity and Identity',
Research on Aging, Vol. 5, No. 4, 473-489
Hazan, H. (1984) 'Religion in an old age home:
symbolic adaptation as a survival strategy',
Aging & Society, Vol. 4, No. 2, 137-156
Hunt, A. (1978) The Elderly at Home, O.P.C.S.,
London
Jerrome, D. (1974) Continuity and change in the
social organisation of the Ibos in London,
unpublished Ph.D. Thesis, University of London
Jerrome, D. (1983) 'Lonely women in a friendship
club', Brit.J. Guidance and Counselling, Vol. 1,
II, 10-20
Jerrome, D. (1984) 'Good company: the sociological
implications of Friendship', Soc.Rev., Vol. 32,
No. 4
Keith, Jennie (1980) 'Old Age and community
creation', in C. Fry (ed.) Aging in Culture and
Society, Praeger, New York
Keith, Jennie (1982) Old People as People, Little &
Brown, Boston & Toronto
Litwak, E. & Szelenyi, I. (1969) 'Primary group
structures and their functions', Amer.Soc.Rev.,
Vol. 34, 465-481
Myerhoff, B. (1980) Number our Days, Simon &
Schuster, New York
Riley, M. et al (1972) Aging and Society, Vol. 3,
Russell Sage, New York
Rose, A.M. (1960) 'The Impact of Aging on Voluntary
Associations', in C. Tibbitts (ed.) Handbook of
Social Gerontology, Chicago University Press
Ross, Jennie-Keith (1975) 'Social borders:
definitions of diversity', Current Anthropology,
16, 53-72
Ross, Jennie-Keith (1977) Old People, New Lives,
Chicago University Press
Sundkler, B.G.M. (1961) Bantu Prophets in South
Africa, O.U.P., London
Unruh, D. (1983) Invisible Lives, Sage, Beverley
Hills
Ward, R. (1979) The Aging Experience, J.B.
Lippincott, New York
Wenger, C. (1984) The Supportive Network, George
Allen & Unwin, London
Wilson, B.R. (1959) 'An analysis of sect
Development', Amer.Soc.Rev., Vol. 24, 3-15
Yinger, J.M. (1946) Religion and the Struggle for
Power, Duke University Press, U.S.A.

Chapter Six

MANAGING EVERYDAY LIFE: THE TRIVIAL ROUND MADE
SIGNIFICANT

Svein Olav Daatland

Abstract

Old people spend a larger part of the day in
their dwelling than do any other adult age group.
They devote most of their time to the repetitive
activities of daily living concerned with personal
needs and household work. More than most others are
they bound to reconstruct their roles and social
identity through the trivialities of daily life, a
fact which ought to make the management of everyday
life a central field of social gerontological
research. The present paper reports from a study on
the self-sufficiency and sex-role differences of
single and couple households in their everyday
living. Samples from two Norwegian communities, a
city and a small town, is compared. How the local
environment seems to be reflected in the
organization of everyday tasks is discussed.

Introduction

Elderly people, aged 67-74, spend an average of
20 hours a day in their dwelling, according to the
Norwegian Time Budget Survey 1980-81 (Lingsom and
Ellingsater, 1983). They devote 11 hours to
personal needs (sleeping, eating, personal hygiene),
another 4 hours to household work (housework,
maintenance, family care), and have 5 hours of free
time in their dwelling, of which 2 hours are spent
in front of the TV, by the way more than any other
age group. It seems a rather private and grey
world, and would have seemed even more so had the
survey included also older persons.
Within this apparently uneventful greyness
lies, however, also true heroism. Included as
household work are for instance the efforts of this

67

woman, aged 70, who lives together with her sick and
bedridden mother of 90. Until recently the daughter
- let's call her Alma - had no assistance from the
public services. As she never married, she has
always lived with her mother, and with her
reputation as a very competent woman and
housekeeper, the home help office in this little
town probably expected her to continue working in
the care and nursing of the mother, as if Alma had
no wishes of her own, and as if she would never
herself get old.

The greatness of their small goals may be
illustrated by the following incidence: The mother
is so weak, and overweight besides, that she can
hardly get out of bed, even with Alma's help. But
the mother has one wish, one goal left in life,
which is to get upstairs one more time before she
dies. There is where the children's rooms are,
where she every night kissed Alma and her eight
brothers and sisters good night. She has this
urge to see the rooms once more. Just be there
for a moment, look out of the window, feel the
furniture.

So they try. By joint effort they manage to
get to the bottom of the stairs. Mother sits down
on the third step. This is their plan: if
mother sits down, back towards the stairs, with
her feet two steps below, she may push while Alma
bends down behind her, her arms under her
mother's arms, pulling. In this way they manage
to get to the fourth step, the fifth, the sixth. A
long break to regain their strength. Then
another effort: the seventh, the eighth. They
realize they won't make it. Mother turns, looks
up in pain. Only another six steps to go, but they
won't make it.

It takes them another hour to get down again
and to get the mother safely to bed in the living
room. Exhausted. But a new plan develops. Alma's
brother will be visiting this summer. He is strong
and three will be better than two. What a relief,
what a joy! Just another three months to wait,
another three months to look forward to.

This kind of struggle is not at all uncommon,
and may also be illustrated in statistical terms,
for instance through the fact that the probability
of being institutionalized at the age of 65 plus is
about eight to ten times greater if you are single
compared to being married (Daatland and Sundström,

1985). A considerable part of this difference is explained by the care efforts of the ageing spouse. Living with a child, like in the case presented, also prevents institutionalization.

The category "household work" includes also efforts put down on self-care. The striving for independence and self-sufficiency in everyday life is probably of major importance for old people's self-respect and dignity when they feel the risk of becoming dependent on others. The attitudes of independence are strong among the aged, and the fear of becoming a burden to their children is prominent (Daatland, 1984).

The 20 hours in the dwelling are thus not uneventful or insignificant. This is illustrated also in an anthropological study among old ladies in Oslo's west-end. These ladies had ritualized their day, and kept up their repetitive activities of their past everyday life; activities which in their present standing and life situation seemed obsolete, but still represented a successful coping strategy of the present (Danielsen, 1984).

All this ought to make social gerontologists more preoccupied with the management of everyday activities in old age. In this paper I shall look at the self-sufficiency in everyday living among single and couple households (1) in two quite different social settings - a small town and a city (2). I am not primarily interested in the activities themselves, but rather in how they are socially organized, and how we may study social structures through these seemingly trivial events.

It is only fair to warn you that I shall feel rather free to speculate on the basis of empirical data. The data are used to illustrate my points rather than as true tests of specified hypotheses. The study is based on two small samples, n = 97 (the small town) and n = 66 (the city), and does not justify detailed analysis of separate results. When I still present generalizations, or rather speculative and hypothetical generalizations, it is only - and if - the tendencies may be judged as integral parts of a larger and more general context. This larger context may be theoretically founded, or it may consist of several details from the present study which build up to a more general pattern, and may be said to constitute a "saturated" whole (3).

Self-sufficiency and help patterns

We interviewed people aged 70 and over living in their own homes. The question relevant for this paper was: Who is it that normally:

(1)   purchases the groceries
(2)   prepares the food
(3)   takes the daily light cleaning
(4)   does the heavy cleaning
(5)   keeps the clothes and linen in order
(6)   maintains the dwelling
(7)   takes care of household bills and paper work

The first three activities are regarded as "daily tasks", activities four and five as "weekly tasks", and the last two as "less frequent tasks".

If others than the interviewed person contributed to these tasks, we asked who this or these others were.

The single household (person) is regarded as self-sufficient if he/she carried out the task by him- or herself, with no outside assistance.

As the household is the unit of analysis, the married couple is regarded as self-sufficient if the interviewed person and/or the spouse are carrying out the activities with no contributions from outside.

The results are presented in diagrams 1 (small town) and 2 (city), separate for single and couple households.

The immediate impression is that these old people are managing well in their everyday life. This is particularly so for the couples. They are - as could be expected - more self-sufficient than are the single persons. For instance more than eight out of ten couples in the small town (diagram 1) are self-sufficient in all tasks except for heavy cleaning. About 1/3 of the couples report they normally have outside assistance with this particular task, while the same goes for about 2/3 of the single households.

The pattern of self-sufficiency is quite similar in the two localities which may be seen by comparing across diagrams 1 and 2. There is, however, one significant difference: city dwellers are in general more self-sufficient than small towners. We may also put it the other way around: small towners have more often outside assistance than have the city dwellers. This is the case for both single and couple households on (close to) all tasks, although the difference is most clearly expressed in the tasks which need not be done on a daily basis. Why is this? The difference seems not to be explicable on the basis of different <u>needs</u> of help. On the contrary - the city dwellers seem to be more self-sufficient despite their <u>higher</u> need of help. That is - the city sample have (in general) poorer <u>mobility</u> than the small town sample, but they are <u>still</u> more self-sufficient in their everyday life.

We are measuring mobility through self-reports. Reporting difficulties when climbing stairs <u>and</u> managing a 15 minute walk at a fair speed is considered as <u>low, or impaired mobility</u>. Having difficulties <u>with</u> one of these activities indicates <u>moderate mobility</u>, while no difficulty with either of the two activities is taken as <u>full mobility</u>.

.When the mobility in general is lower among the aged in the city (table 1), this is probably largely due to their more bothersome physical environment. Many of them live in blocks without elevators, while the small towners live in small houses, often on the ground level.

TABLE 1: Physical mobility[1] in the small town and the city, age 70+. Per cent (n).

	Low	Moderate	Full	TOTAL
The small town	26	19	56	101 (97)
The city	24	33	42	99 (66)

1) Low mobility: Difficulties with stairs <u>and</u> a 15 minute walk in fair speed
Moderate m. :   Difficulties or moderate difficulty with stairs <u>or</u> walk
Full m.   :   No difficulty with stairs or walk

In spite of their poorer mobility, the city dwellers are, as I was saying, more self-sufficient in their everyday activities than the small towners. However, both settings show a clear correlation between mobility and self-sufficiency: the better mobility, the more self-sufficient one is.

This is clearly illustrated when we plot self-sufficiency (4) against mobility in diagram 3 (daily tasks), 4 (weekly tasks) and 5 (less frequent tasks). These diagrams concern the single persons only, as we do not know the mobility of the spouses in the couple households.

It should be noted that self-sufficiency seems to be more closely related to mobility in the city sample. Note also that the city dwellers are more self-sufficient than small-towners in particular when they have full mobility. There is a cross-over effect in the case of daily tasks (diagram 3), implying that city dwellers are more self-sufficient than small towners when they have good mobility, but less self-sufficient when they have poor mobility.

When interpreting these results it should be made clear that self-sufficiency is not an indicator of the ability to perform a particular task, but simply a report of whether or not the household actually performs it. The fact that one receives help, does not necessarily imply that one needs it.

We know from this (Daatland, 1983a) and other studies (Helland et al., 1976) that small towners are closer integrated in their community than are city dwellers. They more often interact with family, friends and neighbours. In the course of such social interaction, one is exchanging also help and services, which are not necessarily, or primarily, need-orientated, but are rather a "natural part" of the interaction itself. It is probably this difference in social structure which emerges in the results. To cut a long story short, it seems to me that the management of everyday living is relatively speaking more of a private enterprise in the city, and relatively more a collective activity in the small town. The closer and tighter social network of the small town seems to be supportive to the management of daily life. With poor mobility, one manages better (are more self-sufficient) than in the city. With full mobility - and this may seem paradoxical - one seems less self-sufficient in the small town. The explanation simply being that one more often (than in the city) receives help also when one does not need it.

Supportive to this speculative conclusion is that the help system of the small towners seems the more complex of the two. The small towners not only receive outside assistance more often, they also receive help from more (types of) helpers, and these helpers are fairly often active at the same time (5). When the city dwellers receive help, they do so mostly from one source only - the home help or the children.

To summarize: I see the social structure of the two different settings reflected in the way the everyday tasks are socially organized. The city dwellers in general higher level of self-sufficiency is to a large extent explained by them being more private, left to themselves, or "alone" in their management of daily living. This is probably also the explanation for the closer relation between mobility and self-sufficiency in the city. As one is left more to oneself, one's personal mobility will affect self-sufficiency more directly.

Management of everyday tasks in marriage

Implied in the interpretation above is that the management of everyday tasks is both a practical and a symbolic activity (Freidson, 1977; Daatland, 1983b). What one does, is done relative to other people and the social relations between oneself and others. One "works" with the tasks and the social relations. One exchanges help within the family not only relative to actual needs for help, but also in order to maintain the family as a social institution. Neighbours offer their reciprocal services maybe first of all in order to "reproduce" the neighbourhood as a social system. Lack of content and mutual help in a particular neighbourhood may be resulting from social values of distance and unreachability rather than personal attitudes (Haugen, 1978).

The double meaning of the everyday activities, as tasks and as symbolic actions, is maybe most clearly seen in marriage. The distribution of tasks between the spouses tells us probably less about the husband's and wife's needs for each others' help, and more about the social relations between them, or rather - their social roles. The wife does not prepare the food or do the laundry because the husband is not able to do it, but because she is the wife and he is the husband.

Let us look at the distribution of everyday tasks within the couple households in this perspective. The wife does, as expected, more then the husband, and the sex-role differences are striking (table 2). She prepares the food and washes the clothes. He is often responsible for the maintenance of the dwelling and the paper work.

TABLE 2: Distribution of everyday tasks between husband and wife, as reported by married women and married men.

Married men : Married woman - ratio[1].

	SMALL TOWN		CITY	
	Men	Women	Men	Women
1: groceries	0.1	1.6	0.5	2.7
2: food	0	0.2	0.1	0.2
3: light cleaning	0	0.6	0.2	0.8
4: heavy cleaning	0.2	1.2	0.8	1.3
5: clothes	0	0.8	0.3	0.4
6: dwelling	5.9	1.8	1.6	1.2
7: bills/papers	0.9	11.5	1.8	∞

1) The ratio is married men's activities (measured in percentage of married men which normally do each task) divided by married women's activities. When the ratio is 1, the tasks are equally distributed in this sense. Ratios lower than 1 mean that women do more than men, ratios higher than 1 - that men do more than women.

The sign: ∞ means that married women do not participate in the task. The sign: 0 means that married men do not participate in the task.

This is a common pattern for the city and the small town. There is, however, one interesting and significant difference between the two settings: the tasks are more evenly divided in the city. In other words - there are less sex-role differences in the city relative to the small town.

I do not think these are primarily attitudinal differences. They are rather produced by structural differences. As the household is more private, or left to itself, in the city, the spouses are more dependant upon each other, which makes it imperative that they help each other out, also by carrying out tasks which traditionally "belong to" the other party.

This is precisely what Elizabeth Bott (1971) has pointed to, when she finds that tight social networks provides each of the spouses with opportunities for outside assistance with their traditional tasks, while a more "open" environment, with less tight network, makes the couple mutually dependant and produce more equal roles.

Another illustration of this point becomes evident when we compare the answers given by married men and married women. Married men report that the wife carries out most of the household work, with the exception of what we have called less frequent tasks. Married women draw a significantly different picture. According to them, the husbands are actively involved also in weekly and daily activities. (See Table 2).

Parts of the difference between what men and women report may be due to both of them being generous to each other. However, we have reports from married men and women in different marriages. The reports from the two are not different angles on the same reality (the same couple). As all interviewed persons were aged 70 and above, and as women usually are married to men who are older than themselves, the comparison between married men's and married women's reports is in fact a comparison between 'younger' and 'older' couples. This probably explains a considerable part of the variation. When married women say their husbands are actively engaged in the daily work, they talk about couples which are older than the one's the married men report about. When married men report that their wives are doing far more than themselves, they are referring to couples who are considerably younger.

The explanation why the division of tasks is more even, and the sex-role differences are less marked, in the oldest couples, lies probably in what Elizabeth Bott concluded. One becomes more dependent upon each other not only in social settings where the couple is "isolated", but also when one gets older. This "forces" the partners to help each other out in daily work, and produces a more equal distribution of tasks.

Concluding remarks

I have argued for the significance of everyday
trivialities, not only in the lives of old people,
but also as a source of information for the social
gerontologist. Through an analysis of the trivial
round, how the everyday activities are distributed
and organized, we may get insight into the social
structure beneath them. The present paper
represents no more than an illustration of ways such
an analysis may go, and the conclusions at
this stage are rather speculative. I still believe
this may prove a rewarding angle for social
gerontology. Things are not as they seem, or
rather - things are not only what they seem. The
trivial round "hides" significant social facts, in
particular for old people, as they are provided with
a social role in which the everyday activities
become their prime way of relating to society.

Notes

1) These two types of households comprise close
    to 80 per cent off all elderly households in
    today's Norway.

2) The city is represented by an older part of
    Oslo which is fairly close to the city
    centre. The small town is situated on the
    south coast including the town centre and the
    environments within a distance of approxi-
    mately three kilometers from the centre.

3) The theoretical basis for this concept is
    given by Bertaux (1982).

4) Self-sufficiency is here considered as self-
    sufficient on each of the tasks grouped as
    daily, weekly and less frequent tasks.

5) F.i. do 1/3 of the small towners which
    receive home help to heavy cleaning also
    report they have other helpers to this
    particular task. Such "co-operation" between
    helpers is far less common in the city
    sample.

References

Bertaux, D. (1982) The Life Course Approach as a
Challenge to the Social Sciences. In T. Hareven
and K.J. Adams (eds.): Ageing and Life Course
Transitions, Tavistock, New York.

Bott, E. (1971) Family and Social Network,
Tavistock, London.

Daatland, S.O. (1983a) Eldres integrasjon og
holdning til hjelp. Paper presented at the
6th Nordic Congress of Gerontology, Copenhagen.

Daatland, S.O. (1983b) Care Systems, Ageing and
Society, 3, 1.

Daatland, S.O. (1984) Holdning til hjelp og hjelpere
- endringer i løpet av 1970-årene, Gerontologisk
Magasin 1, 3.

Daatland, S.O. and Sundström, G. (1985) Gammal i
Norden, Nordic Council of Ministers, Stockholm.

Danielsen, K. (1984) Kultur, identitet og alderdom.
In I. Rudie (ed): Myk start - hard landing,
Universitetsforlaget, Oslo.

Freidson, E. (1977) The Division of Labour as
Social Interaction. In M. Haug and J. Dofny
(eds.): Work and Technology, Sage Studies in
International Sociology, 10.

Haugen, I. (1978) Om forvaltning av
utilgjengelighet, Tidsskrift for
samfunnsforskning, 5/6.

Helland, H., Solem, P.E. and Traeldal, A. (1976)
Integration of the Aged in Six Local Communities,
Norwegian Institute of Gerontology

Lingsom, S. and Ellingsaeter, A.L. (1983) Work,
Leisure and Time spent with Others, Statistical
Analysis no 49, Central Bureau of Statistics,
Oslo

Appendix: Diagrams

Diagram 1:   The Small Town

Self-sufficiency in everyday activities among single
and couple households, age 70+, in the small town

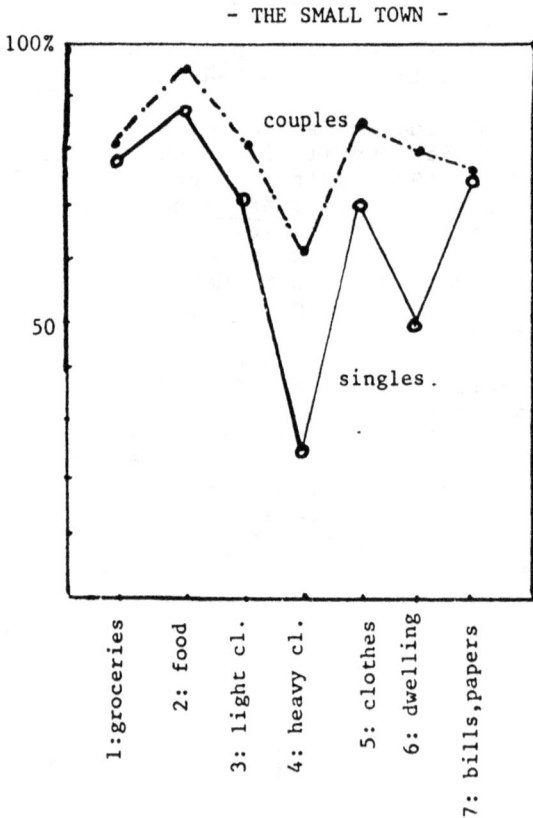

- THE SMALL TOWN -

couples

singles.

1:groceries
2: food
3: light cl.
4: heavy cl.
5: clothes
6: dwelling
7: bills,papers

Diagram 2: The City

Self-sufficiency in everyday activities among single
and couple households, age 70+, in the city

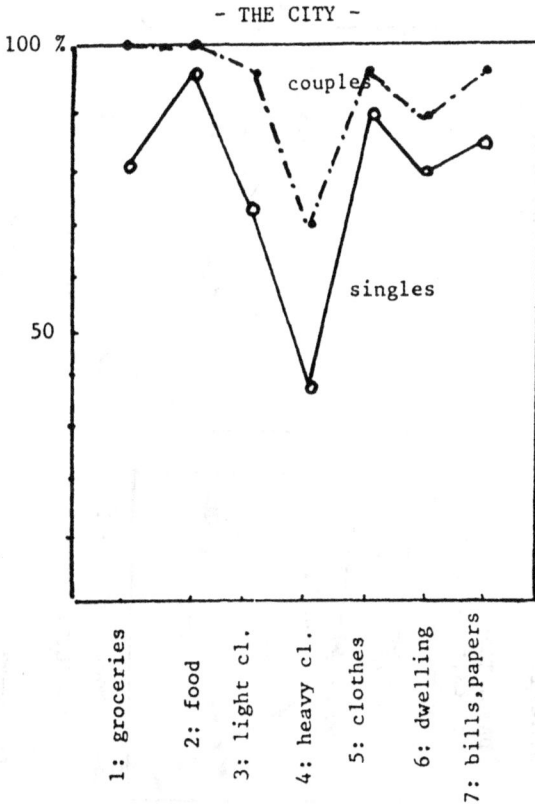

- THE CITY -

100 %

couples

singles

50

1: groceries
2: food
3: light cl.
4: heavy cl.
5: clothes
6: dwelling
7: bills,papers

Diagrams 3 to 5:

Self-sufficiency among the singles, aged 70+, for daily tasks (Diagram 3), weekly tasks (Diagram 4) and less frequent tasks (Diagram 5). (When the plot-point is within parenthesis, n is less than 10)

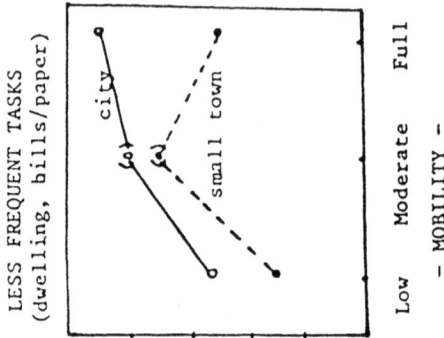

DAILY TASKS
(Groceries, food, light cl.)

Diagram 3

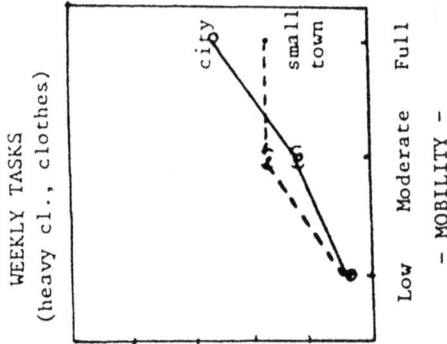

WEEKLY TASKS
(heavy cl., clothes)

Diagram 4

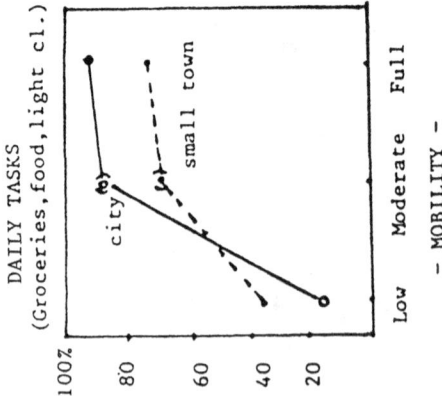

LESS FREQUENT TASKS
(dwelling, bills/paper)

Diagram 5

Chapter Seven

CONSTRAINTS TO CREATIVITY: THE CASE OF LEISURE
FACILITY MANAGERS

Miriam Bernard

Introduction

Over recent years, research into the factors
which determine participation in leisure has begun
to recognise the fact that people cannot, rather
than will not, use available leisure facilities.
This applies particularly to the older age groups,
despite the fact that in terms of time, "leisure is
one thing the elderly apparently have in abundance"
(Long and Wimbush, 1979). However, it is also
apparent that for many older people, there is a
cumulative system of constraints operating on their
leisure lives, and this restricts both the nature
and extent of their involvement. This paper sets
out to briefly explore the nature of that system,
conceptualising it as a series of hurdles which have
to be surmounted before participation becomes
possible. Following this, it then considers some of
the results of a project carried out in early 1984,
in which the managers of a number of sports and
leisure centres were questioned about their
attitudes towards older people and sport (Bernard et
al, forthcoming).

The Hurdles to Participation

Many writers now acknowledge the significance
of a range of factors which inhibit or enable people
to participate in active leisure. In terms of the
time available to pursue activities, older people
are particularly well placed to take advantage of
existing opportunities. However, we also know that
their participation levels are uniformly low, and
thus we need to look more closely at the obstacles
in their path. These obstacles will take many
forms, and will operate with varying degrees of

effect and potency. In order to try and help us understand what the major constraints might be, I have conceptualised them, since we are talking about active leisure, as a series of hurdles (see Figure 1).

The major constraints of age, sex, socio-economic status, health and mobility are familiar to us all. However, there are many important influences which, to date, have been only scantily treated in the literature. Before considering some of them in more detail, it is important to make two points concerning the nature and operation of the constraint system as presented here.

Firstly, it is important to bear in mind that these constraints can operate at two levels: the aggregate or general level, and the individual level. For example, at the aggregate level, those familiar factors such as age, sex and social class will filter out potential participants from non-participants. This is why we find that, in general, older people are less active than younger age groups and hence become classed as a disadvantaged group. But, we cannot say that these factors are causal at the level of the individual, though they will obviously have some effect on an individual's decision to participate or not. Or, as Brian Rodgers (1977) has put it, "no-one is directly disqualified from the chance to participate simply because they belong to what is - in general - a disadvantaged group".

Linked to this, is the naive belief that once we can identify constraints in this way, then simply removing them will inevitably stimulate participation (Talbot, 1979). This is manifestly not the case and suggests that we have an, as yet, inadequate understanding of the complex interrelationships within the constraint system.

Secondly, by presenting constraints as I have done here, I am not suggesting that they operate hierarchically. This diagram is obviously a simplified representation of what is a complex, fluctuating system and indeed, any constraint, operating either singly or in combination, may well prevent an older person from participating.

Turning now to some of the less familiar constraints. Under the individual constraints hurdle, I have noted 'knowledge and awareness'. It seems very obvious to say that one cannot use a facility if one does not know of its existence but,

for people who grew up in a social and educational
milieu in which public leisure provision was
minimal, their lack of awareness is not altogether
surprising. However, such factors are rarely if
ever taken into account by planners when they
estimate the potential catchment of a centre, or
calculate how well served with facilities a
particular population is.
    For older people, this also relates closely to
the constraint termed 'leisure literacy'. Eight
years ago, Rodgers (1977) termed older people
"sports illiterate", and argued that they are as
unlikely to turn to sport in middle age or
retirement, as a true illiterate is to turn to
reading. Moreover, Talbot (1979) has argued that
women are less 'trained' than men, in the kinds of
skills needed to engage in many leisure activities.
She contends that:
    "Their mothers, schools or peers pass on to
    them 'domestic' skills like knitting and
    sewing, but the socialisation process tends to
    miss out gross motor skills, handicrafts in
    wood and metal, informal pub games and
    driving. The ability to take part in many
    forms of recreation depends to a large extent
    on the 'qualifications' of skills of this
    type and this appears to be one constraint
    which precludes women's participation in both
    institutionalised and informal recreation".
It is evident then, that women's participation is
constrained in this way over the whole course of the
life-cycle. Moreover, providers need to be aware
that they are most probably attracting older people
into sport for the first time rather than believing,
as is often the case, that they are attracting them
back to something they did when they were younger.
    The last two hurdles in this system: facility
constraints and managerial constraints, have
received little attention in the literature despite
the fact that it is almost 15 years since Emmett
(1971) first alerted us to the ways in which the
attitudes of managers or 'social gatekeepers', might
exclude certain people from participating.
Recently, programming policies and management style
have come under some scrutiny (Torkildsen, 1983;
Veal, 1981), yet there is nothing which specifically
focusses on these issues in relation to older
people.
    Lastly in this section, it is important to note

the influence of adverse societal attitudes. Such
attitudes and images often suggest that certain
activities are not appropriate for older people
(Johnson, 1978). They then internalise such
beliefs, and come to perceive facilities and
activities as 'not for the likes of us'. Thus, it
is only by exploring and challenging these issues
that we can begin to help overcome them. This then,
was partly what we set out to do in a project
entitled 'Active Leisure in Later Life', to which I
now turn my attention.

Active Leisure in Later Life

This project was funded by the Manpower
Services Commission, under their Community Programme
Scheme for long-term unemployed adults. It lasted
for 12 months, from April 1983 to March 1984. The
problems associated with short-term funding and the
employment of inexperienced personnel, meant that
the scope of the study was of necessity, limited.
The findings presented here, and in the research
report (Bernard et al, forthcoming) merely reveal
something of the situation as it was in North
Staffordshire at that time, and should not be taken
as a general indication.

The project was prompted by a variety of
considerations, not least of which was the fact that
the Sports Council (1982) had identified the over
50s as one of three target groups for stimulating
participation in active leisure over the next ten
years. Moreover, they launched the '50 plus - And
All to Play For' campaign in 1983, at around the
same time as our project received funding. In
addition, the Government White Paper entitled
Growing Older (1981) had made two references to
older people and leisure, which we thought were
worthwhile taking up. Firstly, they called for the
wider dissemination of information on leisure
opportunities available to people in retirement and,
secondly, they stated that:
    "Local authorities might encourage older people
    to make greater use of their leisure and
    recreational facilities, for instance, arrange-
    ments at sports centres - especially those with
    swimming pools and gymnasia - could frequently
    be modified, in small ways and at no extra
    cost, to take greater account of the interests
    and needs of older people."

As a result, our project had two stages. The first stage was to determine the extent of existing provision for indoor leisure in North Staffordshire, and to collate this information into a catalogue (Bernard et al, 1984). The second stage was an exploration of the use older people made of existing facilities. This in turn had three elements to it. Firstly, we chose five centres at which to carry out user counts, in order to determine what proportion of participants were aged 50 plus. Secondly, we held questionnaire interviews with users over the age of 50 and thirdly, we conducted tape-recorded interviews with the managers, which is the element I am concentrating on here. (One centre had two managers, both of whom were interviewed.)

All six managers were men, though they had varying experience and qualifications. They were aged from 30 up to 59 years and four of the six had been in post for eight years or more. In terms of qualifications, two possessed recreation management diplomas, one had coaching qualifications and another had been an instructor in the army.

During the interviews, managers were asked what they thought prevented older people from getting to their centres. Most responses reflected the familiar constraints of lack of company and no transport, illustrated in Figure 1. In addition, poor refreshment facilities were felt to be a particular constraint where actual use of a centre was concerned.

We turn now though, to look in more detail at some of their policies and attitudes. In his review of sports centre user studies, Veal (1981) laments the lack of attention given to how centres are managed, yet this in itself can constrain participation. He also argues that providers of what might be termed universal objectives, believing that they can serve the needs of the whole community. Our managers were no exception, claiming that their aim was to "serve a cross section of the community"; "to offer facilities for everyone" and "to provide a service to the general public."

Moreover, we know that in North Staffordshire, 32.4 per cent of the population are over the age of fifty. However, the managers' guesstimates about the numbers using their centres ranged from two to ten per cent, while the actual user figure was five per cent. Clearly then, they are far from achieving their universal aims and objectives.

If managers are indeed concerned to serve the whole community and provide for a cross section of it, then this has direct implications for policy and the programming of activities. In effect though, what happens is that by default the policy is one of first come, first served and we know that those who 'come first' tend to be the more mobile and affluent sections of the community and not the sections of the community and not the older age groups (Veal, 1981). This was further highlighted when we specifically questionned managers about the programming of their activities in relation to 50 plus users. The following responses illustrate this:

"We have never had a request for facilities for older people ... where would we fit them in? That's the problem"

"Unless they could come in the day time, we couldn't fit them in - could we?"

"It's difficult for us to have any specific time for the over 50s because we are so inundated"

"The problem is that we are fully booked - bursting at the seams - and we cannot fit more people in"

As Veal (1981) again points out, what this means is that the programme pattern at many centres is viewed as a given fact, and attempts to change it often prove very difficult. Furthermore, these policies are reflected in the style of management which, in relation to 50 plus users, was predominantly a passive one. The following comments are representative:

"If the over 50s come, we would accommodate them ... ... but, if they don't come, we cannot go out into the community to get them in"

"I think there is a vast amount for the over 50s to do if they are prepared to come out and do it"

"If the over 50s want to use my centre, I will advise them when to come, and what services are available"

"The facility is there for people to come and use
but its up to them to organise their own
activities"

The attitude revealed in these statements is
very much one of "it's here if they want to use it".
There seems to be little understanding of why older
people cannot, rather than will not, use the
facilities they have on offer.

In addition, we were interested to explore how
far managers were prepared to involve themselves
with this particular age group, given the fact that
the 50 plus campaign was in full swing. With one
exception, they were all adopting a fairly low
profile, saying things like: "we don't get actively
involved ... we help on day-to-day things" or, "I
haven't had any personal involvement with it" and "I
don't really know too much about developments in the
50 plus business."

Not surprisingly then, they felt that the
campaign was having a minimal effect. For example,
one manager remarked: "I never got any increase from
displaying posters ... we didn't get anybody", and
another commented: "I think it's having an effect
... but so are a lot of other things."

As a rider to this, it is interesting to note
that out of our total of 84, 50 plus users 59, (70%)
also said that they had not heard of the campaign.
In addition, students from the local polytechnic
carried out a street survey at Easter 1984, using a
questionnaire based on ours. In their results, 496
out of 577 older people, or 86%, said they had not
heard about the campaign. Consequently, it appears
that in North Staffordshire, there has been little
impact on either the providers or potential 50 plus
users of their facilities.

To sum up - it appears from these results that
managers' attitudes, while not overtly negative, are
at best indifferent. This strong combination of a
passive management style and programming policies
which are viewed as fixed, tends to place
considerable hurdles in the path of older people who
might want to participate. Moreover, the managers'
lack of involvement in what was supposed to be a
national campaign to encourage the over 50s into
activity, accentuates these difficulties.

Discussion

What then, are some of the implications we might draw from the preceeding discussion, and in what ways could the current situation be improved?

Firstly, to consider the managers and policy makers: it is evident that, at least amongst our small sample, there needs to be more sensitive management and greater flexibility of approach and attitude in order to help older people overcome the obstacles in their path. Often, older people are only recognised as a special group in terms of their financial status, but overcoming constraints is about much more than this. Torkildsen (1983), who was the first community sports centre manager in Britain and is now a Recreation Management Consultant, has expressed it in the following terms:

"far from starting with the facility - recreation management needs to start with the people it is intended to serve and their needs ... if we know what motivates people to recreation, then we are better able to plan and manage effectively ... facilities must be both accessible and acceptable."

In order to achieve this, managers have to keep abreast of what is happening in their local community, and Torkildsen (1983) also suggests that they need to blend the skills of both social planner and community developer.

This concept of a community developer, animateur, facilitator, motivator, enabler, activities promoter - call it what you will - is crucial in opening up opportunities for older people. This role is described in the following way by the Rapoports in their seminal work on Leisure and the Family Life Cycle, (Rapoport and Rapoport, 1975):

"This is a pastoral role that involves initiatives in the community - not just setting up facilities and contenting oneself that if people come the facility is successful. This does not imply that people must be constantly active; nor that they should be active if they do not want to be. The activators are important to help those who are inhibited, unresourceful and socially isolated to take the necessary plunges to bring them into contact with sources of development for their potential life interests."

It would be feasible for managers and other key personnel, to take on elements of this role and perhaps adopt a more promotional stance in respect of older people's use of their facilities. There are the beginnings of this kind of 'outreach' approach to sport and recreation (Bernard, 1984). For example, Norwich City Council took a progressive decision in 1981, to appoint an activities promoter for the retired, and eight other schemes have since been established across the Eastern Region. On a smaller scale, centre managers could appoint one particular member of staff to carry out similar co-ordinating and promotional tasks.

However, we need to do more than just exhorting managers and policy makers to be more open-minded and flexible. One of the best ways of changing attitudes, and encouraging participation, is by actually showing people what can be done. Here, the voluntary sector, and the rise of self-help and mutual aid groups, are the forerunners of what is likely to emerge more strongly in the future (Bernard, 1984). Moreover, there is some research evidence to show that if people can be encouraged into such activity, then they will sustain a strong interest in it, despite their lower exposure to sport in earlier life (Rodgers, 1977).

Thus, it is also up to the researchers amongst us to co-ordinate relevant information and evidence and make it easily accessible and available. For example, if we know that older people sustain a strong interest in sport once encouraged into it, this information needs to be passed on to policy-makers. If this does not happen, providers of facilities will continue to assume that because older people have always made limited demands on recreational facilities, they always will. Consequently, they base their plans on extending what already exists. We also know that many more people are retiring while they are still active, and both can, and want to enhance and improve their life styles through active involvement in leisure. Moves towards earlier retirement are likely to accelerate this trend, and over the next 20 years or so we are going to have an increasingly sophisticated and leisure literate elderly population (Kaplan, 1979).

To sum up - ideally, we need to tackle each

Constraints to Creativity

element in the constraint system if we are to overcome the hurdles to participation. Indeed, each could be made a separate policy target. This though is obviously a very tall order. However, what is evident is that there is a role for us all to play whether we are providers of facilities, developers of activities, participants, or researchers. Moreover, we must consciously strive to work together if the current invisibility of older people in conventional forms of leisure provision is to be overcome.

References

Bernard, M. (ed) (1984) Leisure in Later Life: examples of community based initiatives, The Beth Johnson Foundation, Stoke-on-Trent

Bernard, M., Ferns, C., McCulloch, R. and Turner, P. (1984) Active Leisure in Later Life : A catalogue of indoor leisure facilities in North Staffordshire, A Beth Johnson Foundation Research Publication, Stoke on Trent

Bernard, M., Ferns, C., Mculloch, R. and Turner, P. (forthcoming) Active Leisure in Later Life: older people's use of indoor leisure facilities in North Staffordshire, A Beth Johnson Foundation Research Publication, Stoke on Trent

Emmett, I. (1971) 'The Social Filter in the Leisure Field', Recreation News Supplement, 4, July, 7-8

Government White Paper (1981) Growing Older, Cmnd 8173, HMSO, London

Johnson, M.L. (1978) 'That was your Life: a biographical approach to later life', 99-113 in Carver, V. and Liddiard, P. (eds) An Ageing Population, Hodder & Stoughton, Sevenoaks

Kaplan, M. (1979) Leisure: Lifestyle and Lifespan - perspectives for Gerontology, WB Saunders Co, Philadelphia

Long, J. and Wimbush, E. (1979) Leisure and the Over 50s, Sports Council/SSRC Joint Panel on Recreation and Leisure Research, London

Rapoport, R. and R.N. (1975) Leisure and the Family Life Cycle, Routledge and Kegan Paul, London

Rodgers, H.B. (1977) Sport in its Social Context - International Comparisons, Council of Europe, Committee on Sport, Strasbourg

Sports Council (1982) Sport in the Community -
The Next Ten Years, The Sports Council, London
Torkildsen, G. (1983) Leisure and Recreation
Management, E. & F.N. Spon Ltd., London
Veal, A.J. (1981) Sports Centres in Britain -
a review of user studies, CURS, Birmingham
(unpublished)

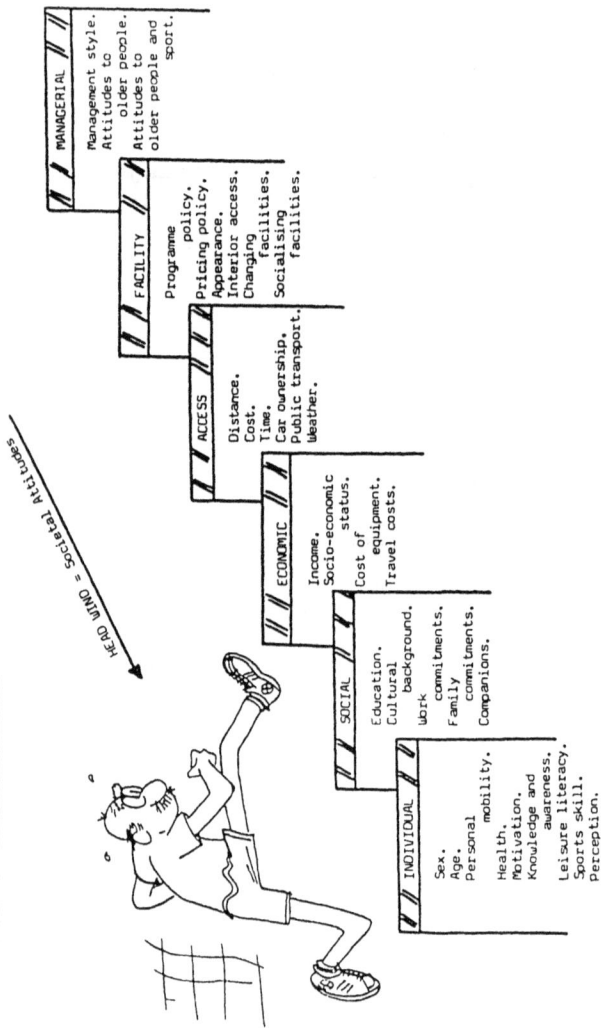

Figure 1: Hurdles to Participation

HEAD WIND = Societal Attitudes

MANAGERIAL
Management style.
Attitudes to
older people.
Attitudes to
older people and
sport.

FACILITY
Programme
policy.
Pricing policy.
Appearance.
Interior access.
Changing
facilities.
Socialising
facilities.

ACCESS
Distance.
Cost.
Time.
Car ownership.
Public transport.
Weather.

ECONOMIC
Income.
Socio-economic
status.
Cost of
equipment.
Travel costs.

SOCIAL
Education.
Cultural
background.
Work
commitments.
Family
commitments.
Companions.

INDIVIDUAL
Sex.
Age.
Personal mobility.
Health.
Motivation.
Knowledge and
awareness.
Leisure literacy.
Sports skill.
Perception.

Chapter Eight

THE ST JOHN'S SENIOR CENTRE: A CREATIVE DEVELOPMENT

Vera Ivers

The St John's Senior Centre sets out to explore a creative response to retirement - initiated by the Beth Johnson Foundation, and based upon recent research material. Drawing upon the life time experience and skills of older people, and showing that such a valuable resource can, when adequately utilised, offer a positive and healthly life style into a great old age.

The Foundation, being a small and independent charity, is perfectly situated to take such an initiative, not having the burden of care of the very frail elderly as laid upon larger voluntary and statutory bodies.

The area chosen in which to work has a predominantly working class population, as the 1981 OPCS Document (O.P.C.S. 1981) showed: 47 per cent of households do not own a car; 60 per cent of women of working age are in paid employment; 43.6 per cent of households live in rented accommodation, 34.6 per cent being council housing.

The population is ageing, having the highest ratio above pensionable age in Staffordshire at 17.6 per cent and the lowest ratio of under 16s at 21.5 per cent.

The concept of a multi purpose Senior Centre is borrowed from the USA where recommendations (Note 1) were made to the Congress in 1981 as follows:

Recommendation 5
Public policy should encourage and promote opportunities for the greater involvement of older people in community and civic affairs and for their participation in formulating goals and policies on their own behalf as a basis for making the transition from work to leisure roles. Society should reappraise the current

life-style sequence of student-worker-retiree roles and promote role flexibility.

Recommendation 9
It should be the responsibility of the federal government, in cooperation with other levels of government, to provide funds for the establishment, construction, and operation of community-oriented, multiservice centres designed for older citizens. Industry, labor, voluntary and religious organizations should assist in the planning and implementation.

The Senior Centre might also be seen to parallel the Youth Centre, where the aims include helping young people to adjust from school to a working life, the senior centre having similar aims at the other end of the working life - helping retired people to adjust to abundant leisure time.
The building is a city centre landmark church - much loved in the area, but in financial difficulties and with a small and dwindling congregation. The criteria that we set ourselves for a senior centre was that it should be near to a main shopping centre, very close to good public transport, large enough to accommodate a very active programme, and a cafeteria, and be offered at a low rent.
St John's Church satisfied all of those criteria, its only drawback being the necessary shared use. This does pose problems from time to time, but they are not insurmountable, and we currently use the building on 4 days per week.
St John's Senior Centre sets about inviting people over 50 years of age to come into the centre for:

1. refreshments - ranging from a cup of coffee to a full meal;
2. advice and information service;
3. activities - ranging from rambling to patchwork quilting;
4. voluntary work - at the centre or at other venues;
5. educational opportunities

Number one of these facilities is often the thing that encourages individuals through the door in the first place. Volunteer users on a rota provide the labour for kitchen and service. To get to the cafeteria, they need to pass the advice desk, where there is always a plentiful supply of up-to-date leaflets and a volunteer adviser. N.A.C.A.B. found that workers on the factory floor were unlikely to seek advice, often because their working hours did not permit, and so set up bureaux in canteens - easily available and accessible. Such people, now retiring after a long working life, are also likely to be pround and reluctant to admit that they need advice, even if anxieties beset them which loom the larger because they have time to reflect and worry. While visitors take their refreshments, all around activities are taking place - perhaps a yoga class, an art class or a course on law as it affects older people. Some users continue to visit because the centre is a convenient resting place while shopping, but many others become curious and decide to try an activity. Some such activities are specifically aimed at improving physical health, but may be unfamiliar, if, as Morris maintains, (Morris 1980), there are strong occupational class trends in recreation and exercise.

Other activities have a broadly educational purpose and in particular a Staying Healthy in Retirement class is proving very popular. Most activities are taught by volunteer seniors who are sharing their life time skills. The health course, though, leans heavily upon health professionals who work happily across professional boundaries at this very local level and in neutral territory (Phillipson).

Other people attend St John's primarily to offer their services as volunteer workers, perhaps unknowingly taking on board the advice of various gerontologists that the harder and longer we work, the more likely we are to stay alive and well. Maggie Kuhn (Kuhn) of the American Grey Panthers not only campaigned for the rights of seniors but believes that resting as a way of life is deadly and that new activities and new goals add life to years, if not years to life.

Many users of St John's Senior Centre have set themselves new goals, and taken up new activities which perhaps they would not have done without such stimulation as the Centre offers. Jonathan Long's work on Leisure and the Over 50s clearly indicates that new activities are not likely to be taken up in retirement without some external initiation being offered (Long 1981).

The benefits of extending life long learning and of sharing life time skills are well documented and at St John's are easily observable (Glendenning and Jones).

An essential element in the creativity, learning and growth of individuals that takes place at this centre is to do with rubbing shoulders with professionals or at least those who have a body of knowledge to pass on and the skill with which to impart it.

Of particular importance in a project which attempts to motivate and facilitate is the key figure or 'animateur'. It was not unusual to find Directors of Senior Centres in the USA who held Masters degrees, and who were paid accordingly. It might be difficult to persuade authorities here that such centres could be as useful as they obviously saw Youth Centres to be in the past. Even more difficult for them to see the need for such skills in an organiser, when the scale rate for Day Care centre managers is usually on offer at £8,000 to £10,000 per annum.

One of the drawbacks of promoting such a project from within a small organisation is that the facilitites necessary for properly documented monitoring are difficult to come by. Also that traditional questionnaires and interviews may be totally inadequate to capture the spirit and dynamism of the operation.

The use of new technology is becoming more familiar in all manner of settings, and perhaps will prove to be the appropriate medium for monitoring and demonstrating such practical projects in the future.

During its first year of operation, St John's Senior Centre was a success if measured by growing numbers of users, and expressed satisfaction with the activities and new companionship experienced; 200 people per week use the centre and the numbers are growing. 40 volunteers give from 2 hours to 6 hours service, and in its first year the advice desk helped 120 people, only six of whom said they would have gone elsewhere for help.

Future plans for the Senior Centre involve further development of health education and, with cooperation from health professionals, a health monitoring and counselling service. Currently a group of uers are attempting to develop an information pack on alternative medicine and similar packs on specific health matters may also develop. Other activities may emerge as demand becomes apparent.

The decisions about development will ultimately depend on users' preferences, after available options and the necessary education and information has been presented to them. Although the Beth Johnson Foundation has responsibility for the Centre at present, the day to day decisions are made by users who will gradually take full responsibility for management. That development will be influenced by the Centre's ability to generate enough income to enable it to be financially viable, and income is rising as numbers of users increase.

References

Glendenning, F. and Jones, S. Education and the Over-60s, Beth Johnson Foundation in association with the Department of Adult Education, University of Keele

Kuhn, M. A New Life - Liberation from Ageism The New Old - Struggling for Decent Ageing, Anchor Press

Long, J. (1981) Leisure and the Over-50s, Sports Council/SSRC Joint Panel on Leisure Research

Morris, J. W. (1980) Equalities and Inequalities in Health, British Medical Journal, 11 October 1980

O.P.C.S. (1981) O.P.C.S. County Monitor, Office of Population Census and Surveys, 1981

Phillipson, C. Developing a Preventive Approach: Health Education, Professional Workers and the Elderly, Health Education Council

Note 1.   The recommendations emerged from the 1971 White House Conference on Aging. Post-White House Conference on Aging Reports, 1973, and Final Report of the Post-Conference Board of the 1971 White House Conference on Aging - June 1973. Sub-committee on Aging of the Committee on Labour and Public Welfare and the Special Committee on Aging, United States Senate, Washington D.C. : U.S. Government Printing Office, 1973, 527-556

Chapter Nine

INTIMACY AT A DISTANCE UNDER THE MICROSCOPE

A. M. Warnes, D. Howes and L. Took

This paper reports the completion of a social
survey which was carried out for an ESRC supported
project into, 'Residential proximity, inter-
generational relations and the support of the
elderly'. It will concentrate on the findings which
relate to residential mobility, residential
separation and visiting. Some details will be
reported of the frequency and distance of the
residential moves undertaken by both the respondents
and their children, which section will lead to an
overview of the extent of the physical dispersion of
parents and their children. Attention will then be
focused on the relationships between physical
separation and the structure of visiting patterns.
        Two levels of objectives are being pursued by
the project. On the one hand an aim has been to
collect information about the contemporary
activities, satisfactions and roles of retirement
in order to promote an understanding of the
implications of demographic, social and geographical
changes upon the circumstances of the elderly. How
are people adapting to a lengthening period of
'third age'? How does the increased likelihood of a
parent of young retired people being alive and of
all children having left home influence social
relationships in late age? Do other social changes,
such as longer distance residential mobility, the
higher educational attainments of younger
generations, or more rapid occupational change, have
an identifiable impact upon retired people? For the
more immediate and specific objectives a focus has
been adopted upon the interactions between spatial
or geographical factors and the frequency and
structure of social relationships among retired
parents and their children. Many commentators have
asserted that longer distance geographical mobility
during the last forty years has led to a greater

dispersal of family members and that, among other things, this has weakened the extended family, led to a reduction in visiting between older parents and their children, and contributed to a growing social isolation of elderly nuclear or single-person households. These assertions are for the most part insecurely founded in observation or measurement: nonetheless they are the common currency of newspaper and magazine comment and are widespread in political and administrative circles. Some accounts recognise compensating influences, such as increased car ownership, improved roads, faster railway services and the arrival of mass access to the telephone (Eversley, 1982, p. 20). The best syntheses by social gerontologists are careful assessments of the net effects of these contradictory trends (Tinker, 1981, pp. 119-132; Wenger, 1984). Theories of inter-personal social exchange and of serial reciprocity through the generations have been elaborated (Bengston, Olander and Haddad, 1975). The consensus now is that the connections of most elderly people with their families and kin networks have been maintained but that there have been substantial changes in the role of extended family members, not least in relation to the health and social services (Rosow, 1968; Stehower, 1968; Sussman, 1965).

Several substantial European studies of the family relationships of elderly people are well known (Rosenmayr, 1968; Rosser and Harris, 1965; Sheldon, 1948; Townsend, 1957; Willmott and Young, 1960). Studies of comparable scope were absent during the 1970s although surveys continued to collect data on residential separation and visiting, while recent years have seen a revival of interest in the subject (Abrams, 1978, 1980; Hunt, 1978; Wenger, 1984). There is also an extensive United States literature on the social interaction of elderly people, often in the form of specialised research papers (Sussman, 1976).

From this substantial body of writing it is possible to identify a small set of cross-sectional influences upon the social relationships of the elderly. Four principal influences emerge; the first being the availability of relatives of different order of closeness. A substitution effect can be described whereby if there are relatives in the same household, social interaction beyond is comparatively weak. If there are children living elsewhere, their households form an important element in social networks; if not, siblings or other 'extended' relatives tend to feature more strongly. If relatives are unavailable or uninterested then friendship interaction takes on greater importance although the further generalisation can be supported that a declining intensity and frequency of interaction accompanies the progressive substitutions from conjugal, friendship or neighbouring interactions.

The second factor which emerges from the empirical research is that of social class and its associations with educational attainment, occupational mobility, geographical mobility, the nature of friendships and, through fertility and mortality, the number of relatives from preceding or following generations that survive at any given age. Thirdly, and particularly associated with the considerable variation in circumstances that applies to any occupational, social class or family-size group, is the important influence of personality and the history of the child-parent relationship. Put in ordinary terms, whatever the socio-economic defining characteristics of a group, within it there will be some cases in which children represent the most important extra-nuclear family focus of social and emotional relationships and other cases where there is neither contact nor a desire for any close relationship.

Finally one identifies in most studies a recognition of the importance of accessibility, whether measured in terms of travel time, geodetic or road distance, as a factor controlling the frequency, duration and nature of visits between separated persons. Further it is widely acknowledged that for elderly or other people with restricted physical capacities and/or low incomes, the 'friction of distance' bears more heavily.

It is not possible to identify a consensus as to the relative importance of these four factors, partly because the answer depends upon the nature of the sample, the scale of the geographical area studied in the analysis and the measurement effects from the manner of representation of the distance variable. For example, general samples will tend to reveal the importance of the social network membership and of social class, while small-scale local studies of homogeneous sub-groups will place more weight on personality differences. The importance attached to the spatial variable often seems to reflect primarily the spatial sensitivity of the observer, not least through the inclusion or exclusion of relevant questions. It is understandable that social gerontologists have previously been little concerned to analyse the spatial influences. Our position is that given the rapidity of mobility and communication change, and with the possibility that social myths are taking root, it is worthwhile to undertake an empirical study.

At least one practical reason for clarifying the role of separation can be briefly described. If separation strongly constrains visiting, it may have an adverse effect on a person's morale and/or social support. Some people may be aware of this locational restraint and wish to lessen the effect by moving house. Because there are monetary, social and psychic costs involved with any residential move, and because there are institutional and organisational impediments to moving, many people will be living in locations at which their interaction with their closest relatives (or friends) will be less than they and the other party desire. If the impediments to moving can be relaxed, then some could not only create a fuller and more satisfactory social relationship in retirement, but also bolster and prolong their residential independence. It is hoped that this study will enable evaluations of the actual extent of these circumstances.

The Research Project

432 married couples were interviewed during 1983, divided approximately equally between Maidstone (Kent), Stockport, the London Borough of Merton and Melton Mowbray and Oakham, Leicestershire. The 'population' to be surveyed was defined as married couples living without others in private households. At least one member had to be of statutory retirement age and there were to be two children surviving and in contact at least once during the last two years. With this demanding specification the construction of a sampling frame and the field-survey procedures were intricate: a description of all aspects of the survey design is available in a working paper (Warnes and Howes, 1984). This also reviews the checks of the sample

in terms of age, housing tenure and occupation which have demonstrated that it is representative of both the survey areas and the English population. Information was collected on the retired couple's previous addresses, occupational histories, home visits, activities during visits, housing satisfaction and attitudes to moving. The educational, occupational and residential histories of the 864 children were also collected, there being gratifyingly few occasions when parents could not provide sufficient details. A follow-up postal survey to 170 of the children was also undertaken, to ask about the location and frequency of visits with the spouse's parents and about the factors which influenced their last residential move. Some consistency questions about visiting with the principal respondents were included.

The Incidence of Residential Moves

The overriding finding of the mobility questions has been to establish the low incidence of moves among retired married couples of the 1980s. Only a minority have ever moved beyond the town or district in which they settled at marriage. 35 per cent of the couples reported no move since 1951 and 80 per cent had not made any move of more than 30 km. Only 28 couples (6.5 per cent) had made more than one move of 30 km or more. A clear but not entirely linear relationship with social class has been confirmed: unskilled manual workers have been slightly more mobile than skilled manual workers so disrupting a simple relationship of a decline of mobility with a decline of social class (Table 1). Put another way, more than half of the couples had lived in their present house for 20 or more years and three-quarters for 10 or more years.

A higher incidence of moves is found among the children; approximately one-half had moved 30 km or more and 27 per cent had made more than one such move. A positive social class relationship with the incidence and the distance of moves is also found among the children (Table 1). Even so, for large numbers of families the combined mobilities of parents and children has not broken the localisation of the related households.

There is of course considerable diversity in people's situations. For over a quarter of the cases, neither parents nor children had moved over

30 km, while in only 49 cases (11 per cent) had both children undertaken more than one move greater than 30 km since leaving home (Table 2). The intermediate situations include the 101 cases where one child had made two or more moves greater than 30 km and the other had made none. The dominant impression, however, is of the relatively small number of families which have experienced dispersion due to a complex combination of numerous long distance moves. Indeed in over 60 per cent of cases neither the parents nor at least one child had moved more than 30 km. The net outcome of the mobility of the related households can be summarised by examining the residential separation of the retired couples and their children at the time of the survey.

Dispersion of Parents and Their Children

A large proportion of children continue to live in close proximity to their parents. Almost 23 per cent lived within 2 km, 38 per cent within 5 km, and half were no more than 10 km from their parents. At the other extreme, 19 per cent lived more than 100 km away. When examined in terms of the distance from the parents of the nearest child, over a third of the couples had a child living within one kilometre and 58 per cent within 5 km. Only 7 per cent of the couples had both children living more than 100 km away. It is therefore evident that for the great majority of retired couples, a close relative lives within a short walk, car, bus or taxi ride.

An unexpected finding is that those children who had made more than one move (independently of their parents) of 30 km or more tended to live closer to their parents than the children who had made only one long distance move. This suggests that second or subsequent long distance moves tend to be towards the homes of parents (Table 3). Direct evidence of this phenomenon comes from the 58 children who had moved more than 30 km when first leaving home and subsequently had made only one further long distance move. Of the 58 children, 41 lived at least 20 km nearer to their parents at the time of the survey than they did upon first leaving home.

The social class dimension is also clearly expressed in the separation of parents from children. One half of the children of parents in the Registrar General's social classes I and II live 20 or more kilometres away compared to 37 per cent of children to parents in social classes IV and V (Table 3). Even with the greater dispersion of the high status families, three in ten of their children live within 5 km of their parents. It is possible to gain a preliminary impression of the relative importance of the parents' and the children's occupational status through a cross-tabulation with the distance of separation. As indicated in Table 4 by the mean separation distances for the various social class groups, there is greater variation among the sub-groups of children than among the sub-groups of parents, suggesting that the child's achieved occupation has a stronger influence than their parental background. This confirms the findings from the mobility analysis, that it is the moves of the children that are most influential upon the proximity or separation from parents. It is interesting to note that on both dimensions, people from social classes IV and V have greater mean separation than manual workers allocated to social class III.

Residential Separation and Family Visiting

It is no surprise that a relationship between residential proximity and the frequency of visits has been confirmed but the strength of the association and the falls of visiting frequency over the shortest distances and with very small increments of separation were not expected. This may be illustrated by comparing the children living within two kilometres of their parents, those living between 5 and 20 km, and those living more than 100 km away. The percentage visiting at least once a week drops from 81 through 47 to 1.6 per cent, while the percentage visiting less frequently than once a month increases from 5 through 14 to 90 per cent (Table 5). It is not only that very high frequencies of visiting (three or more times a week) are almost entirely confined to those pairs living within 5 km of each other, but also that where the separation is 50 km or more (31 miles), 55 per cent of the children see their parents less than three times a year.

Once separation of children from parents is taken into account, social class does not have a significant effect upon children's visiting patterns: the influence of distance is too strong. Put another way, the different visiting frequencies of the different social classes are mostly due to their different levels of residential mobility, particularly among the children, and of their consequential residential separation. Further analysis has explored the influence of such variables as: the presence or absence of grand-children, the sex and age of the child, housing tenure and education attainment; but the only factor which has been shown to have a small independent influence is car ownership.

Discussion

The frequency of visits is recognised as only one, overt manifestation of a social relationship. Not only does the duration and character of visits vary with their frequency, but our survey has confirmed the importance of the telephone as a means of maintaining contact between parents and children. These dimensions of visiting are being explored more thoroughly in further analyses. It is clear however that parent-child relationships are the most important component of the majority of the retired couples' social relationships. A few cases of indifference and of antagonism were encountered but the prevailing norm for both parents and children is to maintain their relationships not only for the immediate practical returns or for reasons of family solidarity, lineage or responsibility, but also because they do provide considerable satisfactions and pleasure.

Approximately one in five of the couples said that they did wish to live nearer their children yet many fewer said that they wished to see them more frequently. The superficial contradiction in these findings arises, it is believed, from the respondents' understanding of the limiting effect of distance and from their realistic approach to adult relationships. While a reluctance to express to the interviewer any dissatisfaction with the relationships with their sons and daughters certainly existed and is understandable, an equally widespread attitude was that the maintenance of family relationships is a shared responsibility. If their residential separation was sufficient to impede a relationship by reducing the frequency of visiting, many accepted that it was their responsibility to move. At the same time it was normally not assumed that to move closer to a child would inevitably result in more frequent visiting. This would only come about by mutual consent and mutual commitment to the relationship. In other words we found a widespread reluctance to make prescriptive statements about an optimum or indeed a different pattern of visiting. The findings reported in this paper demonstrate clearly however that if family members succeed in increasing their residential proximity, then it is very likely that a more intensive structure of visiting will develop and be maintained.

References

Abrams, M. (1978) Beyond Three Score and Ten: A First Report on a Survey of the Elderly, Age Concern England, Mitcham, Surrey

Abrams, M. (1980) Beyond Three Score and Ten: A Second Report on a Survey of the Elderly, Age Concern England, Mitcham, Surrey

Bengston, V.L., Olander, E. and Haddad, A. (1975) 'The generation gap and aged family members', in J. Gulbrium (ed.) Late Life: Recent Developments in the Sociology of Age, Charles Thomas, Springfield, Mass.

Eversley, D.E.C. (1982) 'Demography of retirement', in M.P. Fogarty (ed.) Retirement Policy: the Next Fifty Years, Heinemann, London, pp.14-40

Hunt, A. (1978) The Elderly at Home, Her Majesty's Stationery Office, London

Rosenmayr, L. (1968) 'Family relations of the elderly', Journal of Marriage and the Family, 30, 672-80

Rosow, I. 1967) Social Integration of the Aged, Free Press, New York

Rosser, C. and Harris, C.C. (1965) The Family and Social Change, Routledge & Kegan Paul, London

Sheldon, J.H. (1948) The Social Medicine of Old Age: Report of an Inquiry in Wolverhampton, Oxford University Press, London

Stehower, J. (1968) 'The household and family relations of old people', in E. Shanas, P. Townsend, D. Wedderburn, H. Friis, P. Milhoj and J. Stehower, Old People in Three Industrial Societies, Atherton, New York

Sussman, M.B. (1965) 'Relations of adult children with their parents in the United States', in E. Shanas and G. Streib (eds) Social Structure and Family: Generational Relations, Prentice Hall, Englewood Cliffs, New Jersey

Sussman, M.B. (1976) 'The family life of old people', in R. Binstock and E. Shanas (eds) Handbook of Aging and the Social Sciences, Van Nostrand, New York

Tinker, A. (1981) The Elderly in Modern Society, Longman, London

Townsend, P. (1957) The Family Life of Old People, Routledge & Kegan Paul; (1963 edtn) Penguin, Harmondsworth, Middlesex

Warnes, A.M. and Howes, D.R. (1984) A Social Survey of Retired Married Couples and Their Family Units, Department of Geography, King's College London, Occasional Paper 18

Wenger, C. (1984) The Supportive Network: Coping With Old Age, Allen & Unwin, London

Willmott, P. and Young, M. (1960) Family and Class in a London Suburb, Routledge & Kegan Paul, London

Acknowledgements

The authors wish to thank the Economic and Social Research Council for their financial support and the respondents of Maidstone, Leicestershire, Stockport and Merton who made the research possible. Our enthusiastic and accomplished interviewers were Rodney Bungey, Simon Corley, Geoffrey Crothall, Vivien Crump, Janet Kerber, Christine Ogden, Susan Sayer, Gary Tobiss, Elisabeth Took and Else Zapletal.

Table 1   Mobility of retired couples and their children by social class of retired father

A. Retired Fathers

| | Social class of retired fathers | | | | |
	I	II	III	IV	V
Percentage in social class making since 1951:					
a) At least one move	79	75	60	53	76
b) At least one move over 30 km	46	33	24	7	16

B. Children

| | Social class of child (or husband if child is a married woman) | | | | | |
	I	II	III	IV	V	Housewife (not married)
Percentage in social class making since lived at home:						
a) At least one move after first establishing own household	84	78	68	62	75	65
b) At least one move over 30 km	74	57	48	33	31	45

Table 2   Family mobility behaviour

Mobility of parents	Mobility behaviour of children since first leaving home						
No. of moves >30 km by retired couple since 1951	No. of moves >30 km by one child			No. of moves >30 km by other child			Total
	0	1	2+	0	1	2+	
0	120	65	21	86	22	34	348
1	11	8	7	10	11	9	56
2+	5	7	1	5	4	6	28
Total	136	80	29	101	37	49	432

Table 3 Distance between children and retired parents by mobility behaviour of children since living home and by social class of parents

| | Distance between children and parents (km) | | | | |
	0-1.9	2-4.9	5-19.9	20-99.9	100+
			Percentages		
a By previous moves					
No of moves over 30 km	35.9	24.4	27.3	11.5	0.9
1 move over 30 km	3.5	3.5	9.5	45.0	38.5
2+ moves over 30 km	10.0	7.3	11.0	29.7	42.0
b By social class of parents					
Social classes I & II	19.1	11.3	19.5	22.3	27.7
Social class III	21.4	17.9	18.3	23.1	19.2
Social classes IV & V	27.3	14.0	22.0	10.7	16.0

Table 4   The mean distance separating parents and children by the social class of the parents and by the social class of the children or their spouses

Social class of the parents	Social class of the children or their spouses				
	I + II	III non manual	III manual	IV + V	Totals
	Distance of separation (km), No. of cases in parenthesis				
I + II	90.7(139)	41.9(35)	30.6(47)	28.9(8)	68.8(229)
III non manual	82.2(64)	78.7(30)	37.8(35)	53.2(11)	68.1(140)
III manual	76.4(97)	45.9(41)	23.2(108)	19.6(26)	45.2(272)
IV + V	66.4(43)	21.5(15)	42.9(65)	60.7(17)	50.0(140)
Totals	82.0(343)	50.0(121)	31.6(255)	38.1(62)	57.2(781)

Table 5   Frequency of children's visits to parents by distance from parents

Frequency of visits	Residential separation (km)												Total
	0-1.9		2-4.9		5-19.9		20-49.9		50-99.9		100+		
	No.	%	No.	%	No.	%	No.	%	No.	%	No.	%	No.
3 a week or more	74	39.4	26	19.7	7	4.2	2	1.6	0	0	0	0	109
1 or 2 a week	79	42.0	58	43.9	71	42.5	14	11.2	4	5.7	3	1.6	229
1 to 3 a month	25	13.3	24	18.2	65	38.9	60	48.4	22	31.4	16	8.7	212
4 to 11 a year	5	2.7	11	8.3	12	7.2	34	27.4	24	34.2	45	24.6	131
3 a year or less	5	2.7	13	9.8	12	7.2	14	11.2	20	28.6	119	65.0	183
Total	188		132		167		124		70		183		864

Chapter Ten

LEISURE ACTIVITIES OF THE ELDERLY IN URBAN SHOPPING
CENTRES: A CASE STUDY ANALYSIS

Michael J. MacLean, David Brown and Pieter Sijpkes

Introduction

Recently, there has been considerable research
interest in the leisure patterns of the elderly.
This research has contributed to much knowledge
about how old people use their discretionary time in
later life. It has been found that the leisure
activities most frequently reported by elderly
people are socializing with friends and relatives,
watching television, gardening, reading newspapers,
and sitting and thinking (Harris, 1975, 1981;
Statistics Canada, 1978; Moss and Lawton, 1982). It
has also been suggested that most of these
activities take place indoors and they tend to be
home-based more than community-based (McPherson,
1983). This indicates that, in general, the leisure
activities of the elderly tend to be informal and
individual rather than formal and group-oriented in
that they are not primarily related to organized
activity.
     Since the elderly seem to organize much of
their leisure in an informal way, there may be many
activities that old people would consider as leisure
that may not initially appear as such. Since
leisure could be defined as the use of discretionary
time (McPherson, 1983), several activities in which
the elderly simply use this time could be considered
as leisure. Therefore, such activities as passing
time in public places could be considered a leisure
activity by the elderly. This may be especially
true in an urban area where there are several public
places such as train stations, bus stations,
markets, libraries, parks and squares, among others
which provide an opportunity for elderly people to
pass the time of day. In fact, one could argue that
one of the roles of the city is to provide

opportunities for leisure for its residents.

One of the recent changes in North American cities that has potential to contribute to leisure activities has been the development of "downtown revitalization projects" which include a considerable amount of public indoor space. Montreal is a city that has had several of these projects built during the last twenty years. In fact, Montreal is advertised as being an "indoor city" because of its extensive underground connections between buildings, shopping centres and the Metro system of underground public transportation. If Montreal is truly an "indoor city", people would be using it in the same way they would use other parts of the city. And since most people who live in cities relate their leisure activities to the formal and informal facilities available, there should be a considerable amount of leisure activity in the public indoor space of that city. Further, it would be expected that the elderly population of a city would use some of this public indoor space for their leisure activities.

To assess the extent to which elderly people use the indoor city for leisure pursuits, we focussed on the case study approach to study Complexe Desjardins, which is one of the most recent additions to Montreal's indoor city. Complexe Desjardins has all the facilities of most of these centre-city complexes such as extensive open public space where concerts, exhibitions and other daily events take place. It also has several benches, lots of natural light, foliage, a waterfall, a variety of boutiques and shops, restaurants, business and government offices, public washrooms, and a hotel. It is designed in a circular fashion so most of the activity is in the centre and the shops, restaurants and offices branch off this central area. The centre is connected to the Metro and to bus routes so it is easily accessible from the public transportation system. It has a major front entrance on Ste. Catherine Street, which is the main street in downtown Montreal; it also has a major back entrance on Dorchester Street, another main street of the downtown area. Naturally, with all these shops, offices, restaurants and the hotel within Complexe Desjardins, there is a large number of people passing through it at all times of the day throughout the week. Because it is connected to the Metro, it is also open on Saturdays and Sundays

Leisure Activities of the Elderly

although the majority of the shops are closed.

Method

The methods we used to determine how elderly
people use Complexe Desjardins for leisure pursuits
combined place-centered observation (Ittelson, et
al, 1974), person-centered observations (Zeisel,
1981) and interviews with elderly people themselves.
We observed four main areas in Complexe Desjardins -
the two main entrances, the Metro level and the
central area of the centre. In each area, the
behaviour of people who appeared to be 65 years of
age or older were noted. We differentiated elderly
people by gender and group composition and by
activity these people were doing. Observations were
initially stratified by time of day and day of week
but for the purposes of this paper these data will
be collapsed to weekdays (i.e. Tuesdays), Saturdays
and Sundays. Observations were made during the
weeks in both July and March in order to compare
summer and winter activity. A combination of the
July and March data will be used for the purposes of
this paper.

Results and Discussion

The Elderly in Complexe Desjardins

Elderly people seem to be attracted to Complexe
Desjardins because no matter when we observed this
centre, they were there. We observed a total of
1395 elderly people in this centre during three
Tuesdays, three Saturdays and three Sundays in each
of July and March. Their percentage of the total
clientele of this centre was relatively small but it
is representative of the population of elderly
people in Montreal. On weekdays, the elderly
represented 8 per cent of the clientele whereas on
Saturdays they accounted for 10 per cent of the
population who passed through Complexe Desjardins.
These figures are very similar to the population
statistics of the elderly in Montreal as
approximately 10 per cent of the population of
Montreal is 65 years or older. Thus, the proportion
of the elderly people observed in this centre-city
complex represents the proportion of the elderly in
the city as a whole.

We were surprised to find that the percentage
of the elderly in Complexe Desjardins was as low as

it was. We could have been biased thinking that the
percentage of old people would be greater than it
was simply because we were interested in their
presence and behaviour. The reason there seemed to
be more elderly people than there actually were was
because they were highly visible in this centre as
they were more likely to make use of the seating
facilities and to spend time in the public areas of
Complexe Desjardins than were people of other age
groups. In fact, on Tuesdays of the total
population seated in Complexe Desjardins, 39.3 per
cent were elderly; on Saturdays, 40.5 per cent were
elderly, and on Sundays, 50.4 per cent were elderly.
Therefore, these elderly people seem to be making
more use of the leisure-related facilities provided
in this centre - that is, the seats, the open area
around the seats, and the public viewing area.

In general, elderly people were in Complexe
Desjardins during both summer and winter. More
specifically, we found that there were many more
elderly people (up to four times as many) in this
centre in winter than in summer. This is not so
surprising considering the intensity of Montreal's
winters. From a leisure perspective, this
commitment to come to this centre in winter
indicates considerable motivation on the part of
these elderly people. Since motivation is a
significant component of becoming active, we perhaps
could try to 'tap' some of this energy in our
interests of getting elderly people involved in
leisure pursuits.

Elderly people were also observed in Complexe
Desjardins during the morning, noon, afternoon and
evening of weekdays (N=593) and Saturdays (N=357)
and Sundays (N=445). In a comparative sense, there
tended to be more old people in this centre during
weekdays than during weekends. This probably
reflects the tendency for the downtown population to
be higher during the week than on weekends. In this
respect, the elderly people who were observed in
Complexe Desjardins tend to reflect the ebb and flow
of the general population of the downtown area.
This pattern may also approximate the pre-retirement
work-day schedule of these elderly people.

The observation made on the weekends indicate
an interesting pespective of how the elderly use
Complexe Desjardins in a leisure sense. While there
were fewer old people observed on Saturdays and
Sundays than there were on weekdays, there tended to

be about the same number of elderly people in this centre on Saturdays and Sundays. This suggests that Complexe Desjardins is playing a special leisure role for these elderly people on Sundays since most of the stores are closed then. If we accept the speculation that Sunday may be a very lonely day for many elderly people, perhaps they are coming to this centre as a way of dealing with loneliness.

Naturally, there were many elderly people we observed who were probably just passing through Complexe Desjardins or doing some business there. These people would not be 'regulars' in this centre but they would influence the observations we made. To try to distinguish between these people and those who come to Complexe Desjardins on a regular basis, we interviewed approximately one hundred elderly people in the centre. From these interviews, it is clear that many elderly people use this centre on a regular basis. Approximately 40 per cent of those interviewed stated they come to Complexe Desjardins three or four times per week. They also stated that the length of time per visit is usually between two and three hours. This seems to suggest that a large number of the elderly people observed in this indoor centre spend a considerable amount of time each week in it. It is reasonable to conclude from this kind of information that these older poeple are using Complexe Desjardins as a location for leisure activities.

Sex Differences

There were impressive differences between the numbers of elderly males and females who were observed in Complexe Desjardins. Of the total number of people we observed, approximately 60 per cent were males and 40 per cent were females. A further look at the male/female differences also reveals interesting results. For example, we observed whether the individual was a man alone, a woman alone, men in pairs, women in pairs, men in groups, women in groups, or a couple. We found that men alone represented approximately 40 per cent of the elderly people observed in Complexe Desjardins whereas women alone were only 4 per cent of the total.

It appears that this centre has an attraction for elderly men who are alone. We can only speculate why this is the case - perhaps these men seek the companionship of others without wanting to make a commitment to specific people; by coming to this centre they can be involved in many of its activities and, indirectly, those of many other people who are there. These men may be more comfortable in the centre than women alone would be simply because society has traditionally granted them more of a right to 'lounge around' than it has to women alone.

Men in pairs (i.e. two men) were 25 per cent of the total sample of elderly people observed in Complexe Desjardins whereas women in pairs represented approximately 4 per cent of this total. Men in groups and women in groups accounted for approximately 18 per cent and 4 per cent of the sample respectively which indicates that these older men tend to be involved with groups to a much greater extent than do older women. Finally, couples (i.e. one man and one women) accounted for approximately 4 per cent of the sample of elderly people observed in this indoor shopping centre whereas mixed groups accounted for approximately 2 per cent of the total.

The results of these observations show that both elderly men and elderly women frequent this centre-city complex although men outnumber women; that elderly men alone is the group that is most frequently seen in this centre; and that elderly women tend to come to this centre with others since approximately 90 per cent of the women observed were with someone else. These figures may have some implications for those interested in leisure activities of the elderly. For example, it appears that the activity of going to this centre-city complex is one that men alone may be interested in. It is also obvious that elderly women do not frequent this centre on their own so any leisure activity involving women in these centres must be sensitive to this observation.

Activities

Based on our observations, the elderly seem to be spending a considerable amount of time doing relatively little in Complexe Desjardins. Sedentary activities tend to be the most popular behaviours of the elderly people in Complexe Desjardins. They spend their time doing one or more of the following; sitting and relaxing, sitting and reading, sitting and talking, sitting and eating, standing, strolling, walking briskly, or shopping.

During the week, the elderly in this centre tend to spend most of their time sitting and relaxing and then strolling around the complex. During weekday evenings, they spent time sitting and relaxing or walking briskly through the centre. The elderly spent very little time shopping during the week. Elderly people spent the weekends doing pretty much the same activities as they did during the week. We observed that sitting and relaxing was the most popular activity for these people. This activity was followed by strolling through the complex and then walking briskly. Again, the elderly people we observed spent very little time shopping in Complexe Desjardins on weekends.

We observed that old men and women engaged in different activities both during the weekdays and on the weekends in Complexe Desjardins. During weekdays, men alone tended to be either sitting or walking. Women alone tended to be either walking, sitting or shopping. Men in pairs spend most of their time sitting whereas women in pairs engaged in walking, sitting and shopping activities. Both men in groups and women in groups tended to be sitting. It appears that women were more likely to show signs of shopping behaviour.

On weekends in Complexe Desjardins, both men alone and women also spent their time either sitting or walking. Men in pairs spent most of their time sitting and some time walking; women in pairs tended to be sitting or walking. Both men and women spent most of their time sitting or walking although these women also spent some time shopping whereas these men did not.

These observations suggest that elderly men and women use their time in Complexe Desjardins quite differently. Men spent most of their time sitting or walking and they do virtually no shopping unless they are with a woman. Women also spent most of their time sitting but they also did engage in shopping activities. It is obvious from these observations that these elderly people use Complexe Desjardins for leisure activities much more so than for shopping. Since it was found that some of the elderly spend considerable time in this centre, it is interesting that the leisure activities are relatively simple behaviours. These elderly men and women seem to enjoy coming to Complexe Desjardins to sit or to walk around. Presumably, there is enough gratification in these activities to encourage these elderly people to return to this centre on a regular basis.

While the message may not be crystal clear, there seems to be some implications from these observations for recreationists working with the elderly. One of the implications is that there is a group of elderly people in this urban area that derives considerable significance from spending time in a public indoor environment where there are lots of other people and where there is no fee for the pleasure of being involved in some of the daily activities of urban life. Another implication is that older men seem to be especially attracted to this centre as a place to pass some time. This seems to be one of the few places where older men outnumber older women. Given the demographic fact that there are more elderly women than elderly men, this finding is quite dramatic.

Quotes from the Elderly

Some of the elderly people who come to Complexe Desjardins were interviewed about why they come to this centre. Many of these interviews suggest that the elderly perceive themselves to be coming to this centre to use it for leisure rather than functional activities. This is evident from the interview with a 79 year old man who said:

I come here every morning to pass the time. I never come here in the afternoon or the evening. I feel comfortable here, nobody bothers me.

This man seems to use Complexe Desjardins on a regular basis. This was also the case for another man of approximately 70 years who said:

I come here every day, sometimes in the mornings and sometimes in the evenings. I spend a few hours each day just sitting, walking around, watching people. I like it here very much. It's quiet, peaceful and enjoyable.

Complexe Desjardins is also used as a place for meeting people and just being involved with people. A 75 year old retired watchman said:

I like it here. It's a good place to kill time, a pleasant atmosphere. I meet an old buddy here from time to time. I come here almost every day. I have little else to do. I just sit and watch the people go by.

Leisure Activities of the Elderly

Some people (mostly women) come to Complexe Desjardins together. One woman of a pair of French-Canadian women in their mid 60s said:

> I like this place, it's very pleasing. We often come here to relax. There are many things happening. It gives older people something to entertain them. It's also nice to come here on a hot summer day where it's a good place to relax, stay cool and refreshed.

Finally, some of the interviews suggest that Complexe Desjardins is sometimes seen as having qualities like a park. A French Canadian man of 71 years who comes here four or five times a week stated:

> On ne se sens pas renfermée, il y a beaucoup de lumière et de l'air comme déhors ... des arbres ... de l'eau.

And an elderly woman said:

> It's very interesting here; there are many different types of people around. It's very much like a park and a city rolled into one place.

There are also some old people who seem to like Complexe Desjardins but who do not want to be very expressive about it. One 65 year old man responded to our question by saying:

> Yes, I like this place but go talk to the police if you want to know anything. I don't want to talk.

And another man of approximately 65 years of age who was sitting watching the people go by had the following discussion with a female interviewer:

> - What do you want lady?
> - I wonder if you like Complexe Desjardins?
> - Who are you?
> - I'm a researcher.
> - Go talk to someone else. I don't want to talk.

Conclusions

These observations and quotes suggest that some of the elderly people who frequent Complexe Desjardins have definite leisure interests in being there. In fact, they seem to have more leisure interests than shopping interests. Therefore, it would appear that there may be significant implications for people interested in recreation for the elderly.

These elderly people have adapted an existing

facility, which was designed for commercial purposes, to meet some of their social and leisure needs. In doing so, these elderly people have taught us that there is a considerable potential in the shopping centre environment for old people to be involved in many of the ordinary but essential aspects of life. Now that they have taught us that this public facility can be used in informal and creative ways, we should try to see if we, as professionals interested in the quality of life of old people, can help them expand the use of this shopping centre environment to satisfy more of their social and leisure needs.

References

Canada (1978) Culture statistics, recreational activities, Statistics Canada, Ottawa

Harris, L. et al (1975) The myth and reality of aging in America, National Council on the Aging, Washington, D.C.

Harris, L. et al (1981) Aging in the eighties: America in transition, National Council on the Aging, Washington, D.C.

Ittelson, W.H.; Proshansky, H.M.; Rivlin, L.G. and Winkel, G.H. (1974) An introduction to environmental psychology, Holt, Rinehart and Winston Inc., New York

McPherson, B. (1983) Aging as a social process, Butterworths and Co. (Canada) Ltd., Toronto

Moss, M. and Lawton, M.P. (1982) 'Time budgets of older people: A window on four lifestyles', Journal of Gerontology, 37, (1), 115-123

Zeisel, J. (1981) Inquiry by design: Tools for environment-behaviour research, Brooks Cole Publishing Company, Monterey

PART THREE: ASPECTS OF SOCIAL WELFARE

Chapter Eleven

SHORT-TERM FUNDED PROJECTS: A CREATIVE RESPONSE TO AN AGEING POPULATION?

Averil Osborn

Summary

Short-term funding from Government financed programmes is being taken up by those seeking to provide a creative response to an ageing population. The issues this raises are not being explored within any broader framework of policies for older people, nor are these issues being placed on the agendas of those responsible for the funding programmes. In the meantime, organisations and groups are desperate for resources that will allow them to respond to the requirements of the ageing population. It is understandable that they will continue to adapt themselves and their activities to give the most creative response possible to the funding programmes in order to attract funds, even if the funding programmes were not originally tailored for such purposes. This paper comments on the difficulties and dilemmas facing such organisations and draws out some wider issues.

Introduction

The Government White Paper Growing Older (1981) declared itself to be "the outcome of the first comprehensive review of all the issues which determine the wellbeing of older people". At the time this White Paper was not enthusiastically received by those eager for a creative response to an ageing population. These critics wanted a fuller policy debate and urged that a greater commitment and priority be given to the needs of older people. In fact there has followed a deafening hush; there has been no attempt by Government to put the needs of older people on the national agenda nor to develop a coherent overview of these needs. Hence changes and developments affecting various sectors of the older population are taking place in the absence of a broader based strategy. This paper looks at one such development - the use of short-term funding to provide services for older people - and argues the need to consider the wider issues at stake.

The advent of short-term funding programmes

The environment in which services funded on a short-term basis are coming into being has certain important features. There is, at the very least, retrenchment in the statutory sector: health, housing and personal social services provision is neither expanding nor being significantly redeployed to meet the changing requirements of an ageing population. The voluntary sector is finding local authority grants harder to come by whilst pressure to provide more services, basic or innovatory, is increasing. Both services and service development are struggling for resources. At the same time there are no signs of a concerted attack on poverty in old age; instead a piecemeal and fragmented series of reviews of different components of the social security system is currently generating more concern than hope.

Amongst all this constraint one area of growth and promotional activity stands out. Government funded programmes have been created as responses to the problem of long-term unemployment, the lack of training and planned work experience available to young people and the desire to provide voluntary activities for unemployed people. These programmes, in the main, are operated by the Manpower Services Commission (MSC), notably the Community Programme, the Youth Training Scheme and the Voluntary Projects Programme. A further government fund is administered by the Carnegie United Kingdom Trust - in England as Opportunities for Volunteering and in Scotland as the Unemployed Voluntary Action Fund. Resources are available for a maximum of one year: all funding is short-term.

The resources made available for these programmes are indeed considerable. For example in its first year, 1982, the Community Programme had a budget of about £550 million and was to produce 130,000 "opportunities" or jobs. These resources were not specifically targeted towards work with older people although an amount was actually earmarked in the smaller Opportunities for Volunteering programme: in 1982 Age Concern England administered a half million pound budget. To take a local illustration, in 1983 one local community project for older people using the Youth Training Scheme had an annual budget in the order of £100,000 (Mackay 1983). Another, using the Community Programme had a £90,000 budget for the year (Age Concern Community Enterprise).

Issue is not taken with the general objective of combating unemployment and the fierce debates as to the best means to this end are not the subject of this paper. The issue here is the utilisation of these programmes in an attempt to provide a creative response to the ageing population. In the present climate these programmes offer a rare source of funds. The take-up of programmes designed for one purpose by groups primarily working to a different end, however sympathetic they are to the former, may impinge in unintended ways on the ageing population, its services and the groups seeking to serve its interests.

Short-term funding to help an ageing population

Whilst the programmes are not aimed first and foremost at the needs of an ageing population, nevertheless, work with older people tends to be seen as legitimate or even to be encouraged by these programmes. For example, the Community Programme will give special consideration to projects to help disadvantaged groups such as disabled or elderly people, and Tony Newton, Parliamentary Under Secretary of State for Health and Social Security, said about Opportunities for Volunteering (Hansard 1983), "A key feature of this Government's policies in health and social services is the help that the community can give through volunteers and self help groups to meeting the needs of the elderly ....."

Comprehensive data on the extent of take-up for these purposes is hard to come by. Regrettably there seems to be no available routine analysis of the use of these programmes that will give a breakdown of the proportion of funded projects and programme budgets taken up by work relating to older people. Some indication of the likely take-up by projects working with older people is found in a recent study by Hedges and Hyatt (1984) commissioned

by the MSC. They found 13 per cent of Community
Programme projects in their sample were of this
type. (This will not necessarily mean that an
equivalent proportion of the programme budget was so
used as projects differ greatly in size).

A case of double neglect?

Those responsible for the Programmes have
clearly encouraged applications of benefit to
elderly people and the indications are that those
seeking to develop such initiatives have responded.
This is all the more reason for those looking at the
funding Programmes as a whole to consider the
implications of this particular application; and for
those looking at policies for an ageing population
to explore the impact of such projects.
Neither seems to be happening. No evidence of
recognition of the need for discussion at national
level has come from those primarily concerned with
the wellbeing of older people or from those who are
primarily concerned with the Programmes of short-
term funding. It may be that the former group need
to take the initiative and approach the latter. But
at national level the Government's lack of any
policy overview or forum on the needs of older
people has already been lamented. More locally a
preoccupation by the statutory agencies with their
mainstream services overwhelms consideration of the
implications of the growth of short-term projects.
There may also be reluctance to embark on a
constructive but critical review of the impact of
short-term projects at a time when the statutory
agencies see no adequate alternative source of
funds, are pleased to encourage use of any funds
other than their own and fear to rock the boat.
Is it acceptable to tolerate this double neglect on
the grounds that short-term funded projects of
benefit to older people represent possibly a
relatively small proportion of the use of all short-
term funding and are small when compared to
mainstream services for older people? Surely this
in not a good policy.
The energy and effort demanded in the field of
services for older people by short-term projects is
far in excess of their relative size. Further, a
disproportionate amount of new local development
seems to depend on short-term funded projects. The
effect of this on services and other responses to

meet the needs of the ageing population must be more fully understood.

The double bind facing user organisations

Organisations seeking to provide any response to the ageing population will be acutely aware of the general lack of funds available to them. They will be aware of the resources available via short-term funding and may well be under pressure to undertake 'projects'.

Once dependent on short-term funding programmes they hit Catch 22. Because they urgently need funds they can't argue flat out for the funds they need. Arguments for more appropriate funding could simply threaten present funding on the grounds that the organisation has admitted that such funding is far from ideal for its purpose. Any challenge to this acquiescence, however uneasy, is further impeded by lack of comprehensive data on the amount of short-term funding being used for work with older people and the types of projects funded. Such a context would generalise the debate and reduce the vulnerability of individual organisations who wish to offer constructive criticism. Until improvements are made, those seeking to obtain funds require, in some cases, considerable initiative and inventiveness in order to create apparent harmony between the primary aims of the funding programme and the service and action aims of the project, between the nature and duration of the resources needed to undertake the project and those allowed by the funding programme, and between a realistic project outline and a 'funder-friendly' but over-ambitious one. All this energy has to be diverted from other work desperately needed in the organisation and from straightforwardly planning and operating the best possible project.

Some experience of individual projects

By definition individual projects experience the greatest funding-related problems where the short-term funding is least suited to their aims. Typically such projects are either intent on longer term provision of service or are over-ambitious about the speed at which they can develop new and self sufficient services or other schemes. Service providing projects may also need staffing as well as funding continuity over a longer period, for example, where longer term relationships between workers and older people are a feature of the service. Even where a second project is funded to carry on where the first left off most if not all the original staff have to leave as this is a requirement of the funding programme.

Examples of such projects to be drawn on here include two using the Community Programme to provide essential staff for much needed day care centres, one using the Community Programme to identify needs and create volunteer advice, information and visiting services; one using the Youth Training Scheme to seek out and help elderly people "at risk" in the community.

The first set of problems arose directly from the mismatch of project objectives with the available short-term resources plus the conditions associated with their use. To quote one project, "Were the Project's Central Committee to be given the funds currently invested in the organisation by MSC (£100,000+) to use as they felt best, I doubt very much if they would choose to employ thirty 16 year olds with variable ability and commitment". (Mackay 1983). The Age Concern Community Enterprise project designed to set up volunteer visiting schemes found that the MSC would not allow a budget for crucial expenses for volunteers, nor could project staff fundraise. The day care centre staff developed important relationships with the day care users that threatened to be severed when staff were "terminated", as the jargon has it (A plea from the Heart - Network Notes No.17) The incompatibilty between short-term employed staff and long term relationships is illustrated, for example by the tears of a day care user in a wheelchair, distressed at the thought of losing the staff. The stark choice is however between the above and being able to offer nothing in the short-term.

For all these projects the aim was to try to keep going after the first year of funding. The only real possibility was to apply for a further year of short-term funding. Even when funding did come through, and in all these examples it did, the decision came very late so that the agency could not plan with certainty either for closure or continuation. Understandably, the agencies also had great problems in keeping the older people and others in the community both informed and reassured.

They also bore the brunt of the anger of staff whose contracts came to and end.

A second set of problems faced agencies which had responsibilities in addition to project ones. The project absorbed so much of the parent agency's energy that its wider role suffered, eg. forward planning, critical examination of what would be the most creative response locally to the ageing population. The organisation running the day centre for example was acutely aware that it had a key role in stimulating a co-ordinated approach within the town (See A Crisis in Care - Network Notes No.17). It had ideas as to how to develop from its present large day centre to a 'small is beautiful' pattern of very local integrated centres. It was however overwhelmed with the effort of coping with an under-resourced centre which relied on staff funded on a short-term basis. Paradoxically but inevitably, the treadmill of simply maintaining and keeping going the 'historic' service could not be escaped although the organisation would now prefer to develop and change. This also happened when the visiting services identified a pressing need to develop an advice and information component but found the breathing space, flexibility and resources needed for such a rethink were lacking.

A third set of problems, for a voluntary organisation project, involves relationships with the statutory sector. At its very worst, projects experience this typical syndrome. There is a high level of referrals to the project by the statutory services. These are way beyond the project's resources. At the same time real interest, support and collaboration may be withdrawn as the statutory sector fears (realistically) it will be asked to pick up 'the tab' when short-term funding runs out. Nevertheless, at a time when it is good to be connected with initiatives for elderly people, the statutory sector may not be averse to giving high praise and acclaim to the project initiative, creating the impression that services are thriving and all that can be done is being done. At a recent crisis meeting concerning a day centre, its staff told statutory body representatives that it was tangible resources not pats on the back that were needed, and needed now.

The fourth set of issues concerns volunteers and short-term projects. Often development work in an area is intended so as to create an on-going service which will survive with minimal future funding, by using volunteers. Sometimes a project comes in to support an existing service which already uses volunteers or hopes to do so.

The introduction of paid staff, albeit low paid, into organisations using and often run by volunteers raises many issues and attitudes about the appropriate relationships and balances between paid and unpaid work. This is familiar ground to observers in this field but to many organisations launching into projects for the first time the complex feelings and difficulties will be new.

The large project used young people to promote local visiting schemes. It suffered a loss of existing volunteers and these were not replenished. In this case, mature experienced volunteers were replaced by inexperienced employees with a resultant decline in the service offered. The project in which staff aimed to recruit and support volunteer visitors also had dificulties as this is a sophisticated task for new workers who are anyway keen to do the direct work themselves. In one day centre the key volunteer, the centre co-ordinator, was doing an extremely demanding job which in other circumstances would be paid at a professional rate. It became her task to manage the paid staff. All the projects reported mixed feelings about whether project staff should work for nothing, whether volunteers should really be paid etc. A complex set of issues which were not anticipated or planned for emerge as the projects unfold.

The final set of issues touches on a concern that elderly people are in danger of becoming the fodder of work experience. For example, it seems likely that many 'surveys of the elderly' have provided more in the way of experience for those knocking on the doors than they have provided in terms of subsequent action of benefit to those who answer the doors and answer the long and sometimes personal questions. Given the motivation behind the short-term programmes and the fact that these programmes are not primarily designed with the best interests of elderly people in mind, the danger that the needs of elderly people will be subjugated to the work experience needs of scheme employees must be guarded against. A recent study by Bernard (1964 aimed to assess the impact of Youth Opportunity Programme Schemes on their elderly recipients and seems to be a rare example of research on the elderly person's perspective. Much more information is needed about recipients views.

Concluding Comments

There is an unco-ordinated proliferation of short-term funded developments and services for older people that is not the optimal coherent and creative response to an ageing population. There will be some examples of excellence, but the cumulative effect gives cause for real concern. There are also worries about the "use" made of the good examples, as explained below.

Control of local initiatives is becoming more centralised. Short-term funding programmes are central government controlled. Resources made available by the local authority are declining. Central government has no clear and co-ordinated strategy and overview for service development for older people that it can implement by use of carefully planned short-term funding, nor machinery to oversee such development. Even a continuing commitment to any particular funding programme is uncertain given the past record of unpredictable chops and changes.

In terms of a basic, let alone a creative, response to ageing these Programmes are inefficient and wasteful of resources. Taking as a starting point the actual use of short-term funding, those concerned for the ageing population must be persuaded to argue for funding programmes that better meet the needs of that population. Resources need to be compatible with and supportive of the services and developments that are required and for which short-term funds are currently being used. At a time of particularly rapid growth and build up of numbers of very elderly people the need for an apropriate response has never been greater. Given a sizeable budget, guaranteed for a period of years, some better and more creative response to the ageing population might be possible.

An adequate overview of the needs of the ageing population is needed, plus an overview of the use to which short-term funding is being put in an attempt to respond to these needs. This would both demonstrate the case for more appropropriate funding whilst explaining the double bind in which agencies find themselves when they are intent on providing some action and service now.

The question must also be raised as to where

responsibility lies for the local overview and influence on service and service development. Central government control of short-term funding programmes weakens local authority influence.

A new ad hoc layer of administration and power is being generated with the advent of the Managing Agencies. These need resourcing, perhaps robbing Peter to pay Paul. They do not seem the right location for the missing overview and forward planning activity in terms of a creative response to the ageing population. They are becoming groups with a heavy stake in the present system, more likely to be fighting for more places than for a radically different use of the programme budget money. In the voluntary sector these agencies tend to be part of a larger organisation with a commitment to local community and service development and clearly there will be value but also tension in this relationship. The parent organisations, particularly in the voluntary sector, may themselves have inadequate or insecure funding leading to the possibility that the tail wags the dog. However, not all Managing Agencies have such parent organisations. One organisation created solely to manage the use of MSC funded projects, has now a turnover of £7½ million and is a projects industry - and will consider, for example, any aspects of care of older people, gardening or building.

Short-term funded projects may not be dissuaded from taking on work that has hitherto been seen as the reponsiblilty of the statutory sector. Could this help erode the baseline of services and professional help that the statutory sector can be expected to provide?

All too often, short-term projects are temporary initiatives, yet this is rarely their aim. There can be no built in continuity, yet the project objectives are, in reality, rarely achievable in one year or without some follow on. Where the project itself is designed to fade away some further activity usually requires resourcing and this can be very difficult.

Project initiatives are more likely to highlight shortfall in statutory provision than to provide the total alternative to statutory help yet there is litle chance of stimulating statutory provision, however powerful a case is made.

The presence of a short-term funded project

may serve to discourage collaboration. The statutory sector will be aware of the continuity and funding problems faced by the voluntary organisation running a project and will keep at a safe distance to avoid involvement and commitment lest they ultimately feel obliged to pick up the tab.

With some exceptions there is little evaluation or monitoring of the use made of the programmes by individual projects, apart from financial scrutiny. Where it exists it may take quite inappropriate measures such as body counts of the helpers and the helped to demonstrate "success", and pay little heed to problems of continuity when funding ceases.

They are wasteful and dismissive of the manpower which they temporarily absorb then "terminate". These projects draw in a wide variety of people who develop knowledge, skill and commitment and then have to leave.

Whilst there is a current emphasis on 'volunteering as a good thing' it is not clear that these programmes are designed to allow a real and sensitive contribution, nor has the impact of these programmes on 'old fashioned' volunteering been considered.

Pressure on the voluntary sector to sponsor and manage projects is mounting. This comes from Central government and local authorities including some heavy pressure from local councillors. Slowly (or not so slowly) and by stealth this could change the role and contribution of voluntary organisations, absorbing energy and core resources and weakening the policy and campaigning edge.

This pressure is felt by national and local organisations. A certain amount of local project work can inform the policy and development work of a national voluntary body. However, for organisations with a policy and campaigning role this requires a 'toe in the water' rather than a cross channel swim.

An excess of project work can also skew the type of service and work done locally. Not all voluntary organisations see their role as in projects. Some will not aim for direct service provision but can these survive? A good project track record may become a major selling point or even a necessity when seeking other support, funding or donations.

The scattering of good but possibly ephemeral projects can serve to create an illusion that there is a full and creative response to the ageing population. Over-concentration on projects can act as a decoy unless wider arguments are voiced at the same time. This can camouflage the lack of any real concerted "mainstream" response or disguise the lack of any real interest.

Assuming programmes continue to make funds available, this situation will be self perpetuating and, in the light of cutbacks elsewhere, these programmes will become the major source of money for many voluntary organisations wanting to undertake work of benefit to their community. Hoist by their own petard as, given the 'popularity' of these programmes, why should programmes be modified in response to such muted criticism?

References

Age Concern Community Enterprise Project, various unpublished papers, Age Concern Scotland

Bernard M. et al (1984) The Young and the Old: A study of the impact of Youth Opportunity Programme Schemes on the Elderly in North Staffordshire, The Beth Johnson Foundation

Cmnd 8173 (1981) Growing Older, HMSO London

Hansard 2,February 1983, Written Answers Col. 123.

Hedges and Hyatt (1984) Community Programme Sponsers Survey (1984) p.785, Social and Community Planning Research

Mackay, L. (1983) Community Contact Cares for the Elderly (Unpublished Report, Dundee Association of Social Service, June 1983)

Network Notes No.17 October/November 1984 A crisis in Care, Age Concern Scotland

Network Notes No.17 October/November 1984 Plea from the Heart, Age Concern Scotland

Chapter Twelve

INNOVATION IN THE CARE OF THE ELDERLY: THE ROLE OF
JOINT FINANCE

Ewan Ferlie, David Challis and Bleddyn Davies

Abstract

Joint finance not only represents a significant
source of external funding for innovations in the
community care for the elderly but serves also as a
prototype for an increasing number of incentive led
centrally government financed schemes. It is
therefore important to understand its effects on the
pattern of service provision. Indications of
improvement of efficiency and effectiveness are
derived and used to compare base budget and jointly
financed innovations. The conclusion is that joint
finance does, within the framework advanced, lead to
limited gains in service efficiency and
effectiveness.

Introduction

An examination of the role of joint finance in
stimulating innovation in the care of the elderly is
of interest for two reasons. The first issue
relates to the specific development of community
based services for the elderly. Secondly, it
provides an opportunity to observe the effects of
nationally inspired mechanisms designed to enhance
collaboration between the National Health Service
(NHS) and Social Service Departments (SSDs) at local
level. In the context of arguments about the need
for inter-agency collaboration in community care of
the elderly and appropriate mechanisms to ensure its
achievement, this study examines the nature of joint
finance innovations compared with base-budget
innovations. Of particular concern was whether
jointly financed care schemes exhibit
characteristics associated with a more general view
of community based service development, or whether

they are characterised more by features of short term agency self-interest, and in particular bed-blocking.

PART A: COMMUNITY SERVICES FOR THE ELDERLY

The first issue therefore relates to attempts to develop community based services for the elderly. With the rising number of elderly and very elderly patients, the development of such services has been a long term preoccupation of NHS policy making. NHS complaints about alleged inadequacies in local authority provision for the elderly are as longstanding as the NHS itself (Ministry of Health, 1948), whilst issues of bed blocking and poor patient management assumed prominence as long ago as the 1950s (Boucher, 1957). In the 1970s bed blocking emerged as a major preoccupation in the reports of the DHSS Chief Medical Officer, with the argument for the development of special geriatric services linked to DGH facilities resting in part on patient management grounds (DHSS, 1981a). There has also been periodic emphasis on the development of local authority provision as alternatives to hospital services through planning mechanisms. The ten year planning exercises instigated by Enoch Powell in 1961 and revived in the early 1970s were motivated partly by the need to achieve such substitution. However, attempts to achieve long term planning soon collapsed in the face of the needs of short-term economic management.

As policies of increasingly acute based geriatric hospital care and of high turnover (DHSS, 1976; DHSS, 1981b) were achieved there was greater stress on securing coordinated local authority domiciliary provision. Although the focus on acute intervention was more successful in the geriatrics specialty than any other in reducing the average length of stay in hospital (Chief Officer of the Ministry of Health, 1979), DHSS (1981c) has reaffirmed that a further shift in the balance of resources from hospital to community services is desirable and could be achieved if SSDs were accorded stronger incentives to collaborate. Pressure has been made more severe by the fact that very elderly people (over 75) consume per capita nearly four times the amount of current expenditure as the population as a whole, and six times as much of current expenditure on the personal social services. (Cmnd 8175, 1981).

The demographic pressure of an ageing population, and consequent changes in service types and role, have to be managed at a time of decreasing resource growth. For example, one estimate has suggested that real expenditure on the personal social services rose by 63 per cent between 1970/71 and 1974/5 but by only 8 per cent between 1975/76 and 1979/80 (Webb and Wistow, 1982). As a consequence of this pressure, it is possible to conceive of several different responses by agencies. One defensive strategem might be to rely upon covert mechanisms of dilution and rationing such as a waiting list, as a procedure least likely to increase demands upon agency personnel. A second response would be to restructure patterns of service in order to reach a greater proportion of the more dependent elderly by methods such as screening and early ascertainment of treatable conditions. A third would be to concentrate resources upon intervention with priority sub-groups, such as those most likely to require institutional care.

It is clearly crucial to attempt to distinguish the particular strategic responses which are being made by agencies in the development of community services for an ageing population. This relates to the earlier concern about the utilisation of joint finance as a means of promoting interagency collaboration.

Such collaboration can of course proceed at both agency and client level. The need to link health and social care systems at client level in catering for the elderly with multiple needs seems a common problem in many first-world countries (Hokenstad and Ritvo, 1982) with ageing populations. An interaction of physical, psychiatric, social and emotional difficulties in many elderly patients means that an attempt to manage only one of these difficulties in isolation can offer only a partial solution. For example, Bergmann et al (1978) argue that effective management of demented elderly in the community requires dovetailed SSD support for families. Within geriatric medicine, moves towards multidisciplinary teamwork have been commended (Hodkinson, 1975) as a main focus for development.

The problem with such incremental moves to multidisciplinary working at client level is that the pace of change may be slow. Webb and Hobdell (1980) warn that traditional patterns of professional domination may reproduce themselves within multidisciplinary teams, whilst Evers (1982) argues that genuine team consensus may apply only to a minority of acute elderly cases.

It was for these reasons that the centre became increasingly concerned to push forward more substantial shifts towards multidisciplinary working with the elderly in the localities.

PART B: INTERAGENCY COLLABORATION

The first planning exercises proceeded at a synoptic level through the issuing of national 'norms'. But from the early 1970s onward there was increased interest in securing new forms of administrative machinery. Following preliminary attempts to introduce joint planning in the 1960s (Ministry of Health, 1965), the 1973 NHS Reorganisation Act charged NHS and SSD bodies with co-operating through member based Joint Consultative Committees. Despite periodic attempts to inject life into the system, by 1976 it was clear that the machinery for collaborative planning remained ineffective in many areas (Booth, 1981; Webb and Wistow, 1983a).

Joint Finance was seen as a more modest form of an operationally based, low cost means of carrying forward DHSS priority group policy in the mid seventies period of increasing pressure on public expenditure. By 1975 difficulties in securing collaboration between health and social services through the setting up of formal coordinating machinery were already evident. Mrs. Castle put on record her disappointment as the Secretary of State concerned at a speech to the inaugural conference of Area Health Authorities in 1975, but went on:

> 'to plead with (health authorities) to regard cooperation with local authorities as a high priority, for without it the concept of community care to which we are all commited will become an empty cliche.'

The 1976 Public Expenditure White Paper (Cmnd 6393, 1976) contained details of the new mechanism of joint finance. A 'modest' sum of money was to be allocated to AHAs to be used to finance high priority social services expenditure 'where it is accepted by both sides that this would yield a

better return in terms of total care.' The spending
criterion was clarified in a 1977 circular (HC77/17,
para 6) as follows:

> 'The criterion by which an AHA will use the
> money allocated to it for joint finance will
> be that the spending is in the interest of the
> NHS as well as the local authority and can be
> expected to make a better contribution in
> terms of total care than if directly applied
> to health services.'

Joint Finance has been extensively used to develop
services for elderly people: DHSS (1981c, para 5.1)
estimates that about 40 per cent of expenditure has
been on services for the elderly. However
reservations have also been apparent concerning the
use to which joint finance has been put. The Care
in the Community circular summed up the position as
follows:

> 'By a careful blend of projects, including
> capital schemes (where the use of joint
> finance saves local authorities having to
> incur loan charges) and short term projects,
> many local authorities have made good use of
> joint finance, often improving services in
> imaginative ways, with manageable long term
> revenue consequences. In other places, the
> combined effect of the build up of joint
> finance projects incurring long term revenue
> consequences, and current financial
> constraints, has led to authorities being
> increasingly reluctant to agree to schemes for
> which they will eventually be required to
> assume full financial responsibility.' (DHSS,
> 1981c).

Important criticisms were made by the House of
Commons Public Accounts Committee (1983) which found
in an investigation of seven Area Health Authorities
that the NHS side had played a reactive role in the
joint finance process with little consideration of
objectives, monitoring or evaluation. The Committee
argued that 100 per cent long term grants could
badly distort service development:

> 'The dangers are those of undermining the
> incentive toward efficiency in the specially

assisted schemes and of distorting local
priorities in favour of those schemes as
compared with others which might be more cost
effective but would mean a greater cost for
local ratepayers'

This reflects the perception that Joint Finance was
a significant new departure as it was based on
creation of incentives for implementors rather than
on an expectation that it was sufficient to define
policy for implementing authorities. Although the
intellectual origins of the concept have not been
explored, specific grants have long been made to
local authorities to provide incentives to adapt
spending patterns. this was, for instance, the
theme of the review of the Grant System carried out
by the influential IMTA study group in the 1950s
(Lees, 1956). Reservations about the efficacy of
joint finance have centred on the disincentive
generated by tapering and the potential of bias
towards capital rather than revenue based schemes.
Local authority reservations might be expected to be
most acute in areas where the direct rather than
indirect model of joint finance predominates.
The analysis of the role of incentives and
revenue sharing in promoting service shifts is more
developed in the American context (Stein and Miller,
1973). A massive expansion of specific federal
grants was a characteristic feature of the so-called
'creative federalism' of many Great Society
programmes in which federal government sought to
fund new social policy programmes at state level.
Over two hundred new grant programmes were enacted
during the five years of the Johnson presidency (Lee
and Benjamin, 1983). However, an analysis of the
effects of title 1 of the 1965 Elementary and
Secondary Education Act providing for federal grants
for the development by the states and localities of
education facilities for deprived children (Cohen et
al, 1973) found little real impact: 'lacking
counterpressures, federal officials are relatively
powerless to impose standards on state and local
school systems' (p.103). Partially as an outcome of
these implementation studies, greater emphasis was
put on providing incentives which would directly
reward implementors with the achievement of policy
goals. Much effort was concerned with assessing the
relative utility of regulatory and incentive methods
in the containment of environmental pollution and in

industrial policy (Schultze, 1977; Douglas and Miller, 1974; Kneese and Schultze, 1975; Majone, 1975). In health policy in particular, Americans proposed schemes for the incentive reimbursement of nursing homes and hospitals. So the efficacy of incentive led implementation processes has already been a subject of American debate.

The British literature is much weaker. However, the Joint Finance model may well pave the way for a proliferation of smaller incentives led schemes. Westland (1983) calculates that the money available under eight small scale DHSS programmes launched between 1980 and 1983 is set to rise from £0.65 m in FY 1982 to £21.65 m. in FY 1985.

There are therefore two questions which arise from the development and utilisation of joint finance as a prototype of an incentive led model of change:

1) To what extent has joint finance been used to fund conventional rather than innovative modes of provision?

2) Is the provision of Joint Finance targetted upon narrow bed blocking concerns (the direct self interest of the NHS) or has it been focussed upon the development of more general forms of services for care in the community (the indirect approach)?

PART C: AN APPROACH TO SCHEME ASSESSMENT

An examination of the impact of joint finance upon the type of care scheme in which it has been catalytic can considerably illuminate the two policy issues of the impact of incentives-led collaboration and the extent and nature of community service development for the elderly. The data base for this study was derived from a collection of information relating to innovative schemes in the care of the elderly, some of which were developed with joint finance (Ferlie, 1982). There were 222 schemes on which information was available. The 222 schemes were those which had SSD base budget finance but no joint finance (146 schemes) and those which had joint finance but no SSD base budget money (76 schemes). Table 1 provides information about the types of scheme and sponsoring organisation. The sponsoring organisation was defined as that which reported the innovation. It is important to note that schemes based upon NHS, Housing or Voluntary Organisation finance alone have been excluded from the analysis. As a result, the remaining schemes emphasise domiciliary care rather more than the overall collection of schemes.

TABLE 1
TYPE OF SCHEME AND SPONSORING ORGANISATION

1.1 Sponsoring Organisation

	Number
SSD	170
NHS	14
Housing Department	16
Voluntary organisation	22
Total	222

1.2 Basis of Scheme

Domiciliary care	69
Social worker based care	14
Day care	26
Neighbourhood care	16
Sheltered housing	26
Hospital based care	5
Other	66
Total	222

The method used to obtain the information was a postal trawl for documentation on innovation from the relevant agencies. One limitation was that information tended to be of a 'snapshot' rather than historical nature. Secondly, although a substantial amount of information was received, as might be expected, little related to the direct measurement of impact on clients. Consequently an evaluative approach to the different schemes based upon, say, the comparison of outcomes for people receiving the new provision with those receiving a standard range of services was not possible. However, although measurements of outcome are of great importance, indicators of the structure and process of care may be good indicators of intent if not of achievement (Donabedian, 1980). Such process evaluations based on efficiency and effectiveness has been developed (Davies and Ferlie, 1982) and elaborated (Ferlie, Challis and Davies, 1983) elsewhere but the major features can be summarised. They derive both from a content analysis of the reports received and from major features of the case management process (Challis and Davies, 1983). The following exposition tackles the problem, for convenience, by taking first 'effectiveness' and second 'efficiency'.

Effectiveness

Reports were analaysed and information on the following features recorded.

(i)   whether schemes are clearly targeted on priority subgroups. Patterns of need and of requisite response are likely to differ markedly from one subgroup to another. In order to fulfil the initial objective of lessening pressure on NHS resources, joint finance will be used best when concentrated on tightly defined high risk subgroups. The following definitions of target populations were included in the final analysis:
   a.   those elderly on the margin of admission to institutional care
   b.   elderly in need of post discharge care
   c.   elderly with insufficient informal carers
   d.   the elderly mentally infirm
   e.   stressed relatives
   f.   the elderly physically handicapped

(ii) whether the innovation promotes horizontal target efficiency (Bebbington and Davies, 1983) An alternative model of joint finance is that it will be used for indirect rather than direct provision, building up a general preventive and early warning infrastructure which can act as a buffer zone. Such a model could be especially vital if rapid deterioration is to be avoided. Higher horizontal efficiency can be promoted in a number of ways. Uptake can be improved through expansion of service, removal of charging barriers or localisation of provision. Good outreach to particular subgroups will attempt to draw them into service receipt. 'Open' or simplified referral channels also reduce the possibility of cases being lost across service boundaries. Information was thus recorded on the following 'signs':
   a.   increased uptake
   b.   preventive surveillance (good neighbours)

    c.   enchanced referral policy on discharge from institutional care
    d.   enhanced referral policy pre admission to institutional care
    e.   move to more 'open' referral policy
    f.   outreach to socially isolated elderly
    g.   outreach to the elderly physically handicapped
    h.   outreach to the elderly mentally infirm

(iii) whether the scheme increased vertical target efficiency (Bebbington and Davies, 1983). Schemes which focus tightly on high risk sub groups will need improved assessment procedures as a means of defining needs more sharply. Of particular interest are:
    a.   enhancement of the assessment instrument or process
    b.   multidisciplinary assessment procedure

(iv) whether there are explicit arrangements for the performance of core case management tasks. One of the ways in which joint finance could promote a better spend is through the integration of previously fragmented inter-agency and indeed inter-service decision making. At the level of the individual elderly person receiving services this indicates an enhanced system of total case management and of monitoring care. Information was recorded on the following signs of an explicit case management perspective:
    a.   monitoring
    b.   the provision of direct work
    c.   a follow-up service
    d.   a policy of immediate admission to institutional care (eg. geriatric units)
    e.   care packaging
    f.   service arranging (changes in the authority to prescribe services so as to enhance care packaging)
    g.   audit or review mechanisms
    h.   the presence of a key worker
    i.   the presence of a special care review on discharge from institutional care

(v) whether the service content is made more flexible or varied. A legitimate use of joint finance would be to 'bend' SSD provision at ground level towards the care of high risk subgroups. This will often take the form of provision for tasks of daily living (Isaacs et al, 1972) which demand forms of service more intensive than conventional home help. More flexible responses would also be important. Information was recorded on the following items:

a. enhanced physical support for the elderly physically handicapped (aids and adaptations; very sheltered housing
b. domestic care
c. personal care
d. basic nursing tasks (dressing, medicine, pressure sores)
e. provision of improved communications systems or warden cover in sheltered housing
f. out of hours or emergency service

We now turn to process indicators of efficiency.

Efficiency

(i) whether there is provision for short term service. This dimension clearly relates to the direct 'bed unblocking' role of joint finance through the provision of short term post discharge support schemes. Crisis intervention could aim at preventing admissions in addition. The following features were identified as of interest:

a. short term post hospital discharge service
b. short term post Part 3 discharge service
c. short term relief care service
d. short term crisis intervention service

(ii) whether there is provision for rehabilitation. Pressure on beds might in some instances be reduced by rehabilitative regimes designed to correct initial misplacement and prevent a drift into long term care. These would include physiotherapy and specific rehabilitative regimes for stroke patients. Information was also recorded on interventions designed to promote coping mechanisms in the care of the mentally infirm:

a. rehabilitation (social skills)
b. rehabilitation (physical)
c. coping mechanisms for the elderly mentally infirm

(iii) whether there is evidence of a switch from institutional to community care. This relates directly to the original function of joint finance in priority group policy. Do the schemes report an intention to move the boundary between institutional and community care? Do schemes appear to be moving towards lower cost forms of provision? Information was collected on the following 'signs':
   a. report of a shift in the boundary of care from institutional to community care
   b. support for informal carers
   c. use of volunteers
   d. greater use of basic grade staff for basic grade tasks (eg. nursing auxiliaries)

(iv) whether there is support for informal carers. One of the indirect roles of joint finance could be to support the informal sector where much of the caring for elderly people takes place and so prevent the possible collapse of informal caring networks under excessive strain which could result in requests for emergency admissions (Isaacs et al, 1972). Relative support is often seen as one of the distinguishing features of geriatrics and psychogeriatrics as medical specialities. Support can be offered in a number of ways:
   a. domiciliary support
   b. residential care or rotating care support
   c. day care support
   d. volunteers
   e. Relative Support Groups

(v) whether there is promotion of technical efficiency. Even within a given system mode, there are a variety of methods of production which result in the adoption either of localised or centralised production systems according to whether large scale production results in economies or diseconomies of scale for the service under consideration. The meals on wheels service is a good example of an area in which such questions assume significance. Productive efficiency might also be expected to increase along with the level of staff skill and management support which together constitute an important part of the stock of human capital. The use of low cost or adapted premises indicates lower capital costs as does the creation of more flexible methods of using existing residential facilities for short term intervention. Information was recorded on the following items:

    a. creation of new short term places in residential care

    b. economies of scale

    c. removal of diseconomies of scale

    d. enhanced managerial support or training

    e. low cost adaptation

(vi) community development. Part of the 'indirect' role of joint finance schemes could be to interweave with informal care and indeed to create new forms of care. Such community development activities can take a number of different forms:

    a. formation of new voluntary groups

    b. creation of new forms of neighbourhood care

    c. increasing outside social input into day care

    d. attempt to involve relatives or neighbours in care

PART D: DIFFERENTIATING JOINT FINANCE AND BASE BUDGET DEVELOPMENTS

The objective of the study was to examine whether it was possible to discriminate between two distinct groups of care schemes, those funded by Social Services base budget and those initiated by joint finance, using the efficiency and effectiveness characteristics of those schemes discussed earlier. In this way, evidence of the efficacy of joint finance in tackling the two policy issued discussed earlier, inter-agency collaboration and enhanced community support of the elderly, could be sought by the extent to which certain characteristics differentiated base budget developments from joint finance schemes.

The statistical procedure adopted was discriminant function analysis which weights and seeks a linear combination of the scheme characteristic variables so as to most distinctly separate the two groups. The dependent variable was whether a particular scheme was provided by base budget or not and the independent variables were the 62 indicators associated with effectiveness and efficiency outlined in the previous section. A stepwise discriminant function was computed using an inclusion/exclusion criterion of F-values greater than 1.6 to exclude the more trivial associations.

Results

The discriminant function which was derived is shown in Table 2.

TABLE 2
DISCRIMINANT FUNCTION

Variable	Standardised Coefficient	F
1. Factors associated with Joint Finance		
Basic Nursing	-.54	15.22***
Enhanced Post-discharge Referral Process	-.28	10.78**
Domiciliary Care based	-.57	6.62*
Voluntary Organisations sponsored	-.35	8.67**
Multidisciplinary Assessment	-.15	6.73**
Increased Uptake	-.28	4.12*
Shift away from Institutional Care	-.17	4.73*
Housing Department sponsored	-.41	4.51*
Formation of new voluntary groups	-.22	4.43*
Direct work (social work/therapeutic)	-.33	3.78
Rehabilitation/new coping skills (EMI)	-.39	3.38
Support for informal carers (volunteers)	-.27	2.74
Neighbourhood care	-.20	2.34
Enhanced pre-admission referral policy	-.26	2.02
Targeting (post-discharge care)	-.19	1.63
Outreach (elderly physically handicapped)	-.26	1.60
2. Factors associated with Base budget provision		
Monitoring	.41	6.49*
Follow up	.31	3.39
Staff training	.35	3.01
Outreach (socially isolated)	.22	2.05
New types of residential care (short stay/rotating care)	.19	1.89
Support for informal carers (day care)	.19	1.87

Statistics

Canonical Correlation	.61	Significance Levels
Wilks Lambda	.63	*** p= .001
		** p= .01
Significance	.000	* P= .05

The signs of the coefficients provide the basis for interpreting the meaning of the relationships: a negative coefficient indicates that the particular characteristic is association with joint finance and a positive coefficient is associated with base budget developments. It can be seen that the equation was reasonably successful in different-iating the two groups since 78.4 per cent of cases were correctly classified (χ^2 = 71.51 p= .000). Table 3 provides further details. This suggests that there were significant differences between the two modes of finance in developing services.

TABLE 3
PREDICTION OF CASES

		Predicted Group	
Actual Group	No. of Cases	Base Budget	Joint Finance
Base Budget	146	113	33
Joint Finance	76	15	61
Total	222	128	94

78.4 per cent of cases correctly classified

χ^2 = 71.51
Sig. = .000

First of all, joint financed schemes were more likely to produce basic nursing or 'tending' care (outside conventional medical settings), which Cang (1978) has argued is unfairly neglected in attempts to professionalise nursing. This development is especially relevant to the question of the mass delivery of basic nursing care to elderly patients and the recognition in many Joint Finance schemes that tending tasks may offer key forms of support to elderly people in addition to more technically skilled forms of nursing is welcome. Gibbins (et al) (1982) report a scheme involving home care and home nursing care inputs as a means of maintaining elderly patients at home. The nursing staff consisted of a nursing officer, two nursing sisters, three state enrolled nurses and two nursing auxiliaries. It may well be that such forms of service-mix would prove worthy of further development.

Joint Finance schemes were more likely to display other key features. An interest in easing bed blocking was demonstrated by provision of enhanced post-discharge referral policies by, for example, the automatic assessment of all patients being discharged from hospital to identify the need for post-discharge care. The provision of short term intensive care is geared to acutely rather than chronically ill elderly and reflects recurrent concern about poor communication between agencies on discharge (Amos, 1973; Centre for Policy on Ageing, 1980) and about early readmissions. Joint finance schemes were more likely to report a shift from institutional to community care for clients on the margin of admission, reflecting a greater concordance with priority group policy than base budget innovations.

Other signs suggested a more indirect use of joint finance, resulting in the creation of a community based 'buffer zone'. Jointly financed schemes were also more likely to involve voluntary and housing departments and to lead to the formation of new voluntary groups. They appeared more likely to display multidisciplinary assessment procedures, although whether this is likely to lead to a genuine concensus on service provision is unclear given the different concerns of groups of staff (Plank, 1977; Heuman and Boldy, 1982). Horizontal targeting by increased uptake appeared to be promoted by the absence of charge for many jointly financed short term schemes, even in those areas in which charges are made for the mainstream home help service. The deterrent effects of charging may indeed be a principal reason for introducing a special jointly financed scheme, for example in the case of the scheme developed in Kensington and Chelsea (Ferlie, 1980).

Second, whilst a number of characteristics appeared to be significantly associated with joint finance, the only feature significantly associated with base budget schemes concerned monitoring as part of the repertoire of the social work task with elderly people. It is difficult to be clear to the extent to which this was the more passive and traditional form of review-visiting (Goldberg and Warburton, 1979) or a more active part of overall case management. However, this emphasis on monitoring could represent the budgetary influence of elderly clients as significant consumers of long-term care resources of the Social Services Department and the concern to ensure that increasingly scarce resources are used to maximum effect. It could also reflect the marginal position of base budget innovations on pilot money, resulting in an emphasis on monitoring not apparent in more securely established mainstream programmes.

Third, it was clear that most 'signs' did not manage to distinguish between the two sets of schemes. Multidisciplinary assessment was the only variable associated with case management processes to discriminate significantly. Joint financed schemes did not seem to be more likely to change line management hierarchies perhaps by delegating resources to facilitate care packaging or service arranging. Joint finance did not appear significantly more likely to be used to develop services for priority groups such as the elderly mentally infirm. It is of interest in this regard to note that the DHSS have now decided to set up a separate fund for psychogeriatric initiatives separate from mainstream joint finance. Although the first equation derived indicated joint finance was not more likely either to be targeted on post discharge clients or to provide short term post hospital discharge care, it was clear that this finding is in part a product of multicollinearity in the data. The variable measuring enhanced post discharge procedures (REF2) was unsurprisingly found to be highly associated both with targeting on post discharge cases (X^2=15.06: p=.0001) and on the provision of a short term post hospital discharge service (X^2=20.04; p=.0000). Thus whereas 7 per cent of base budget schemes operated a short term post hospital discharge service, 18 per cent of jointly financed schemes did so.

PART E: DISCUSSION

Many joint finance schemes ease bed blocking through enhanced SSD post-discharge care, confirming the self-interest model of innovation (Glennerster et al, 1982). However, although it is impossible on the basis of this evidence to speculate about the motivations of actors, there do also appear to be wider consequences. A second function of joint finance has resulted in a more general buffer zone protecting institutional facilities from bombardment. Thus joint finance schemes are more likely to involve voluntary organisations and Housing Departments, more likely to provide basic nursing care in new contexts and more likely to 'pump prime' the creation of new voluntary services. Elaborate forms of service integration are not present, although multidisciplinary assessment may be used at least to manage conflicts over allocation criteria.

On the other hand, joint finance does not appear to have resulted in any more systematic shift of resources to such groups as the elderly mentally infirm than that associated with base budget schemes. There are two main reasons for this. First, joint finance is in many cases seen as a means of funding the transfer of patients into local authority care through the provision of short-term bridging mechanisms rather than to provide for long term support (Webb and Wistow, 1983b). However, frail elderly clients will often require just such long term support (Morris, 1977). Second, existing incentives do not seem strong enough to elide the different views and preferences held by different actors operating within a pluralist welfare system. Voluntary organisations will, for example, often place stress on localist provision and relative support, with the result that there may be poor linkage with the goals of public agencies.

It is important to bear in mind other evidence about the relative power of incentives in producing change at local level.

Inner Cities policy (Department of the Environment, 1977) similarly proposed a central/local government partnership (involving DHSS money). In the absence of clear central guidelines, the following pattern emerged according to Ham, Towell and Underwood (1981): little emphasis was placed on 'bending' main programmes, a preference was shown for capital rather than revenue expenditure, stress was not placed on integrating health and personal social service inputs, and many schemes focussed on basic provision rather than service enhancement. In terms of services for the elderly, few schemes promoted further service innovation, area based strategies or specific community development approaches but rather built up basic domiciliary and day care services.

Such findings reflect general problems of achieving changes desired by funders in the absence of criteria for allocation and monitoring. It seems that general incentives are not always enough to shift local patterns of decision making and that further development of incentives-led planning is necessary. Perhaps marginal client groups which require both long term social and medical care could be best serviced by an agency which linked health and SSD personnel and which had its own budget. Changes in some authorities towards management partnerships and joint user establishments suggest that some areas at least are willing to move in this direction. If there were an independent budget for marginal client groups, however, there might be more of an incentive to spend rather than to argue.

However, although such organisational changes might promote shifts in patterns of service development, incentives cannot act in isolation from changing perceptions amongst agency personnel themselves. Role changes can be accelerated but not caused by joint finance, but depend on a much more fundamental value consensus on the need to shift resources to particular client groups and to value caring rather than curing roles (Webb and Hobdell, 1980). Glennerster et al (1983) found most officers and professionals engaged in joint planning still thought in terms of departmental expansion rather than creation of joint services.

The introduction of joint finance can on the evidence of this study be justified in terms of producing limited and local improvements in service within the framework advanced with shifts away from continuing institutional care and towards earlier discharge, basic nursing care and multidisciplinary assessment. The joint finance innovations appeared to be adopting both the "direct" and "indirect" roles already discussed. It was therefore not possible to reject either of our initial hypotheses. What is also clear is that this evidence certainly does not support the more severe criticisms of the efficacy of joint finance. Indeed, these innovations were significantly more likely to display key indicators of good practice. However, there was no evidence of a systematic shift towards priority groups such as the elderly mentally infirm and the high bargaining costs associated with such innovation also have to be taken into consideration. Although best use is not always made of joint finance; nevertheless without such incentives there would probably be even less collaboration. An

important question is whether the pattern of
incentives and central inputs can be changed to
promote such collaboration further and to develop
the opportunities opened up by the Joint Finance
initiative.

References

Amos, Geraldine (1973) Care is Rare, Age Concern,
    London
Bebbington, A.C. and Davies, B.P. (1983) 'Equity and
    Efficiency in the Allocation of the Personal
    Social Services', Journal of Social Policy, 12
    (3), 309-330
Bergmann, K., Foster, E.M., Justice, A.W. and
    Matthews, V. (1978) 'Management of the Demented
    Elderly Patient in the Community', British Journal
    of Psychiatry, 132, 441-449
Booth, T. (1981) 'Collaboration between the health
    and Social Services: A Case Study of Joint Care
    Planning', Policy and Politics 9(1), 23-49
Boucher, C.A. (1957) 'A Survey of Services Available
    to the Chronic Sick and Elderly in 1954-5',
    Reports on Public Health and Medical Subjects, 98,
    HMSO, London
Cang, S. (1978) 'Full time and part time patients:
    an analysis of patient need and their implications
    for domiciliary and institutional care', in E.
    Jacques (ed) Health Services, 204-224, HEB, London
Centre for Policy and Ageing (1980) Organising
    Aftercare, CPA, London
Challis, D.J. and Davies, B.P. (1983) Matching
    Resources to Needs in Long Term Care, PSSRU,
    University of Kent
Chief Officer of the Ministry of Health (1979) On
    the State of the Publich Health, HMSO, London
Cmnd 6393 (1976) Public Expenditure to 1979-80,
    HMSO, London
Cmnd 8175 (1981) The Government's Expenditure Plans
    1981-2 to 1983-4, HMSO, London
Cohen, D.K., McCann, W.J., Murphy, J.T. and van
    Geel, T. (1973) 'Revenue Sharing as an Incentive
    Device' in Stein and Miller, op. cit. (1973),
    93-116
Commons, House of (Public Accounts Committee)
    (1983) Session 1982-1983, HCP, 160 and 160-i
Davies, B.P. and Ferlie, E.B. (1982) 'Efficiency
    Promoting Innovation in Social Care', Policy and

Politics, 10 (2), 181-203

Department of the Environment (1977) Policy for the Inner Cities, Cmnd 6845, HMSO, London

DHSS (1976) Priorities for Health and Personal Social Services, p.41, HMSO, London

DHSS (1981a) Growing Older, Cmnd 8173, HMSO, London

DHSS (1981b) Care in Action, HMSO, London

DHSS (1981c) Care in the Community: A Consultative Document, London, DHSS

Donabedian, A. (1980) The Definition of Quality and Approaches to its Assessment, Health Administration Press, Ann Arbor, Michigan

Douglas, G.W. and Miller III, J.C. (1974) Economic regulation domestic transport: theoried policy, The Brookings Institution, Washington DC

Evers, Helen (1982) 'Professional Practice and Patient Care = Multidisciplinary Teamwork in Geriatric Wards', Ageing and Society (2), 1, 57-77

Ferlie, E.B. (1980) A Directory of Innovations in the Community Care of the Elderly, PSSRU, University of Kent

Ferlie, E.B. (1982) A Sourcebook of Initiatives in the community Care of the Elderly, PSSRU, University of Kent

Ferlie, E.B., Challis, D.J. and Davies, B.P. (1983) A Guidebook to Innovations in the Care of the Elderly, PSSRU, University of Kent

Gibbins, F.J., Lee, M., Davison, P.R., O'Sullivan, P., Hutchinson, M., and Murphy, D.R. (1982) 'Augmented home nursing as an alternative to hospital care for chronic elderly individuals', British Medical Journal, 30.1.82, 330-333

Glennerster, Howard; Korman, Nancy; Marslen-Wilson, Frances and Meredith, Barbara (1982) Social Planning : A Local Study, LSE, London

Glennerster, Howard; Korman, Nancy and Marsler-Wilson, Frances (1983) 'Plans and Practice: The Participants' Views', Public Administration, Autumn, 253-264

Goldberg, E.M. an Warburton, R.W. (1979) Ends and Means in Social Work, Allen and Unwin, London

Ham, Chris; Towell, David; and Underwood, Jacky (1981) Inner Cities : Community Services, SAUS, University of Bristol, Working Paper 15

Heumann, C. and Bolby, D. (1982) Housing for the Elderly, Croom Helm, London

Hodkinson, H.M. (1975) An Outline of Geriatrics, Academic Press, London

Hokenstad, K.C. and Ritvo, R.A. (1982) Linking
     Health Care and Social Services - International
     Perspectives, Sage, Beverley Hills
Isaacs, B., Livingstone, M. and Neville, Y. (1972)
     Survival of the Unfittest, Routledge & Kegan Paul,
     London
Kneese, Alan and Schulze, Charles L. (1975),
     Pollution crisis and public policy, The Brookings
     Institution, Washington DC
Lee, P.R. and Benjamin, A.E. (1983)
     'Intergovernmental Relations: Historical and
     Contemporary Perspectives', in C. Estes, R.
     Newcomer et al, Fiscal Austerity and Aging, 59-82,
     Sage, London
Lees, D.S. et al (1956) Local Expenditures and
     Central Grants, IMTA, London
Majone, G. (1975) 'Standard setting and the theory
     of institutional choice: the case of pollution
     control', Policy and Politics, Vol. 4 No. 2, 35-
     52, December
Ministry of Health (1948) Circular 87/48, Ministry
     of Health, London
Ministry of Health (1965) Circular 18/65, Ministry
     of Health, London
Morris, R. (1977) 'Caring for (vs.) caring about the
     people', Social Work, 22, 353-359
Plank, D. (1977) Caring for the Elderly, Greater
     London Council Research Memorandum, 512, London
Stein, B. and Miller, S.M. (1973) Incentives and
     Planning in Social Policy, Aldine, Chicago
Schultze, Charles E. (1977) The Public Use of
     Private Interest, The Brookings Institution,
     Washington DC
Webb, A.L. and Hobdell, M. (1980) 'Coordination and
     Teamwork in the Health and Personal Social
     Services', in Susan Lonsdale, Adrian Webb and T.L.
     Briggs, Teamwork in the Personal Social Services
     and Health Care, 97-110, Croom Helm, London
Webb, A. L. and Wistow, G. (1982) Personal Social
     Services: Trends in Expenditure and Provision, in
     House of Commons Select Committee on Social
     Services (1982), '1982 White Paper : Public
     Expenditure on the Social Services' Session 1981-
     82, HCP 306-ii, 168-189
Webb, A.L. and Wistow, G. (1983a) Power Rationality
     and Social Planning : Collaboration in the Health
     and Personal Social Services, University of
     Loughborough, draft
Webb, A.L. and Wistow, G. (1983b) 'Public

Expenditure and Policy Implementation', <u>Public</u>
<u>Administration</u>, Spring, 21-44
Westland, Peter (1983) 'No sense of direction',
<u>Community Care</u>, 17.11.83
Williams, Alan and Anderson, Robert (1975)
<u>Efficiency in the Social Services</u>, Basil
Blackwell, Oxford

Chapter Thirteen

WELFARE BENEFITS AND THE ELDERLY: SOME PRELIMINARY
RESULTS FROM THE G.L.C. TAKE UP CAMPAIGN

Christina R. Victor

INTRODUCTION

    Poverty and low income are a characteristic
feature of old age in Britain as social commentators
from Charles Booth onwards have documented. Using
the supplementary benefit scale rates (currently
57.10 pounds per week for a couple and 35.70 for a
single person) laid down annually by Parliament,
which may be taken to approximate to society's
notion of a minimum standard of living, 20 per cent
of all pensioners have incomes below the poverty
line.   A further 44 per cent have incomes which are
on the margins of poverty i.e. less than 40 per cent
above the relevant S.B. scale rate (Townsend, 1979).
Thus 5.2 million pensioners in Britain live in or on
the margins of poverty. Additionally although the
elderly constitute approximately 15 per cent of the
total population they account for 32 per cent of the
population defined as poor.
    The incidence of poverty is unequally
distributed within the elderly population.   The
fraction classified as poor, or on the margins of
poverty, increases significantly with age from 56
per cent of those aged 65-69 to 86 per cent of those
aged over 85. Additionally poverty is concentrated
amongst those elderly classified as disabled or who
are widowed.   Particularly strong is the
concentration of poverty amongst elderly women.
    Several factors explain this concentration of
poverty in old age. The elderly have access to few
financial or other assets. Townsend reports that in
his survey only 21 per cent of the elderly had
assets of over 1000 pounds.   Additionally the
elderly are less likely to possess consumer
durables and more likely to live in poorer quality
dwellings than the rest of the population (Hunt,

1978).   Thus   the   elderly   are   reliant upon State
benefits,   notably   the   retirement pension, for the
majority   of   their   income.   20   per   cent   of all
pensioners are reliant upon state benefits for their
total   income   and this fraction increases with age.
Thus   70   per   cent   of   those over 80 have no other
income   apart   from   that   provided   by   the   State.
Occupational   pensions are paid to less than half of
the   retired population (Walker, 1980).   Although it
is   the primary means of support for the majority of
elderly   the   retirement   pension   has   remained low
relative   to   earnings.   The   pension   for a single
person   has   fluctuated at about 20 per cent   of the
average   gross   manual   workers wage and 30 per cent
for couples.

The elderly and means-tested benefits

The   low   level of the retirement pension means
that the elderly with few other assets, which is the
majority,   are   eligible   for Supplementary Pension.
However   take-up   rates   (i.e. the fraction of those
entitled   who are actually claiming the benefit) for
this   benefit remain low amongst the elderly.   Table
1   shows   that   in   1981 2.4 million pensioners were
eligible   for   supplementary pension but that it was
being   claimed   by   only   67 per cent.   Thus 810,000
elderly were not claiming a total of 210 million per
annum; or an average payment of 5 pounds per week.
Take-up   rates for other means tested   benefits
remain stubbornly low amongst the elderly.

TABLE 1   Estimates of take up of supplementary
                        pension

	1979	1983
Total Eligible (000's)	2590	2480
% Receiving	65	67
Number eligible but not receiving (000's)	900	810
Estimate benefit unclaimed (million pounds per annum)	145	210
Average weekly amount unclaimed	3.10	5.0

Source: Hansard written answers 30th November 1983

Reasons for the non-take-up of benefits

Three major explanations have been proposed for the low take-up of specific means-tested benefits by all age groups.
It has been suggested that many people fail to claim means-tested benefits because of the stigma and negative feelings involved. This is thought to be particularly strong amongst the elderly who vividly remember the pre-war household means test (Deacon and Bradshaw, 1983).
The second perspective suggests that low take-up is a result of claimants (and potential claimants) lacking information about the availability of benefits; the rules for eligibility or the method of claiming. The third view suggests that the difficulty, or perceived difficulty, of actually claiming may deter many potential claimants.
In addition to these 3 main explanations perceived need, the low monetary value of many benefits and a previous refusal of a claim have also been suggested as discentives reducing the level of benefit take-up.
Using data derived from the evaluation of a take up project currently being sponsored by the G.L.C. this paper explores how relevant these explanations are in trying to understand why the elderly do not claim all the benefits to which they are entitled.

The G.L.C. benefits project

In response to the estimate that at least 100 million pounds per annum in benefits is not claimed by Londoners the G.L.C. has initiated a project which aims to increase take-up by providing information and portraying claiming in a positive way as a right or entitlement. This project is multi-faceted including specific geographically based local campaigns, extensive media advertising and T.V. programmes. The data used in this analysis derive from the evaluation of the local take-up campaigns which is being undertaken at Surrey University. A series of local campaigns have been undertaken in various parts of London. Each area, which aproximates to an electoral ward, is selected because it is thought, upon the basis of census and other data, that they will contain a high proportion of potential claimants. Each address receives a leaflet which describes simply a variety of benefits, contains a specially designed claim form and timetable of the Benefit Bus, a mobile advice centre, and gives the number of the special freephone benefits advice service.

METHOD

To evaluate the effectiveness of this strategy in meeting its objectives of providing information about benefits and encouraging more positive attitudes towards claiming a quota sample of 200 potential claimants are interviewed before the campaign. Given the difficulty of operationalising the definition of a potential claimant, the evaluation used the major categories of underclaimers; the elderly, the sick/disabled, single parents and unemployed, to define the study population of potential claimants. Using a simple screening question to exclude households not falling into the categories of potential claimants a target quota of 50 per claimant group is specified. The interview is conducted with the person in the household who is responsible for managing the finances. This person was selected as the respondent because the project team considered that this was the individual within the household that they wished their publicity to most influence. The interview schedule used in the evaluation was based upon questionnaires used in previous studies of welfare benefits and upon the results of unstructured interviews carried out in a pilot survey. The questionnaire examines subjects's levels of knowledge about the availability of welfare benefits and their claiming history. Attitudes towards claiming and the welfare state are explored using a series of Likert style attitude measures which require subjects to agree or disagree with a series of statements. Additionally a series of open ended questions further explore attitudes towards claiming and subjects suggestions for improving the method of claiming welfare benefits and improving take-up. After the local take-up campaign has been completed a second sample of subjects is selected and interviewed and the responses between the two groups are compared. The evaluation will be repeated in 6 areas of London; the data presented in this paper, which examines the attitudes of the elderly towards benefits claiming, are based upon 3 surveys completed in Wandsworth and Tower Hamlets.

RESULTS

Characteristics of the study population

Of the 602 subjects interviewed, 167 were classified as pensioners i.e. the head of the household exceeded statutory retirement age; 168 were classed as unemployed: 165 as single parents and 102 as sick/disabled. Of the elderly 55 per cent lived alone and 40 per cent were female and their ages ranged from 60 to 91 years of age. 57 per cent reported that they suffered from a limiting illness/disability.

Current receipt of benefits

Over half of the elderly interviewed had an income of less than 50 pounds per week compared with 75-79 pounds for younger subjects. In addition to the State retirement pension 43 per cent of the elderly were receiving supplementary pension and 25 per cent were receiving housing benefit. Only 6 per cent were receiving an occupational pension.

77 per cent of pensioners and 11 per cent of other subjects had previously received supplementary pension or benefit respectively. A variety of extra weekly payments (known officially as additional requirements) are available to those receiving supplementary pension/benefit with specific exceptional needs such as extra laundry costs because of incontinence or special dietary requirements. 4 per cent of pensioners and 7 per cent of others had previously received such payments. 11 per cent of elderly subjects and 38 per cent of others had previously been awarded a supplementary single payment for such things as household equipment, bedding or clothing.

Attitudes to claiming and welfare

Before examining the utility of the major explanations of non-take-up the attitudes of the elderly towards welfare generally are compared with those of younger subjects.

78 per cent of the elderly agreed with the

statement that the welfare state was something which we could be proud of in Britain compared with 58 per cent of younger subjects. However the elderly were significantly more likely to consider that some of those receiving welfare benefits were scroungers. 86 per cent of pensioners felt that such people existed compared with 64 per cent of younger subjects. Respondents were then asked to estimate what fraction of benefits receipients were scroungers. The median fraction suggested by the elderly was 50 per cent compared with only 15 per cent quoted by younger subjects. Subjects were then asked to nominate those groups which they considered most and least deserved to receive welfare benefits (Table 2).

TABLE 2   Groups most and least deserving
               of welfare support (%)

	Most Deserving	
	Elderly	Others
The poor	15	16
Poor families	11	10
Single parents	3	23
Sick/disabled	27	14
Elderly	100	17
Unemployed	13	34
N	167	435

	Least Deserving	
	Elderly	Others
None	22	30
School leavers	19	3
Lazy/workshy	9	14
Black economy	10	11
Scroungers	7	3
Immigrants	10	5
Large families	5	2
N	167	435

NB: %'s do not total 100 as each individual could give more than one answer.

The elderly were much less likely to nominate single parents and the unemployed as deserving welfare

than younger subjects. However with the exception
of school leavers both young and old subjects were
in close agreement about the groups who did not
deserve welfare payments; the lazy, scroungers and
those participating in the 'black' economy.
    Table 3 describes the responses provided
by subjects to a series of general statements about
the provision of welfare payments.

TABLE 3   General attitudes towards welfare provision

	% agreeing with statement	
	Elderly	Others
The welfare state is still something we can be really proud of	78	58
It's so difficult to get welfare that many people don't get all they are entitled to	72	81
If there weren't so much social security people would learn to stand on their own two feet	71	41
Poor people only have themselves to blame, so there's no reason why society should support them	20	7
People who get social security get dependent on it and stop trying to help themselves	62	32
People who claim social security should feel guilty about living off taxpayers charity	27	11
Everyone who is poor should be given help	76	83
People should only be given money from the government if they've paid for it in the past	59	27
People who live on social security have a really hard struggle to make ends meet	58	88
N	150	391

The majority of subjects, both young and old, considered that all the poor should be helped regardless of why they were poor. Similarly the majority of elderly and young felt that the difficulty of claiming benefits precluded many people from gaining their full entitlement. However significantly fewer older subjects agreed that those living on welfare had a struggle to make ends meet. In contrast to younger subjects the elderly were also significantly more likely to agree that people would learn to look after themselves if there were less state help and that the provision of state help stopped people from helping themselves. Thus it seems that the elderly, whilst generally in favour of the provision of welfare benefits, consider that a substantial fraction of recipients are scroungers and are more likely to consider that provision of benefits reduces personal initiative and independence.

Explanations of low take-up

Having considered general attitudes towards welfare provision the 3 major explanations for low take-up are now considered individually.

1) Lack of information

Table 4 describes the fractions of subjects who were aware of the existence of a series of welfare benefits and additional weekly and single payments which are available to those receiving supplementary benefit/pension. Pensioners were consistently less aware of the existence of benefits than the other groups. The only exception to this generalisation being attendance allowance. Within the two groups there were further variations in the levels of awareness; women being consistently more aware of benefits than men. Those receiving supplementary benefit/pension were no more aware of the availability of extra weekly payments (additional requirements) or single payments than non recipients. These data demonstrate a significant lack of knowledge by the elderly about the provision of welfare benefits. However even where subjects were aware of the existence of a benefit this does not mean that they understood the criteria for eligibility. It was not possible to investigate this topic area in this particular study. However anecdotal evidence from the fieldworkers suggests

that few subjects, if they were aware of a benefit,
understood the rules for eligibility or claiming.
Subjects were also asked where they would go if they
wanted advice about welfare benefits. 30 per cent
of the elderly did not know where they would go to
seek advice compared with 9 per cent of younger
subjects. However there were few differences in the
types of agency which the two groups would consult;
namely the DHSS or the C.A.B.

TABLE 4 Knowledge of Benefits

| | | % of subjects heard of benefit | |
		Elderly	Others
Supplementary benefit		91	100
Supplementary pension		37	40
Additonal Requirements	diet	25	30
	baths	5	8
	heating	37	59
	laundry	15	21
	clothing	19	38
	hp	0	7
	fares	26	56
Single payments	furniture	13	50
	bedding	11	55
	clothing	11	48
	fuel bills	24	39
	lagging	6	11
	removals	26	54
	baby things	17	54
Attendence allowance		44	37
Mobility allowance		39	56
Invalid care allowance		39	47
NCIP		11	17
HNCIP		4	9
Housing Benefit		94	98
N		167	435

NCIP = Non Contributory Invalidity Pension
HNCIP = Housewives Non Contributory Invalidity
        Pension

Thus compared with younger subjects the elderly
were both less aware of the availability of benefits

and where to go to get advice about benefits.

2) Notions of stigma and pride
     Subjects were given a series of statements which, they were told, had been given as reasons why people might not claim all the benefits to which they were entitled. They were then asked how pertinent these explanations were to them. The responses given by the two groups to a series of 5 statements which related to general notions of pride and independence as explanations for not claiming benefits are shown in Table 5. The elderly were more likely to agree that claiming benefits involved a loss of independence and that benefits were synonomous with charity. However, there were no differences between the two groups in responses to the questions about visiting DHSS offices, enquiries about financial circumstances and the effect of claiming benefit upon an individuals pride.

TABLE 5   Attitude statements relating to
                         pride/stigma

	% agreeing with statement	
	Elderly	Others
I feel I would lose my independence	60	47
I would feel my pride would be affected	51	48
I wouldn't want people asking about my personal affairs	47	51
I would feel I was accepting charity	46	31
I don't like going to social security or other benefit offices	78	78
N	152	426

     Thus whilst there were some differences in responses to these questions between the two groups these were not as great as some previous studies had lead us to expect.

3)   The claiming process
Attitudes to the claiming process are shown in Table 6. The elderly were significantly more likely to agree that claiming benefit was straightforward, that   DHSS   staff   were   helpful   and   that   DHSS literature was helpful than were younger subjects. Although there were no differences between the two groups in the fractions agreeing that making a claim involved a long wait at the DHSS office the elderly were more likely to agree that claims were dealt with promptly and less likely to agree that a claim involved filling in a long form.

TABLE 6   Attitudes to the claiming process

	% agreeing with statement	
	Elderly	Others
Claiming benefit is straightforward and uncomplicated	54	29
DHSS counter staff are helpful	66	40
DHSS leaflets explain clearly what benefits are available and who is entitled to them	52	33
Claiming benefit involves filling in long and complicated forms	63	84
If you claim benefit you have to wait a long time in DHSS offices	77	76
If you make a claim it is dealt with promptly and efficiently	56	28
N	160	425

Thus the elderly were generally less critical of the claiming procedure than other respondents. This difference may reflect a difference in the way young and old claimants are treated by the DHSS. Alternatively it could have arisen because older people are less willing to criticise the bureaucratic machinery of the state than younger clients of the welfare services.

4)   Perceived need

It has been suggested that perceived need is an important stimulus to making a benefit claim, particularly where the elderly are concerned (Kerr, 1982). Thus a series of 4 statements relating to this parameter were included in the present study (Table 7). These responses show that the elderly were more willing to agree with the notions of managing within their present budget than younger age groups. They also were less willing to ask for extra money and to make a claim where they were unsure of their entitlement.

TABLE 7   Attitudes to perceived need and entitlement

	% agreeing with statement	
	Elderly	Others
I would rather manage without if I could	81	72
I would only claim if I were sure I was entitled	94	76
I don't feel I need the money enough to make a claim	39	18
I wouldn't like to ask and be turned down	83	65
I would not like to ask for extra money	72	54
N	161	430

These data provide some evidence which supports the notion that perceived need is an important stimulus to claiming. For many elderly, who are classified as poor by the standards of the rest of society, the reference by which they set their standard of living is the 1930's rather than the 1980's. Thus they may not perceive a need for more money. Considerable evidence to support this hypothesis was forthcoming in the pilot study conducted before the evaluation was started. Additionally these data also demonstrate that uncertainty about entitlement is probably a powerful disincentive to claiming.

FURTHER INVESTIGATIONS OF TAKE-UP

The attitude statements described above have the disadvantage that subjects have to agree (or disagree) with a preselected list of topics. There is no scope to express themselves in their own words about aspects of take up not included on the list. Thus a series of open ended questions were included about potential entitlement to benefit and the changes which subjects would like to see in the way benefits were claimed.

1) Potential entitlement
50 per cent of the elderly and 45 per cent of others felt that they might be eligible for a benefit they were not currently receiving. They were then asked if they could think of any reasons why they might not claim for this. Even given the methodological problems inherent in asking hypothetical questions the responses listed in Table 8 are interesting. For both groups a previous refusal of a claim was a strong disincentive to submitting a further claim. However for the elderly it is evident that uncertainty over entitlement was the biggest barrier to claiming. Very few elderly thought they might not apply for reasons which could be interpreted as pertaining to notions of pride or stigma.

TABLE 8   Suggested reasons for not making
                 a claim (%)

	Elderly	Others
None	23	26
Uncertain of entitlement	58	50
Previous refusal	19	19
Don't need extra money	5	4
"Pride"	2	1
Other	3	5
N	82	258

2) Changes to the system of claiming benefits
The less critical perspective of the elderly towards the welfare system was reflected in responses to the question which asked subjects if, in their opinion, there should be changes made to the system of benefits claiming. 55 per cent of

elderly replied yes to this compared with 92 per cent of other subjects. Their respective suggestions for change are shown in Table 9 and show very few differences between the two groups. The most popular change with both groups involved notions of automatic assessment i.e. that it was the job of the DHSS to notify all potential clamants of their entitlement to all relevant benefits rather than the onus being on claimants to find out about benefits and prove their eligibility. Other popular suggested improvements were a quicker service, fewer forms to complete, more and more helpful DHSS staff and improved DHSS offices and publicity.

TABLE 9   Suggested changes to the system
           of claiming benefits (%)

	Elderly	Others
Automatic assessment	47	32
Improve publicity	33	19
Fewer forms to complete	30	16
More helpful attitude of DHSS staff	27	30
Improve DHSS offices	27	36
Quicker service	23	25
Simplify leaflets and forms	18	32
Employ more DHSS staff	13	15
Increase value of benefits	8	9
N	91	400

NB: %'s do not total 100 as subjects could give more than one answer

3) Suggestions to improve take-up
Subjects were also asked how more people could be encouraged to claim their full benefits entitlement (Table 10). The most popular suggestion amongst the elderly was for home visits from DHSS officers (or other qualified individuals) to explain benefits and the rules for eligibility. Improved publicity via T.V. and media advertising were also popular suggestions with both groups as was the establishment of specific advice desks within DHSS offices.

Responses to these questions indicate that potential claimants feel that the system of claiming benefits requires modification to make claiming easier and that advice and information about benefits should be more readily available.

TABLE 10   Suggestions for increasing benefits take up (%)

	Elderly	Others
Home visits from DHSS or benefits advisors	26	18
Advertise on TV	15	25
Advice centres in DHSS offices	13	15
Home delivery of special	10	15
Advertise entitlement more widely	10	19
Put forward claiming in a more positive manner	8	6
Advertise in papers	7	6
Simplify forms	7	6
Automatic notification of benefits and entitlement	7	9
Wider availability of leaflets	5	11
Make DHSS staff more helpful	4	12
Improve DHSS offices	2	7
N	160	430

NB: %'s do not total 100 as subjects could give more than one answer

DISCUSSION

167 elderly persons resident in the London Borough of Wandsworth and Tower Hamlets were interviewed about their attitudes towards claiming welfare benefits. These responses were compared with those provided by younger subjects to establish if under claiming was precipitated by different sets of factors in the various age groups.

Welfare Benefits and the Elderly

Using a series of attitude statements general views on the provision of welfare were elicited. This revealed that the elderly were more likely to feel that the provision of welfare reduced personal initiative than younger subjects. They were also more likely to feel that some of those claiming benefits were 'scroungers'. Additionally the elderly were less willing to see groups such as single parents and the unemployed as worthy of welfare support than younger subjects. However there was considerable unanimity between groups about the undeserving beneficiaries of welfare payments; the lazy, workshy or those participating in the "black" economy.

Lack of knowledge, the complexity of claiming and feelings of pride/stigma were the 3 explanations for the non-take-up of benefits tested in this preliminary investigation. Neither group displayed a great awareness of benefits but the elderly were particularly handicapped by their low levels of information. Additionally a substantial minority did not know where advice about such matters could be obtained.

The elderly were less critical of the claiming process than younger subjects particularly in responses to the preset attitude statements. They were also much less likely to feel that the system for claiming needed alteration. This may be because the elderly are less willing to be critical of state institutions than younger subjects. Alternatively it may be that the elderly encounter fewer problems in their dealings with the benefits system than do younger subjects. Thus the complexity of the claiming process may be less of a disincentive to claim for the elderly compared with other groups of potential claimants. However in the open ended questions elderly subjects stated that they felt that modifications could be made to assist them, particularly the introduction of domiciliary visits to discuss benefits; a previously routine practice which is now being suspended by the DHSS. They also felt that the forms which they needed to complete could be made less complex and that there should be fewer of them.

The elderly demonstrated a higher level of agreement with several of the statements which related non-take-up of benefits to feelings of independence and pride. However this difference was not as marked as was expected suggesting that these factors are only of limited value in explaining the non-take-up of benefits. Of greater importance in this study seemed to be the disincentive to claiming if the subject was uncertain of their entitlement. Amongst both young and old alike the fear of having a claim rejected was also important. Amongst the elderly there was also evidence that the level of perceived need was lower than that characteristic of younger respondents. Until they feel the need for money acutely they will not apply for any available benefits. This finding supports the work of Scott Kerr (1982).

Thus our findings demonstrate that for both old and young alike, underclaiming seems to be strongly related to the low levels of knowledge about benefits and the uncertainty about eligibility which this generates. This seems to support the findings of Meacher (1972) who suggested that 70 per cent of underclaiming was a result of either inadequate or incorrect information about benefits and the rules for entitlement. The complexity of the claiming process seemed to be less of a disincentive for the elderly. Notions of pride were also of less importance than expected which is in line with the work of Allison (1982).

Additionally our data also demonstrate that a previous refusal of a claim can also be a powerful disincentive to submitting a further claim, especially for the elderly.

These findings are, however, preliminary as the evaluation of the GLC campaign has not yet been completed. However these data suggest that take up campaigns which attempt to promote a greater understanding of benefits via greater publicity are well founded. Additionally for the elderly more domicilliary benefits advice and promotion would seem to be a useful way of encouraging a greater take-up of benefits by one of the poorest and most deprived groups in the community.

References

Allison, F.M. (1982) The non-take-up of welfare benefits - the would be claimants obstacle course, M.Sc. thesis, University of Bath.

Deacon, A. and Bradshaw, J. (1983) Reserved for the poor, Martin Robertson, Oxford.

Hunt, A. (1978) the elderly at home, HMSO.

Kerr, Scott, A. (1982) Deciding about supplementary

pensions: a provision model, Journal of Social Policy, 11, 505-507

Meacher, M. (1972) Rent rebates : a study of the effectiveness of the means test, Child Poverty Action Group, London.

Townsend, P. (1979) Poverty in the United Kingdom, Penguin

Walker, A. (1980) The social creation of poverty and dependency in old age, Journal of Social Policy, 9, 49-75.

Chapter Fourteen

SHELTERED HOUSING: SOME UNANSWERED QUESTIONS

Graham Fennell

Introduction

The main publication of the Leeds University study of sheltered housing (Butler, Oldman and Greve, 1983) has focused on a range of social policy issues. Our understanding has been enhanced by the authors' illuminating discussion of what they see as the seven conventional rationales for providing sheltered housing. But while no one would dispute the importance of these issues, there remain other questions of considerable sociological interest relating particularly to the tenants of sheltered housing and how they function in their social world and these could not satisfactorily be answered in the short compass of the seventeen page chapter devoted to them in the book. In this paper, I examine some of these questions by reference to intellectually antecedent studies and describe a forthcoming research project among Anchor sheltered housing tenants which may cast some light on them.

Family Ties

The first issue is the exchange of services in social networks and whether study of such exchanges in any sort of 'natural' setting affords the basis of an argument for grouping elderly people together in sheltered housing. To summarise a welter of evidence, we know that the primary locus for the services throughout a lifetime is the family: this still heavily outweighs any other source. Advantages of family supplied services are that they are flexible and tailormade to a person's needs, individuated, covering a vast range of different types of needs, including over a lifetime exchanges of intimate bodily care and of financial support,

both of these being properties, as it were, too hot
to handle in many friendship or neighbourhood
networks; and these exchanges may be of long
duration or moving on long cycles, longer than can
generally be sustained or countenanced in non-
kinship settings.

The questions which immediately suggest
themselves about sheltered housing include: (1) does
living in a sheltered housing scheme (or having a
relative living in one) facilitate or inhibit the
flow of services in the family and, if so, how and
why, or is it neutral in its effect? (2) given that
different cohorts of elderly people passed through
different historical phases of family-building
patterns, are the tenants of sheltered housing drawn
from the conventional universe of kinship types, or
are they untypical in either of two ways: they
might be distinctively lacking in kinship ties as
Peter Townsend (1962) argued for the residents of
old people's homes, being disproportionately drawn
from the single, the childless, or the very elderly
who had outlived their kin; alternatively, since we
know that 'moving near relatives' is often a reason
given for going into sheltered housing, perhaps the
tenants might be better endowed with relatives than
the general universe of the elderly?

The Leeds study tells us that 95 per cent of a
sample of tenants claimed to have existing relatives
with whom they generally maintained contact, with 69
per cent claiming they were visited at least once a
week by 'a relative'. But the term 'relative' is
very broad: we could be talking about brothers and
sisters, sons or daughters, grandchildren, nephews
or nieces. Townsend (1957) has informed us that
different sorts of services are exchanged between
different sorts of kin; for instance, daughters
perform more services and of a different type than
either sons or sisters. The way responsibilities
are divided up, shouldered or evaded by kin is an
interesting and complex area. We need data for a
national sample of sheltered housing tenants
comparable to that presented by Shanas et al (1968)
to tell us what surviving relatives they have in
general; and then more data about the exchange of
sociability and services among what one might call
'relevant' or 'significant' relatives (Fennell et al
1981). The Leeds team report that 20 per cent of
tenants had moved closer to significant relatives
whilst 14 per cent had moved further away, and 20

per cent said that frequency of visiting had increased since the move, as opposed to 10 per cent who felt that it had declined, but we need to know more about what sort of relatives and whether they are doing more than simply visiting; this is vital to our understanding of whether or not sheltered housing contributes to, or prevents, 'structured dependency' (Townsend, 1981).

Neighbours and Friends

From kinship, we move to contact with neighbours. Classic socio-architectural studies such as those by Festinger et al (1950) and Leo Kuper (1953) give some general pointers, and consideration of the work of Irving Rosow (1967) shows why sheltered housing might be regarded as a natural laboratory for investigating academic hypotheses about social contacts which could have marked pratical and policy implications.

In a study of temporary housing for mature students at MIT, Festinger, Schachter and Back suggested that

> the architect who builds a house or who designs a site plan, who decides where the roads will go and will not go, and who decides which directions the houses will face and how close together they will be, also is, to a large extent, deciding the pattern of social life among the people who live in those houses.

Indeed, these authors find that the main determination of friendships among previously unacquainted residents were firstly how physically close the dwelling units were, people being most likely to know their next door neighbours, then the people one dwelling removed and so on in ever decreasing frequencies; and secondly, how close they were to one another in terms of 'functional distance': dwellings situated on common pathways where residents frequently met accidentally being functionally closer than physically close dwellings where residents set off from home in different directions. Differences of physical or functional distance as little as twenty feet affected friendship choice in this fit, young age range, and we might speculate that even slighter differences might be significant in a frailer population.

An extreme statement of architectural determinism is to be found in Whyte (1960).

> The location of your home in relation to the others not only determines your closest friends; it also virtually determines how popular you will be. The more central one's location, the more social contacts one has ... it would appear that certain kinds of physical layouts can virtually produce the 'happy' group ...

English studies have tended to qualify, but not entirely reject, this highly deterministic, and perhaps over-optimistic, position. Leo Kuper in Coventry, for instance, set himself an objective which sheltered housing researchers might emulate, namely

> to understand what happens to residents when they are suddenly thrown together in a residential unit within a planned neighbourhood, and to analyse their behaviour from the point of view of the influence of the planned environment on social relations

Examining a variety of indicators, Kuper found that even minimal knowledge of neighbours was essentially restricted to the occupants of two or three houses on either side of the subject and hardly anyone was known outside a particular cluster of dwellings. Very little evidence was found of joint sociable activities and, what little there was, took place within a small compass. In general, people were most likely to know and interact with people whose back doors faced theirs (close functional distance), and then the people on the other side of the party wall (close physical distance). Kuper concludes in favour of a modified form of physical determinism. Proximity is a necessary, but not a sufficient condition to promote contact between strangers.
Support for this modified position is to be found in Carey and Mapes (1972). Studying a variety of private housing developments, the authors conclude that explanations of the varying levels of visiting within different layouts 'cannot be found in the planning characteristics of the estates', though proximity to neighbours in forming contacts was 'unquestionably' important: more important was

perceived age homogeneity or compatibility.

> Some effort is made to form and sustain
> relationships with adjacent neighbours,
> regardless of perceived compatibility; but the
> strong relationships, as indicated by their
> reciprocal nature, result from, or are
> supported by similarity of age. (emphasis
> added)

The strongest theoretical argument for grouping
people together on this principle is, of course,
Rosow's Social Integration of the Aged (1967). It
matters less, in some ways, what Rosow actually
said, than what he was perceived as saying. Derek
Fox (1971), for instance, then an adviser on housing
management at the Department of the Environment,
cited Rosow's research, when addressing a conference
as follows:

> The view that elderly people are best housed as
> part of the normal community is now losing
> ground and there is even some support for the
> belief that complete segregation is desirable,
> as adopted in the large scale colonies found on
> the Continent and in the U.S.A.

This embodied a double irony, firstly in that
Rosow did not study such colonies, but only certain
apartment blocks in Cleveland which he noted were
very hard to find and completely untypical of most
apartment blocks in the city so that the
generalisability of his findings is debatable, and
secondly because Fox's speech came only 10 years
after Professor Wilma Donahue (1961), after a tour
of Western Europe, had taken back to an American
conference almost exactly the opposite message:

> An appraisal of the practices in the housing of
> old people in the Western European countries
> and Great Britain indicates that the trend is
> definitely away from developments which bring
> together relatively large numbers of old people
> in varying states of physical and mental health
> ... older family members should be housed in
> proximity to their children who can then more
> easily give them daily assistance. (emphasis
> added)

Space does not permit a detailed exposition of what construction can legitimately be built on the basis of Rosow's impressive statistical analysis or a textual critique of his recommendations. Whatever he did not say, he certainly does say that:

i)   there is a 'strong pervasive social barrier between generations which propinquity does not dispel'.

ii) working class elderly people are particularly affected by what Rosow calls the 'age density' of the local environment.

iii) 'the integration of older people into local friendship groups, especially the most socially dependent, is susceptible to planned intervention and social policy'.

Rosow argues that 'significant inroads' on the socially isolated can be made in age-dense environments (where minimally 40 per cent or more of the residents in a block are elderly).

Rosow's work has been cited to give theoretical colour to some well-known case studies of groups of old people living together and interacting intensively (Carp, 1966) (Hochschild, 1973) (Johnson, 1971) (Ross, 1977). Elsewhere, I have tried to examine some of the nuts-and-bolts of this interaction to try to explain why we do not seem to observe such intensity in English grouped schemes (Fennell, 1982). Points to check include:

are mail, milk and newspapers delivered to individual front doors, or do the residents congregate regularly as some central distribution point?

is there some other focus for communal activity as, for instance, in Les Floralies (Ross, 1977) the residents all ate together at least once a day in a communal dining hall?

do the tenants have any knowledge of one another which facilitates interaction, as for instance in Merrill Court (Hochschild, 1973) there was a regular newsletter which introduced new residents to one another through the medium of a reporter who interviewed them and wrote up a mini biography?

Analytical Variables

In speculating about contacts with neighbours
in English sheltered housing schemes, we might think
in terms of:

<u>cultural</u>   variables to do with neighbouring
<u>scheme</u>   variables
<u>social</u>   variables affecting the tenants
            such as class
<u>individual</u> variables such as health, person-
            ality and previous life history

Under the heading of <u>cultural</u> variables, we might
conclude that there are significant variations
between American and British samples about what
value to assign to neighbouring and where to draw
the boundaries of intimacy. It seems plain from the
American studies that a high volume of neighbourly
sociability - to the extent of regularly meeting in
one another's homes, regularly playing cards,
regularly sharing meals, regularly going on outings
together, is accepted and valued. In English
samples, the reverse seem to be true. Too much
contact with neighbours is viewed with mistrust; the
appropriate number of neighbours to know is more
circumscribed; what it is appropriate to do with
those one knows is even more narrowly restricted -
an occasional cup of tea being near the upper limit
of what is culturally permitted.

It may also be the case that there are cultural
variations <u>within</u> the British working class about
neighbouring behaviour which explain why some people
report 'all the neighbours are very nice, they'll
give you a "good day"', and some report them as
being 'stand-offish', 'unfriendly' or 'clannish'.

Norman Dennis (1963) speaks of 'close' and
'distant' styles of neighbouring. In the closer
style:

neighbours are your sort. They will rally
round when you are in trouble. A continuous
change of petty services takes place in the
locality. Interpersonal relationships are
based on the assumption that there are a few
firm important qualities of friendship and
decent heartedness, or directness and openness
of dealing,

but he feels this close style is being replaced by a
more privatised mode. In a more distant style of

neighbouring, there is less 'popping in and out of one another's houses', and less regular 'change of petty services'. The range of contacts is more restricted, and neighbours will be looked to for stop-gap help in 'real' emergencies (i.e. summoning relatives, holding the fort briefly in the case of sudden illness or accident), but not in lesser crises such as running out of sugar.

Peter Mann (1954) observing a council estate near Birkenhead, speaks of two styles of neighbouring and two camps of housewives:

The higher degree of manifest neighbourliness exhibited by some was not acceptable to other housewives who considered such action to be below their dignity ... It became clear that there were two camps of housewives on the estate - those who chatted, gossiped, lent and borrowed etc., and those who did not do such things and, furthermore, did not approve of them. The division of thought on the forms which manifest neighbourliness took resulted in a strain on the latent neighbourliness in some cases, and help in a crisis or emergency would not have been given with much enthusiasm.

It is this generation of housewives from whom contemporary sheltered housing tenants are drawn, so we might expect to see such tensions reproduced. But it is also possible that what we see nowadays is what we might call an embourgeoisement of the neighbouring style of the 'rough' working class, such that it is safest for the new tenant in a sheltered housing scheme to restrict, rather than encourage, contacts with neighbours and for the general level of contacts to be lower than we would expect from Rosow's arguments about age density.

By scheme variables, I have in mind direct properties of the sheltered housing scheme such as whether or not there is a common room, a luncheon club, covered access ways, a central congregation area near a lift shaft, etc., and also emergent properties of the group made up of the social characteristics of the individual tenants, or what writers in the traditions of Zena Blau (1961) would call the status congruence of the scheme. Blau argued that someone of incongruent status (relative to a group of status equals) such as a bachelor in a group of widows, a widow in a group of married couples, a younger elderly person in a group of the very aged and so on would tend to be excluded from interaction. The aggregate status congruity of the group could change over time, for instance converging towards the modal type of high age, all female, all widowed and in such situations one would expect to find higher levels of interaction than formerly, assuming health permits them.

By the social characteristics of the tenants, I refer to their sex, age, marital status and social class distributions and conceivably variations in styles of life (and perhaps resources) within the working class - as, for instance, differential ability to furnish a flat or bungalow nicely, to keep it clean and redecorated, whether or not one has 'a bit of money' over and above the basic pension. These are only some of the possible sources of differentiation in a group we are too prone to regard as homogeneous.

Finally, there is a cluster of variables of a more individual nature such as personal health - which may allow one a degree of independence from the scheme ('using the place like a hotel'); or ill-health, restricting one's interest and energies for interaction, including mental ill-health such as paranoia which makes people reluctant to interact, or verbal aphasia or depression which makes others reluctant to initiate contact.

Age Group Preference

Somewhat related to the issue of social contacts with neighbours is that of age group preferences. This is not the easiest question to investigate. In his paper for the DHSS conference Alan Butler (1983) tells us that only 37 per cent of their sheltered housing sample would choose other old people as neighbours, with 45 per cent being agnostic, and this is very similar to my own findings in Newcastle (Fennell, 1982).

Yet the picture of the general preferences of elderly people in grouped housing is made more obscure than it needs to be by uncritically citing the work of the Building Research Station reported by Hole and Allen (1962) where a high figure of 70 per cent preferring their own age group as neighbours was reported. Such findings are highly sensitive to methodological bias, in particular the bias arising in respondents from a preference for the existing environment, whatever its age density.

Hole and Allen report this, but do not control

for it, and their sample was severely skewed in the direction of 'segregated' environments.

When Haynes and Raven (1966) did a related but different study for the Building Research Station, they came up with quite contrary conclusions, reporting overall a figure of 38 per cent favouring 'age dense' environments and 62 per cent 'mixed ages'. However, on one estate (a segregated one) preferences for 'segregation' rose to 71 per cent. Re-examination of Hole and Allen's data by these authors showed that only 16 per cent of the original sample was drawn from 'mixed' environments, and the high figure reported to prefer 'age dense' situations should, therefore, be discounted.

To throw some more light on this type of problem, we require at least statistical controls in the data analysis, setting preference for elderly neighbours against variables such as size of scheme, length of tenure, age and sex - as well as multivariate analysis in which intervening variables, such as ill-health, which could affect attitudes and be related to age, can be partialled out.

The Anchor Study

An impending study of the tenants of Anchor sheltered housing schemes may permit some of these questions to be analysed.

With the British Legion and Hanover, Anchor is one of the three largest national housing associations for the elderly in the U.K., providing accommodation in flats and bungalows for approximately 17,000 tenants in 450 schemes across the country. A representative random sample of 1,000 tenants drawn from 45 schemes will be interviewed in November 1984 by Social and Community Planning Research.

Anchor has a reputation for sensitivity to the needs of its clientele, and it is hoped that results from the study will feed into the housing management process and the design brief for new schemes. Abandoning the distinction between Category One and Category Two schemes allows for a more flexible approach to design: how seriously do tenants value, for instance, the common room facilities which have had to be provided hitherto in Category Two schemes?

Pilot interviews seem to show a certain ambiguity at the heart of sheltered housing. If the ideology states that the object is to preserve independence and tenants much enjoy privacy behind their own front doors, they must not be 'organised' into activities because that smacks of residential care and is an invasion of privacy - then what is the logic of providing extensive common room facilities, particularly if these are little used?

If I were to risk a trend projection at this stage, I would surmise that, as ideas clarify about what sheltered housing can and cannot do, we might see an inherently more privatised type of scheme developing.

Tenants might expect higher standards of provision in their flats and more minimal communal facilities. They might prefer, not merely a refrigerator and a three-ring cooker, but in addition, a freezer, a four-ring cooker, a microwave oven, a small built-in washing machine rather than a large machine in a laundry room; perhaps a more luxurious bathroom suite. If the trend proves to be towards less communal actitivy and more private domestic activity, tenants might prefer slightly larger flats - a room big enough to have a dining table in around which to seat the family; perhaps a spare bedroom - rather than the under-utilised quiet rooms, large common rooms and hobbies rooms.

This projection, however, is making assumptions about the health of tenants and their capacity for self-care which may be wrong. The picture of the health of sheltered housing tenants as it emerges from the Leeds team is slightly confusing. The authors suggest that tenants are fitter than one might expect and seem to endorse the 'why so much for so few?' position. They 'could not help concluding that most "emergency" signals were engendered by tenants attempting to switch on the lights at night'. Yet in their 'reasons for moving' section 'poor health', leading to a desire for more suitable accommodation and to move closer to a relative, is cited as one of the most common complexes of reasons given by tenants for seeking sheltered housing in the first place.

The authors mention that tenants may be the fitter surviving partner of a couple, but this can apply at most (one would guess) to only half the tenants since 52 per cent are described as living alone before they entered sheltered housing. Also, the fact that a fifth could do no shopping and between a third and a half had required warden help when ill, 21 per cent had been ill recently and 12 per cent had been in hospital in the previous year, suggests that there are objective health reasons for seeking sheltered housing.

The issue of emergencies is an interesting one: it may be that the move into sheltered housing is often a prophylactic one: it is not necessarily that the tenants are ill now, or prone to fall, but that they sense an increasing probability that these things will occur: the sense of the professional literature is surely that prophylactic moves are sensible rather than a misuse of resources.

Anchor's policy is not to organise communal activities and to encourage non-interventionist wardens (and the Leeds team provide evidence to show that housing association wardens are in aggregate less interventionist than local authority ones). But, as I have tried to show, communal activity is hardly likely to flourish in English schemes without additional inputs.

This perhaps undermines the logic of building in features found in residential care like a common room and a scheme front door locked at a fixed time and only opened by ringing the warden. The trend is perhaps more towards greater gadgetry in the flats (such as intercoms and entry phones and tenants having their own telephones), larger flats and more self-contained residents, with the issue of who the neighbours are being less relevant than how close you are to your family and convenient facilities such as shops.

Conclusion

There have been many piecemeal and small-scale studies of sheltered housing or analogous local environments for the aged and suggestive pointers have arisen from them. Large sample surveys are necessary to generate the statistical data required satisfactorily to test some of these ideas, and it was not possible within the compass of the book on sheltered housing arising from the Leeds study to investigate questions of sociological, as contrasted with social policy, significance. A plea is entered for more basic sociological research as well as for putting elderly consumers of services at the forefront of the analysis. A new study of Anchor sheltered housing tenants is described which has these as two of its main objectives.

References

Blau, Z.S., (1961) 'Structural Constraints on Friendships in Old Age', American Sociological Review 26, 429-439

Butler, A. with Tinker, A. (1983) 'Integration or Segregation: Housing in Later Life' in DHSS Elderly People in the Community, Their Service Needs HMSO, London

Butler, A., Oldman, C. & Greve, J. (1983) Sheltered Housing for the Elderly, Policy, Practice and the Consumer, George Allen & Unwin, London

Carey, L. & Mapes, R. (1972) The Sociology of Planning, a Study of Social Activity on New Housing Estates, B.T. Batsford, London

Carp, F.M. (1966) A Future for the Aged: Victoria Plaza and its Residents, Austin, University of Texas

Dennis, N. (1963) 'Who Needs Neighbours?', New Society, July, 8-11

Donahue, W. (1961) 'Housing the Aged in Europe', in Burgess, E.W. Retirement Villages, University of Michigan, Ann Arbor

Fennell, G., Emerson, A.R., Sidell, M., Hague, A. (1981) Day Centres for the Elderly in East Anglia, Centre for East Anglian Studies, University of East Anglia

Fennell, G. (1982) 'Social Interaction in Grouped Dwellings for the Elderly in Newcastle upon Tyne', Ph.D. Thesis, University of Newcastle upon Tyne

Festinger, L., Schachter, S. & Back, K. (1960) Social Pressures in Informal Groups: A Study of Human Factors in Housing, Harper and Brothers, New York

Fox, D. (1971) 'The Needs and Ways of Meeting Them' in "Housing the Elderly, Report of a Housing Centre Conference", Housing Review July-August, 96-106

Haynes, K.J. & Raven, J. (1966) 'Old People, Study of Living Patterns' Architects' Journal, October, 1051-66

Hochschild, A.R. (1973) The Unexpected Community, Prentice-Hall, Englewood Cliffs

Hole, V. & Allen, P.G. (1962) 'A Survey of Housing for Old People' Architects' Journal, May, 1017-26

Johnson, S.M. (1971) Idle Haven, Community Building Among the Working Class Retired, University of California Press, Berkeley

Kuper, L. (1953) 'Blueprint for Living Together' in

his Living in Towns: Selected Research Papers in
Urban Sociology of the Faculty of Commerce and
Social Science, University of Birmingham, The
Cresset Press, London

Mann, P. (1954) 'The Concept of Neighbourliness',
American Journal of Sociology, 60, 163-8

Rosow, L. (1967) Social Integration of the Aged, The
Free Press, New York

Ross, J-K. (1977) Old People, New Lives: Community
Creation in a Retirement Residence, University of
Chicago Press, Chicago

Shanas, E., Townsend, P., Wedderburn, D., Friis, H.,
Milhoj, P., & Stehouwer, J. (1968) Old People in
Three Industrial Societies, Routledge and Kegan
Paul, London

Townsend, P. (1957) The Family Life of Old People:
An Inquiry in East London, Routledge and Kegan
Paul, London

Townsend, P. (1962) The Last Refuge: A Survey of
Residential Institutions and Homes for the Aged in
England and Wales, Routledge and Kegan Paul,
London

Townsend, P. (1981) 'The Structured Dependency of
the Elderly: A Creation of Social Policy in the
Twentieth Century', Ageing and Society, 1,5-28

Whyte, W.H. (1960) The Organization Man, Penguin
Books, Harmondsworth

Chapter Fifteen

SHELTERED HOUSING: THE WARDEN'S VIEW

Chris Phillipson and Patricia Strang

The paper reports on a small section of the
work of a project concerned with developing a health
education strategy for older people. The study
provided an assessment of the work of a range of
paid carers and reviewed the possibilities for more
innovative work aimed at people from middle age
onwards. Interviews were carried out with community
nurses (health visitors and district nurses), social
workers, sheltered housing wardens and home helps.
(Phillipson and Strang, 1984).
This paper will describe the results of our
interviews with wardens of sheltered housing. The
reasons for including wardens in the study were
rather speculative. We reasoned that sheltered
housing was itself a preventive concept; a form of
housing for (in theory at least) relatively 'fit'
and 'active' elderly people, with facilities which
might assist in reducing some of the anxieties
associated with the later stages of ageing. But how
did this work in practice? How did preventive care
operate within the context of individual schemes?
Did health education have any place in the
organisation of sheltered accommodation?

The Sample

For the empirical side of our enquiry we
collected information, using a structured face-to-
face questionnaire, from wardens in 52 sheltered
housing schemes in North and South Staffordshire.
Because of time shortage we restricted our work to
Local Authority schemes (although it should be
pointed out that Alan Butler et al (1983) found few
differences between local authority and housing
association schemes). We approached the wardens
employed by four local authorities: Newcastle-under-

Sheltered Housing: The Warden's View

Lyme, Stoke-on-Trent, Staffordshire Moorlands and Stafford. This produced a total of 55 wardens (excluding deputy and relief wardens). Of this group, two refused to be interviewed, and one was too ill to be seen.

The Wardens: Background Data

Most studies of wardens indicate a group which is predominantly middle aged, married and female. Our sample is consistent with these findings. The average age of the 52 wardens was 51 years; 40 (77 per cent) were married and all were female. As with the research by Butler et al (1983), the age range was wide: 7 wardens were in their 30s and 10 were in their early 60s.

Although few of the wardens had any formal qualifications, a majority (36/69 per cent) had some previous experience of working with elderly people: nurse, care assistant and home help being the most popular occupations.

The wardens had been in their present post for an average of nearly 5 years (the figure in Butler et al's (1983) study was 5½ years). They were each responsible for an average of 35 tenants. There was a considerable spread in terms of the ages of the youngest and oldest tenants. The mean age of the youngest tenant was 66.8 years and the mean age of the oldest tenant was 89.7 years. However, a majority of the schemes had the bulk of their tenants in the 75 plus age group. The implications of this for the work of the wardens is an aspect to which we shall return at various points in this chapter.

Visiting Elderly People

Regular visits to tenants is seen as one of the key elements in the work of wardens. This was confirmed by the group we interviewed, all of whom did once or twice daily rounds of their schemes:

'I start at 7.45 and check on emergencies and those who can't make a cup of tea. I have my own breakfast then and I do my full round. If someone is ill I send for the doctor or I do things myself. I am on 24 hour call for emergencies.'

'I do two calls per day - morning and early evening to make sure they're OK. You use

your judgement to see whether they need a
GP, relatives or a social worker. They are
all different - different moods, dispositions
and moans and groans.'

The vagueness of the warden's formal job
definition was a point highlighted in some of the
comments:

'I go in of a morning and check they're OK
and walk out ... that's what it says in
the contract, but that's not what happens.
I get pensions, shopping, dry their washing
... I do a round every morning to check they
are alright. It took me almost three hours
this morning. Sometimes you get back and
your head is throbbing!'

'We do a lot more than is in the contract ..
With it being a large scheme there are many
clashes between tenants. There are cliques.
Loneliness is a problem ... so many miss
their families ... they want to belong.'

We asked the wardens what they saw as the main
purpose of their work with tenants. The majority of
responses could be classified either in terms of a
surveillance role (27 mentions), or acting as a
'good neighbour' or friend (19 mentions). The
following comments are representative:

'You're there if they need anyone, if they
fall and need anything. They know there's
someone here - it's peace of mind.'

'To see there are no accidents which you
find in ordinary houses and streets. 24
hour surveillance so I am always here if
something happens during the night.'

The wardens varied, however, as regards their
involvement in the various illnesses and conditions
affecting tentants:

'I care for them ... I look after them when
they are sick. I organise social
activities ... they won't do it themselves,
they fall out with each other. The elderly
are like children really.'

'I try to care and give advice. You know
their ailments and what drugs they are on
... they are my chicks and I am the mother
hen.'

By contrast, other wardens were careful to
stress their role in maintaining independence
amongst the tenants:

'I see that I'm here to look after each one

differently, they're all individuals and have to be treated as such. I'm here to help in emergencies, to help in any way I can and to maintain their dignity and independence.'

'Not so much caring from physical side we help on mental side. A lot of people tend to treat elderly like children. But I don't think they should be looked upon that way. They aren't just a carcass that has got old they need understanding.'

The majority of wardens (45/87 per cent) said they would, if the need arose, provide direct care for an individual tenant. The typical activity was to do shopping or prepare meals for sick tenants; a few mentioned going with a tenant to hospital or helping those who had experienced a stroke. Some of the wardens we interviewed appeared to be going well beyond the superficial brief provided by their job description:

'I had a new tenant recently who has had 2 strokes, she could hardly walk or talk. Fortunately, I'm winning with her and have helped her as much as possible. But I can't do it all. I have two with senile dementia here ... one with no family.'

'I increasingly provide nursing care where services have been reduced and families are not available.'

'I work according to the family situation. What else can you do? I spend a lot of time with a diabetic lady who is often upset. I was companion and friend to a lady who has just died after 18 months with cancer. I've sat with three now who've been dying.'

The surveillance role is brought out in the finding that 48/83 per cent said that they frequently checked whether tenants were eating regular meals. In addition, 29/56 per cent of the wardens frequently checked that tenants were taking drugs as prescribed by their GP. The extent of their involvement in this area was somewhat surprising. Thus, whilst the contracts of most wardens had forbidden involvement in the drugs field, a majority had found this unrealistic. It is fair to say that many distinguished between checking and explaining the right amount of drugs which a tenant should take, and actually administering drugs. However, the dividing line was a narrow one. Some wardens reported being asked by doctors to check whether their patients were taking tablets; others felt pressure from the over-prescribing of tablets; some felt worried that they would get the blame if tenants either did not remember or took the wrong dosage. As a result of these factors, a minority of wardens became heavily involved in monitoring the use of drugs:

> 'I usually collect prescriptions for drugs the GP has prescribed. I will tell the old person what is in the bottle - although we are not supposed to. I will give old people their drugs if they are confused.'

> 'I write down everything they're on and check how long they should last and don't re-order until they're supposed to. I often keep them and give them one at a time. I've made enquiries about the strength of one lady's tranquillisers and she was re-assessed and put on to a lower dosage.'

Another warden was involved in rationing tablets for a patient dying of cancer, because 'I worry that he will take the lot.' For others, it was a case of taking responsibility for a confused tenant, rather than face trouble if anything went wrong.

The drugs example is symptomatic of the breadth of activity of the wardens. In part, this had arisen from the gradual ageing of the schemes - they had been open an average of nearly 11 years. It also reflected the limited training received by the wardens (see below). A further difficulty, however, was the limited support given to the wardens by other groups concerned with the elderly.

Co-ordination with Professional Carers

There was some evidence from our study that wardens experienced considerable isolation in their daily work. Many reported only limited support from line management. As one warden put it: 'The attitude of the Council is that if things are running smoothly, they don't bother us.' In the absence of any regular meetings amongst wardens, there was only a limited occupational identity. Few wardens reported having the opportunity to visit other schemes or to talk to other wardens about their work. In this situation, contact with other carers could be crucial in providing support and stimulation. Unfortunately, evidence from our research showed that any sort of liaison was limited in frequency (see Table 1) and often superficial in content. GPs and district nurses provided the most regular source of contact. Social workers, by contrast, had only a limited involvement with wardens in sheltered housing schemes (see Bowling and Bleatham (1984) for similar findings concerning the support given by professional carers).

TABLE 1:   FREQUENCY OF LIAISON WITH AGENCIES
                 ABOUT ELDERLY TENANTS

		F		O		R/N	
		n	%*	n	%*	n	%*
No. of schemes with GP visits	51 **	19	37.3	20	39.2	12	23.5
No. of schemes with HV visits	40	12	30.0	15	37.5	13	32.5
No. of schemes with DN visits	50	23	46.0	17	34.0	10	20.0
No. of schemes with SW visits	50	14	28.0	16	32.0	20	40.0

Note:

F = Frequently; O = Occasionally; R/N = Rarely/Never

(*Percentages expressed as a proportion of schemes with agencies visiting)
(**One warden excluded due to recent appointment)

There are some complex issues surrounding the question of the warden's relationship with other carers. Middleton (1982) makes the point that tenants my feel that the arrangements they have with health and social services are their own affair. However, there is the quite separate issue of support by professional groups for an isolated and untrained warden - a measure which can be supported at least as much for its preventive value as for the subjective benefits to the individual carer.

The isolation experienced by the wardens had two consequences: first, it may have increased their sense of anxiety and concern over problems affecting individual tenants; secondly, it limited the possibilities for exploring innovative approaches to their work. Both these aspects were reinforced by the limited training undergone by the wardens; a by-product of the superficial view of their work held by the warden's employers.

Training

In Alan Butler et al's (1983) survey, only 24 per cent of wardens said they had experienced any form of training, either before or after starting work. For those who had received training, most reported finding it a useful experience. For the wardens in the 52 schemes we visited, none had received any introductory training; 28 (54 per cent) had received a limited amount of general training (usually a 5 or 6 day course). Some of those we interviewed were highly critical of the absence of any initial preparation:

'It took me years to understand I was going about things the wrong way - I was trying to mother them. You've got to make them independent. I think they might have prepared you for that.'

'Once you're on the job no, but initially you should get some sort of preparation to let you know that you do more than they state in the contract.'

'I think we should have training before we start ... people are dumped here and left ... we get a lot with emotional illness and depression. Someone who writes up the contracts and tells us what to do should come and spend some time with us and then think what a warden's job consists of.'

Training, in respect of the counselling aspects of the warden's work, was covered only superficially by the courses. It was also disappointing to find limited attention to areas such as exercise and fitness in old age. Medical problems amongst the elderly were, by contrast, covered by virtually all those interviewed (see Table 2).

It is important to underline, however, that the 'one-off' course was virtually all that the wardens were likely to receive. This would have been less serious if they were receiving regular support on the social and medical aspects of their work. Unfortunately, our research findings suggest that this was not the case. For example, the majority of schemes had tenants with hearing problems of varying degrees of severity. Yet hardly any of the wardens had received advice on either the psychological problems associated with deafness or the equipment and aids which can help deaf people. Similarly, most wardens had clients who were blind or partially sighted, yet few reported receiving advice on how they could help this group. Finally, despite the close involvement of many wardens in the drugs area, just 15 (29 per cent) felt they received sufficient information on the possible effects of drugs on elderly people.

TABLE 2: TOPICS COVERED IN GENERAL TRAINING

	Y		N		CR	
	n	%*	n	%*	n	%*
Nutrition	22	78.6	5	17.8	1	3.6
Emotional needs	16	57.1	10	35.7	2	7.1
Exercise	11	39.3	13	46.4	4	14.3
Home safety	23	82.1	3	10.7	2	7.1
Pensions, benefits etc.	13	46.4	12	42.8	3	10.7
Medical problems	26	92.8	1	3.6	1	3.6
Organisation of Social Services	18	64.3	7	25.0	3	10.7
First Aid	16	57.1	10	35.7	2	7.1

Note: Y = Yes; N = No; CR = Can't Remember

(* Percentages are expressed as a proportion of the 28 who had received general training)

Responding to change: The Warden's View

Our impression from the visits to the 52 schemes was that wardens faced increasing pressure both with the ageing of their schemes and with the later age of entry of tenants to their accommodation. What emerged from the interviews was, first, the variety of emotional pressures on the wardens as they faced a range of chronic and acute illnesses in their schemes; secondly, their involvement in the management and support of ill-health.

The emotional pressures were described in a number of ways. Getting used to the regularity of death was one problem, as one warden commented 'We have had 55 deaths on this scheme in the past 12 years'. And helping people come to terms with death was a source of tension:

'I have one man who never married who causes difficulties because he is frightened of dying alone.'

The experience of depression amongst tenants also required skilled intervention by the wardens. They reported struggling to deal with comments such as: 'Is it worth going on?'; or trying to 'jog people out of their depression'; or worrying about the tranquillisers which people were taking.

At another level, however, they were also involved in the management of conditions and illnesses in old age; working with tenants who had suffered strokes; alerting doctors about patients who were taking tablets which had been suspended or banned; making suggestions about diet for people with eating difficulties; advising residents to change GPs where they had experienced negative attitudes or where the doctor had failed to attend them promptly.

In these examples we see the warden acting as a surrogate health counsellor, often stepping into the vacuum created by the withdrawal of other services. Yet there were problems resulting from this type of involvement. Her skills may have been stretched on occasions to near breaking-point by the succession of demands. She may also have accrued excessive control and influence in the daily life of schemes. One illustration of this was her hold over social activities. Twenty-three of the wardens reported organising activities exclusively on their own; 9 reported varying degrees of help from tenants; 4 relied upon a committee of tenants; 16 said that there were no organised activities. When questioned about the social life of the schemes there were some disturbing comments:

'The tenants committee has caused a lot of

arguments. I found it better if I do it
and then ask individuals to help.'
'The tenants aren't that bothered.'
'I haven't organised much recently, they are
happy now just sitting around.'
'Initially, we organised a lot of
activities. But as the workload has
increased we have tended to neglect these.
Also, it is difficult getting some of the
residents down to the common room.'
Where activities had been developed they were
of a strictly traditional kind (e.g. bingo or pie
suppers). Two of the schemes had run keep-fit
demonstrations; four had organised cookery
demonstrations.
The overall impression from the schemes was
that an opportunity had been missed for developing
activities and interests which would give a sense of
empowerment to tenants. For most wardens, the day-
to-day run of illnesses and minor and major crises
formed the main pre-occupation, and developing other
kinds of activities became something of a luxury.

Conclusions

There are a range of reforms which are now
urgently required to relieve some of the pressures
facing wardens. We shall mention two of these:
first, developing long-term planning for individual
schemes, secondly, collaboration with paid carers.
It was clear from our research that little
thought is given to developing long-term plans for
individual sheltered housing schemes. We think this
to be a major deficiency, one which results in an
accumulation of problems which creates considerable
pressure both on wardens and managers. One
suggestion from our work is that health education
might play a valuable role in the field of sheltered
housing.
The facilities in sheltered accommodation offer
many advantages to health education programmes.
Common rooms, for example, provide an ideal venue
for activities such as yoga and other forms of
exercise. They could also be used for 'pensioner
health days' - for both tenants and people in the
surrounding community. These could provide
demonstrations, stalls and books and leaflets,
illustrating various aspects of health in old age.
Another feature of health education concerns

self-health care (individual activities) and self-help (group activities). Both of these could be developed to some advantage in sheltered accommodation. Self-health care, for example, could entail teaching simple diagnostic skills which the individual can practice in making an estimate of his/her health status; providing skills needed to treat chronic illness; teaching skills relevant to simple acute conditions.

Developing work in the health education field might have a number of benefits for wardens and managers: (1) it may relieve some of the pressures experienced by wardens when coping with chronic and acute illnesses in housing schemes; (2) it may stimulate thinking about the long-term future of schemes - particularly as regards the health needs of very elderly people; (3) it may lead to preventive action amongst tenants, paid carers (health visitors, district nurses, etc.) and relatives. These developments may lead to a reduction in problems arising from the ageing of the tenant population in particular schemes. This is an issue which concerns many involved in sheltered accommodation: health education offers some creative policy options for this situation.

Secondly, we think that the absence of collaboration with professional carers (health visitors, social workers, etc.) is a major drawback. Managers of schemes (whether local authority or housing association) must play a more prominent role in ensuring that wardens receive support from these groups. There are a number of ways in which this might be achieved: wardens (or their representatives) could participate in relevant district health authority or area social services meetings; health visitors could play a monitoring role in relation to individual sheltered housing schemes; sheltered housing managers could talk on half-day release courses (attended by general practitioner trainees) about the aims and objectives of sheltered accommodation.

In general terms we think that this important area of housing provision is evolving with insufficient support from neighbourhood services, and in the absence of firm ideas about future problems which may affect individual schemes. Some solutions to these problems are urgently required if the potential of sheltered accommodation is to be realised.

Acknowledgements

This chapter draws from material produced whilst the authors were in receipt of a grant from the Health Education Council. A full report of the research for the HEC is contained in Phillipson, C. and Strang, P. Health Education and Older People: the role of paid carers, Health Education Council in association with the Department of Adult Education, University of Keele, 1984, 173pp, £9.95.

References

Bowling, A. and Bleatham, C. (1984) 'Beyond the Call of Duty', Community Care, October 4

Butler, A., Oldman, C. and Greve, J. (1983) Sheltered Housing for the Elderly, George Allen and Unwin

Middleton, L. (1982) So much for so few: a view of sheltered housing, Merseyside Improved Houses

Phillipson, C. and Strang, P. (1984) Health Education and Older People: the role of paid carers, Health Education Council in association with the Department of Adult Education, University of Keele

Chapter Sixteen

REPORT OF PILOT STUDY OF DELAYED DISCHARGES FROM
HOSPITAL: LIVERPOOL 1983-84

R. M. Eley and L. M. Middleton

Introduction

Patients who require no further medical
treatment, and are declared fit to leave hospital by
the medical staff sometimes remain in hospital for
what are broadly termed as "social reasons":
unsuitable housing, lack of domiciliary services,
shortage of places in residential homes etc. The
aims of this six month pilot study were to
establish:

1   the extent of the problem in terms of non-
     medical use of beds
2   the reasons for the delayed discharge from
     hospital
3   the kinds of environmental changes and/or
     service input that might have permitted
     discharge had they been possible/available

LOCATION OF STUDY

We conducted two kinds of survey:
1   A longitudinal one over six months, which took
     place on a geriatric ward and an orthopaedic
     ward in the Royal Liverpool Hospital
2   Snapshot surveys of two rehabilitation wards in
     Mossley Hill Hospital

METHOD

(1) Longitudinal Survey

  i) We obtained on a weekly basis from the
     Registrar or Senior House Officer the names of
     any patients (of whatever age) deemed fit for
     discharge but unable to leave hospital for

other reasons. Only patients deemed to have been in the delayed discharge situation for 7 days were included in the survey.

ii) We noted the progress of these patients until they were discharged.

iii) Each patient was approached for interview on an informal basis (that is, without a standard questionnaire) about their perception of their situation. During this interview we tried to establish whether the patient shared the professionals' perception of the situation, and what their own private plans were.

iv) We interviewed the social worker involved with each patient, using a standard, but open ended questionnaire.

(2) Snapshot Survey

i) On a day chosen at random we asked the senior medical officer on each of two rehabilitation wards to identify which of the patients on that ward at that time were in a situation of delayed discharge. Short histories were taken of patients so identified.

ii) These patients were approached for interview on the same basis as those in the longitudinal survey.

iii) A record was kept of the patients' progress until discharge.

FINDINGS

On the acute wards a total of 13 patients were identified. This represented 9 on the geriatric unit and 4 on the orthopaedic unit. On the rehabilitation wards, in the one day snapshot survey, a total of 10 patients out of 33 were identified.

The number of patient/days affected is shown in Table 1. The individual periods varied from 14 to 63 days, on the geriatric wards and from 20 days to 162 days (that is, the whole period of the survey) on the orthopaedic ward.

If these kinds of figures were extended to a full year, it would represent roughly the wastage of 2 beds per 24 bed ward per year.

The sample size in terms of numbers of patients turned out to be surprisingly low, and did not match the numbers we had expected, given initial reactions by medical staff when we first explained our intentions. That "bed-blocking" is apparently more significant in terms of its perceived troublesomeness than its actual numbers in terms of patients has been a finding of other, more quantative studies than this one (Rubin and Davies 1975; Hall and Bytheway 1982). Although the number of patients is small as a proportion of the total ward population, the "bed-blocking" problem arises because those few who do become stuck tend to do so for long periods of time. 7 out of the 13 patients were blocking beds for over a month; of these 1 was there for over 2 months, 1 for 4 months and 1 for 5 months. This latter patient was in hospital at the beginning of the survey period, and still there at the end.

Table 1:

	Patient - Days Affected	
	Geriatric Ward	Orthopaedic Ward
Period of survey - days	209	162
No. of beds	24	24
Total No. patient/days	5016	3888
No. patient identified	9	4
No. patient/days affected	323	352
% of total patient/days	6.4%	9.1%
Mean period occupied	35.9	88

INTERVIEWS

Small numbers did however, permit a more detailed case analysis than would otherwise have been possible. Out of a total of 23 patients, however, only 16 interviews could be conducted because of the mental or physical state of the patients.

REASONS FOR DELAYED DISCHARGE

The medical reasons for delayed discharge were compared, where possible, with the social worker's version and both were compared with that of the patient.

We separated the replies into those that were identical or broadly consistent reasons, those that showed minor differences, and those that were completely different. These are presented as Tables 2 to 4.

The first obvious point to note is the lack of

occasions when the professional and patient opinion are consistent. The doctors never fully agreed with the patients' perception and the social workers rarely did so.

Table 2:   Reasons for Delayed Discharge
Social Worker/Doctor:

Broadly consistent	4
Minor differences	3
Major differences	4

Table 3:   Reasons for Delayed Discharge
Doctor/Patient:

Broadly consistent	0
Minor differences	2
Major differences	8
No patient data	3

Table 4:   Reasons for Delayed Discharge
Social Worker/Patient:

Broadly consistent	2
Minor differences	2
Major differences	5
No data	4

Another point to add is that, while the sample was defined by the medical staff, there was no reason why either the social worker or the patients themselves should agree that they were appropriately defined as occupying beds for non-medical reasons. In four cases the social workers felt the patients were not fit enough for discharge, either to home or residential care. Two of the patients felt strongly that they were not fit to leave, while others displayed some fear or ambivalence about the future.

A similar pattern emerged on the rehabilitation ward between the medical and patient perception of the reason for the prolonged stay in hospital, as is shown in Table 5.

Table 5:   Reasons for Delayed Discharge
Rehabilitation Unit
Doctor/Patient

Broadly consistent	1
Minor differences	2
Major differences	3
No data	4

SOME EXAMPLES

Some examples of the sort of disagreements we found will add a little flesh to the statistics. An example of a minor difference was when the medical reasons given were that there were stairs in the home, and repairs were needed to make the downstairs rooms inhabitable. The patient's version was not totally inconsistent but added a new dimension. She said her house was a mess, and she hoped to hang on as long as possible while it was sorted out. She believed the hospital social worker, and her own illness, were useful levers in pressing for the repairs to be effected.

The areas of major disagreement were varied. In one case the medical reason was given as a patient who needed some help at home, which the family, for reasons of their own ill health, were unable to provide. The social worker felt the patient was unfit to leave the hospital, was suffering from depression, and that, even if the family had been in good health, the discharge would have been inappropriate. The social worker did not, in fact, agree with the medical definition of this patient being in the sample. Another instance was of the doctor saying the patient was too confused and her home too dirty. The patient claimed her landlord was preventing her return home because he wanted to make improvements to the property. In another case the medical staff gave the reason as that the patient cooked on a coal fire, which she could not manage since having a plaster on her leg following a fractured femur. The patient felt she was not well enough to leave hospital as her leg was too weak, and there were, moreover, 46 steps to her flat: a much more troublesome factor than the lack of a suitable place to cook. Another patient felt herself too unwell to leave, and the social worker also considered her mobility too poor even for a residential home. The medical version was that the neighbour was unable to continue past support (a factor which the social worker considered irrelevant while the patient was unable to walk), and that therefore a place should be sought in a residential home. In one case the stories were not so much inconsistent as incomplete, and we felt that, between them, the social worker and the doctor might have a picture which was broadly consistent with that of the patient. This lack of full communication was unusual however, and there was more likely to be agreement between the professionals than not. The areas of disagreement are worth noting however. In three of the four cases where there was a major difference between the social worker and the doctor, the social worker felt the patient was not fit enough to leave hospital. One of these was a candidate for residential care. The difference here seems less that the social worker is querying medical knowledge than that the social worker is highlighting the implications of physical or mental disabilities in the proposed setting. Both the doctor's attitude, in considering the use to which medical skills and the facilities of the hospital are put, and that of the social worker, who is considering the fate of the patient on discharge, are entirely consistent with their own position, but the need for care resources beyond hospital is very clear, if the patients discharged in such precarious fashion are not to continually bounce back.

PLANS FOR DISCHARGE

Having examined the reasons for the delayed discharge we next took the slightly different issue of whether or not there was agreement about the plans for discharge. In other words, was everyone working toward the same goal? See Table 6.

Table 6:	Plans for Discharge:	Acute	
Social Worker		Doctor	Patient
1. OPH		OPH/Home	Undecided
2. HCP		HCP	OPH
3. OPH	Home, when cleaned		Home
4. Home, when cleaned	Home, when cleaned		Home
5. UFD		OPH	Confused
6. Home now	Home, when repaired		Home now
7. Home later		Home	Home
8. OPH		OPH	Home
9. UFD		OPH	Depressed, wouldn't discuss
10. OPH		OPH	Confused
11. Home for the blind	OPH		Undecided
12. No data		OPH	Convalescence then home
13. No date		OPH	Not sure

Note:
UFD = Unfit for Discharge; OPH = Old People's Home; HCP = Home Care Programme – an extended home help service

As a general point, medical staff appeared more definite about the option of residential accommodation than the social workers or patients.

On the rehabilitation unit the doctor recommended a local authority old people's home in seven out of the ten cases. Only one patient, and she reluctantly, agreed with the plan. Others wanted sheltered housing, to go home, or to stay in hospital. These areas of confusion cannot help in making plans for patients.

RESOURCE IMPLICATIONS FOR THE STUDY

We were anxious to find out from the key witnesses what the resource implications behind the delayed discharges were. Was there simply a need for more of something? Or was there a need for different kinds of services?

Social workers were therefore asked to tell us what kind of resources, had they been available, would have aided the patient to be discharged. We were seeking for evidence of gaps in the existing resource network, and hoped for some imaginative responses. We were disappointed. Social workers were generally unable to think beyond the constraints of existing resource availability. In some cases the resources were not criticised, but the problem was seen as too long waiting lists. In one case the resource was seen as not being available at the right times of day: in other words it was not flexible enough. This last instance was the only one in which the social worker offered any suggestions for services beyond what was already in existence. What made the lack of imaginative thinking all the more disturbing was that the type of cases we were concerned with were not untypical, but the sort of problems dealt with every day by social workers in a general hospital.

It might be a valuable exercise if social workers (and other professionals) were asked to produce assessments for patients on the same model which is required of LEAs in respect of children under the 1981 Education Act: that is, a statement of needs regardless of what is actually available. Social work intervention is currently based on knowledge and utilisation of what is available, and new services typically take months to build up a clientele, even when they meet a real need, because of the time it takes for social workers and other professionals to incorporate new services into their mode of operating.

PATIENT OUTCOME

A further question we asked ourselves was whether the actual discharge matched the plans for discharge made by the doctor, social worker and patient. We compared the discharge arrangements that were finally made for patients with the plans that had been made by the professional staff, and, where possible, the patient's own plans. This is illustrated in Table 7.

Table 7:	Discharge Outcomes Compared with Plans for Discharge			
Acute n = 13	DA	CP	DDP	DU
Medical plan	13	7	4	2
Social Work plan	11	9	0	2
Patient plan	6	4	2	-
Rehab. n = 10				
Medical plan	9	6	1	2
Patient plan	6	1	3	2

Note:
DA = Data Available;
CP = Corresponded with plan;
DDP = Discharges which differed from plan;
DU = Discharges which were still unresolved

Where the outcome differed, from the medical plans 3 patients destined for an old people's home went home, 1 patient destined for home went to an old people's home and another died suddenly while waiting for an old people's home. Where social work data was available the social work plan matched the actual outcome in all cases. Only 12 patients of those interviewed gave clear opinions as to their plans for discharge. Five of these matched the actual outcome. Of the 5 where the outcome differed 2 wanted to go to an old people's home and went home, 1 wanted to stay in hospital, but went to an old people's home and 1 wanted sheltered housing but went to an old people's home.

CONCLUSIONS

We have divided our conclusions into two sections. Firstly, those conclusions which we have been able to draw from our own findings. Secondly, recommendations for further investigation, since this was originally designed as a pilot study.

(1) Conclusions from our own findings

The first impression is that delayed discharges occur in so few cases that the problem is not particularly important. Although the number of patients in the sample was small, however, the time periods spent waiting in hospital for some patients is worrying, and seen as a proportion of total bed/ patient time, delayed discharge becomes an issue.

Although it appears at first reading that the delayed discharge problem is greater on the orthopaedic unit, we would be cautious about giving any great weight to the actual figures produced as a result of this survey. This is because the history of one patient who may be delayed for a long time, can make an enormous difference to overall figures in such a small sample.

Routine social work assessment enables the early identification of problems which may delay discharge. Otherwise, problems may not be discovered until the point of discharge, and may necessitate a prolonged stay in hospital. Working to solve social problems ought to dovetail with, rather than follow on from, solving medical problems.

The patient who finds herself in this situation becomes passive in decision making. While many of the patients suffered from degrees of mental confusion, this was by no means universal, and in any case, it appeared that professional plans tended to be pursued regardless of whether they coincided with patient wishes. This is not to suggest that these plans were always achieved. The patient who "refuses to go home", is stubbornly rejecting the professional plans. The language explaining her situation is more commonly like this than, for example, "Mrs Brown does not yet feel well enough to go home" (an explanation never heard).

The medical assessment that a patient is ready for discharge is not always accurate, but the readiness to include other professional opinions in that assessment is not always apparent. In 4 out of the 13 cases on the acute wards the social worker disagreed with the medical view that the patient was ready for discharge because they were not fit enough. The patient therefore acquires the status of "bed blocker" in medical terms, but may be deemed as not yet ready for discharge if a broader view is taken. This therefore brings into question the status of beds in hospital. Are they to be regarded as having a purely medical function, or a broader function of restoring a patient to a level of wellbeing at which she is able to manage successfully after discharge (wherever that may be)?

The difference between the social worker and the doctor may result from different perceptions of what is meant by "fit". The doctor will tend to mean "I can improve their condition no further by medical treatment". The social worker will relate the patient's level of functioning to the actual conditions to which the patient would be discharged. Definition of fitness would therefore vary according to whether or not the patient was returning to their own home with no inside toilet, home with relatives, to a warden controlled flat or to an old people's home.

(2) Recommendations for further investigation

We are well aware that it is insufficient to carry out a survey of delayed discharge on only two acute wards over only six months. Our pilot study confirms our view that a full scale research project is justified in this area, not simply to look at delayed discharge in terms of numbers, or bed wastage, but to investigate the communication and co-operation between medical and other professional staff, and the position of the patient in decision making regarding her own treatment and future.

Further study need not necessarily be over a much longer period, but should include more wards, and different types of wards. Patients should be interviewed on more than one occasion and followed up for six months after discharge. More detailed interviews with medical staff are also required. If our finding on the snapshot survey was typical, about a third of beds on the rehabilitation unit were not being used for that purpose. While one snapshot survey is insufficient to draw firm conclusions, the level of inappropriately used beds on that day does seem to merit further investigation. This may be a problem with admission. It may be that doctors tend to take risks with rehabilitation, giving patients the benefit of the doubt as to whether they will achieve some "independence", and thus building in a high, but justifiable failure rate. On the other hand, it may be that initial admissions are for non rehabilitation reasons. On our survey 2 our of the 10 respondents had been admitted for reasons other than rehabilitation. We would, therefore, suggest a longer term survey is undertaken on the rehabilitation unit, looking at the philosophy behind the unit, assessment procedures before admission, reasons for admission, patient histories, and the involvement of para medical staff.

References

Hall, D. and Bytheway, B. (1982) 'The blocked bed: definition of a problem', in Soc.Sci.Med. (16), 1985-1991

Rubin, S. and Davies, G. (1975) 'Bed blocking by elderly patients in general hospital wards', Age and Ageing, (4), 142-147

Chapter Seventeen

AGEING IN TURKEY: PATTERNS, PROVISIONS AND PROSPECTS

C. J. Gilleard, A. A. Gurkan, and Esen Gilleard

Abstract

The elderly in Turkey present a growing section of a growing society. Within the country there can be observed marked inter provincial variation in the "age" structure, while historically the impact of the creation and development of the republic willhave affected the lives of Turkey's 'new elderly' at many different points in their own lives. Against this background of geographical variety and historical discontinuity, there can be seen emerging in recent years a policy of increasing state provisions for the elderly aimed at securing some degree of economic and social well being for this section of society.

Introduction

In 1960 the elderly (over 65 years) population in Turkey numbered under 1 million and constituted approximately 3.5 per cent of the total population. By 1980, the elderly made up 4.7 per cent of the population and number more than 2 million. Because of the overall growth of the population in the last two decades, the proportionate rise in the elderly population has not reflected the very significant growth in absolute numbers of this age group. Nevertheless the changes reflect a transition from a young to a mature population (United Nations, 1956), and a growing awareness of the rise in the numbers of elderly has, in the last five years especially, resulted in increased consideration of the social and economic needs of this group in Turkey. Because of the country's geographical position and historical development, Turkey reflects a mixture of

European and Asian social and demographic
structures. In order to place the present
demographic structure of Turkey, it is helpful to
draw some international comparisons. Table 1
presents details of age structure and life
expectancy in Turkey in comparison to some other
European and Asian countries.

TABLE 1

Proportion of population aged 65 and over, and life
expectancy at birth: some international comparisons

Country	Population 65+	Life expectancy at birth	
		M	F
Turkey	4.7%	60.3	61.6
England and Wales	15.3%	70.4	76.6
Scotland	14.1%	68.6	74.9
Yugoslavia	9.4%	65.4	70.2
U.S.S.R.	8.5%	64.0	74.0
Iraq	4.0%	53.6	56.7
India	3.5%	46.4	44.7

Source: U.N. Demographic Yearbook 1982

It is evident from these figures that Turkey
remains part of the developing world, closer in
demographic structure to Asian rather than European
countries. Nevertheless overall national data
conceal considerable differences in the proportion
of the elderly people across Turkey's sixty-seven
provinces. In 1970, the proportions varied from
2.4 per cent in the eastern province of Bitlis, to
7.3 per cent in the Black Sea province of Kastamonu
By 1980, this variability had actually increased
- from 1.9 per cent in Bitlis, to 9.3 per cent in
Kastamonu. Sections of the country thus
reflect both 'young' and 'aged' populations.
We have collated data from all 67 provinces
from the 1980 census, and calculated the
proportions of elderly people in each of the
provinces. The interprovincial variation is shown
in the Figure 1.
From this information it is possible to see a

Figure 1

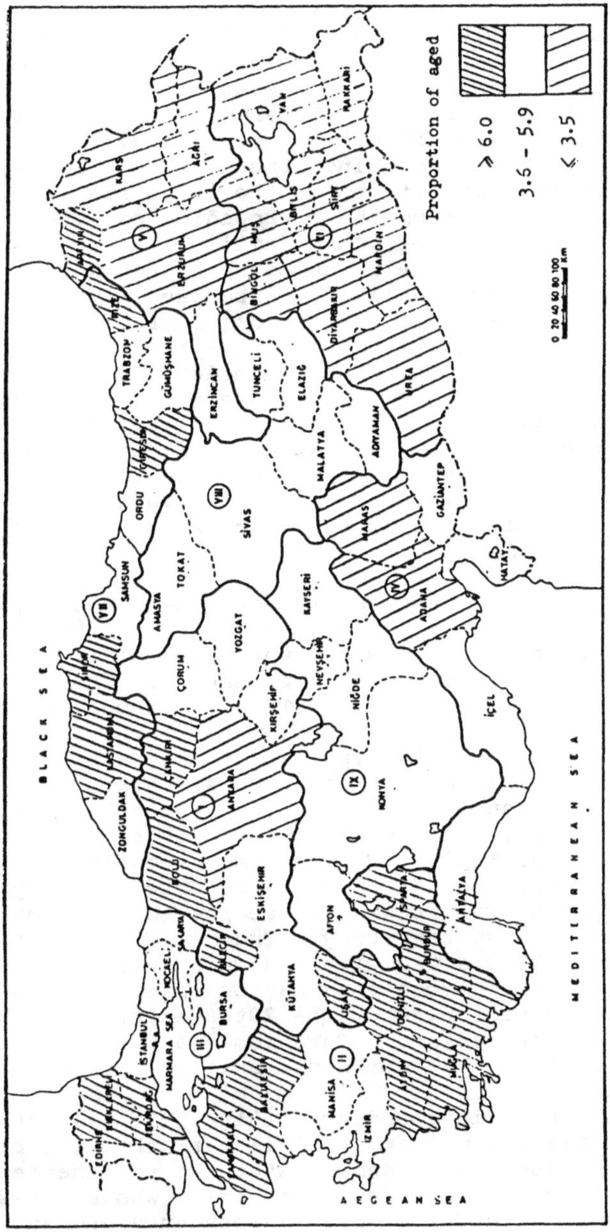
BLACK SEA
AEGEAN SEA
MEDITERRANEAN SEA
MARMARA SEA
Proportion of aged
≥ 6.0
3.5 - 5.9
≤ 3.5
0 20 40 60 80 100 Km
EDİRNE
KIRKLARELİ
TEKİRDAĞ
İSTANBUL
ÇANAKKALE
BALIKESİR
BURSA
KOCAELİ
SAKARYA
BİLECİK
KÜTAHYA
MANİSA
İZMİR
UŞAK
DENİZLİ
AYDIN
MUĞLA
BURDUR
ISPARTA
ANTALYA
AFYON
ESKİŞEHİR
BOLU
ZONGULDAK
KASTAMONU
ÇANKIRI
ANKARA
KONYA
SİNOP
SAMSUN
AMASYA
ÇORUM
YOZGAT
KIRŞEHİR
NEVŞEHİR
NİĞDE
İÇEL
KAYSERİ
TOKAT
SİVAS
ORDU
GİRESUN
TRABZON
GÜMÜŞHANE
ERZİNCAN
TUNCELİ
ELAZIĞ
MALATYA
ADIYAMAN
URFA
GAZİANTEP
MARAŞ
ADANA
HATAY
DİYARBAKIR
MARDİN
SİİRT
BİTLİS
MUŞ
BİNGÖL
ERZURUM
RİZE
ARTVİN
KARS
AĞRI
VAN
HAKKARİ

broad East-West division of the country from the young populations in the eastern provinces, to the mature/aged provinces in the west. However, the most developed regions (Istanbul, Izmir, Ankara, Antalya and Bursa) are not the most aged, but rather the provinces surrounding these areas. It may be that internal migration to the industrialised and urbanised areas from the surrounding provinces has reduced the numbers of young families in the latter, while increasing their numbers in the most highly developed (industrialised, urbanised) provinces. Our own analysis of rates of increase in the proportion of elderly in the 67 provinces between 1970 and 1980 suggest that high levels of internal migration are indeed predictive of lower rates of provincial ageing. We hope to publish the results of these analyses in full at a later date. For the present it is important to recognise the fact that quite marked inter-provincial variations in demographic structure do exist at present in Turkey.

Historical perspectives

Aside from the geographical perspective, the historical context also provides an important consideration in viewing the position of, and provisions for, the aged in present day Turkey. In three years' time, the Turkish republic will celebrate its 65th birthday: the history of the republic is very much part of the life history of Turkey's present generation of pensioners.

The beginning of the first World War saw the Ottoman Empire in a state of imminent collapse. At that time the Empire had seen the secession of most of its Christian European territories, and by the end of that war it was to see the loss of most of its Islamic Arab territory. The declaration of the Republic in 1923 arose within a much more culturally and ethnically homogeneous nation than had been the case at the beginning of the 20th Century. Turkism replaced Ottomanism, Turanism and Pan-Islamic ideologies as the dominant uniting force in the country.

The war of independence (1919-1923) was both an anti-imperialist war and a civil war; the victorious elite headed by Kemal Ataturk represented a military-bureaucratic intelligentsia, whose views of nationhood gained increasing ascendency and support amongst the Turkish people. The 1923 Grand National Assembly was dominated by 'official' and 'professional' groups who made up 74 per cent of its members (Frey, 1965, p.181), an indication of the orientation of the new government.

The reforms that followed the creation of the republic - the abolition of the Caliphate, the replacement of Islamic law with the Swiss Civil Code, the introduction of the latin alphabet, the Gregorian calendar, European style surnames, compulsory primary education for both sexes, and the granting of universal suffrage - took place at an extremely rapid pace and have been seen by some commentators as a determined attempt by Ataturk and his government to replace the allegiance to "the idiocy of traditional community oriented life" (Mardin, 1981, p.213) with an individualistic and autonomous responsibility to the nation state. Thus Mardin sees these reforms as a consistent effort to replace the supremacy of the "mahalle" or neighbourhood community, with a more modern world view embodied in the state. This transfer of responsibility can be seen in one of the last pieces of legislation overseen by Ataturk, the 1936 Labour Code. Under article 100, it was decreed that "public assistance for employees in case of an industrial accident or occupational disease, maternity, old age, unemployment, sickness and death shall be organised and administered by the State. A worker's insurance organisation shall carry on these tasks" (quoted by Eren, 1965, p. 149). Thus the state asserted its responsibility for the welfare of its citizens.

The impact of these reforms no doubt varied from social group to social group. While most pensioners from the educated classes can now determine their date of birth by reference to the present calendar, it is probable many of the uneducated elderly cannot; this factor may well contribute to the enormous unreliability of age records in the census data, and resultant 'age heaping' in official statistics (cf. Shorter and Macura, 1982).

Lerner writing of life in rural villages in Turkey at the beginning of 1950 considered that the majority of villagers remained 'traditional' bound to the immediate environment of family, village and mosque, for whom public policy impinged little if at all upon their personal affairs. Since 1950, urbanisation, increased social mobility and improved communication networks have probably shifted all but a minority into the status of 'transitionals' with an "ambivalence, incompleteness and inconsistency of attitudinal structures" (Lerner, 1958).

Thus it is possible to see the elderly in present day Turkey as made up of groups or classes whose separation from a neighbourhood world view has occurred fully or in part at different points in their own personal development. The ideal, if not the reality of the extended family, is being replaced for each new generation of elderly persons by the nuclear family with its more direct relationship to the state. As the state's role in the care of the elderly expands so it may be seen that the succeeding generations of the over 65 year olds reap both the rewards and penalties of the Kemalist revolution of over sixty years ago.

Pension and Social Security Schemes

As was noted in the preceeding section, the introduction of state pensions and social security was an important benefit of the Kemalist regime. The origins of contributory social insurance schemes can be traced back to the early years of the republic, when a limited social insurance programme was instituted for the miners in the Ereğli region, in 1921 (Pamir, 1983). By 1950 employees in state organisations, local authority and local council workers were all brought within the framework of an obligatory social insurance scheme operated through the Workers' Insurance Organisation. Since 1961, two contributory pension schemes have operated - the government Retirement Fund (T.C. Emekli Sandiği) for state employees, and the Social Insurance Organisation (Sosyal Sigorta Kurumu), taking contributions from employees and their employers, primarily in the private sector. In 1971 Bağ-Kur, a third insurance scheme, was established, covering self-employed tradesmen, workers and independent businesses. By 1981, approximately 30 per cent of the economically active population were contributors to such insurance schemes (Pamir, 1983).

Eligibility varies between the various schemes, but at present extensions downward have meant that most contributors aged over 50 years, who have worked and contributed for at least ten years can claim retirement pensions. Earlier retirement is possible for those in heavy industry and those whose ill health and premature ageing can be related to their working conditions.

Between 1975 and 1981 there has been almost a threefold rise in the number of people receiving social insurance pensions - from 301,962 to 867,717 (Pamir, 1983). In the rural/agricultural sector however there are few recipients of pensions, though this sector still contains the majority of the population. Established in 1968, law no. 2022 provided for a state welfare pension for both the elderly and the disabled who are otherwise without means of economic support. Applications for this non-contributory pension are made by the elderly, or on their behalf, through local officials in district centres or villages, to the General Directorate of the government's Retirement Fund (T.C. Emekli Sandiği), where decisions concerning eligibility are made. Pensions are then paid out every three months through the recipient's nearest branch of the Agricultural Bank (T.C. Ziraat Bankasi). Receipt of this old age pension guarantees free treatment in state hospitals and dispensaries. The system has met with a number of difficulties (Çuruk, 1983) notably in decisions of eligibility and need, and in ensuring the regular collection of the pensions by the recipients; substantial numbers of elderly people in rural areas are still probably financially dependent upon their families. At present (1983) 630,995 elderly people receive a pension from this legislation, but there is no information yet available concerning the numbers of elderly who are eligible but have not claimed this benefit.

Of course it must be recognised that in many villages the elderly male members of the family often retain economic control of land and property and thus retain an important and respected position in the family and in the community. Retirement is less common in rural areas and elderly people are more likely to remain economically active even late in old age. Beller and Palmore (1974) in a study of elderly Turkish nonagenerians found that almost all were socially active and one fifth economically still active. Eighty per cent felt "honoured formally or informally by their community" (p. 375). It seems probable that in the absence of such economic independence (in terms of ownership of property and land), the provision of an old age pension under law 2022 provides not only some form of economic support to the elderly, but also a source of self-esteem and sustained social status in the community.

Residential and Institutional Provisions

Before 1963 all residential homes and nursing homes for the elderly had been run by local authorities, or voluntary and charitable organisations. This dated from legislation passed in 1930 during the early days of the republic. Despite legislation passed in 1963, which effectively handed over responsibility for residential homes to the Ministry of Social Security, the situation did not change remarkably over the next twelve years. In 1975, the total number of residential places for the elderly was approximately 2,500, for a population of 1.85 million aged 65 and over. Over 50 per cent of the places then available were in local authority homes, and almost 40 per cent in the voluntary and private sector, with only 8.5 per cent in homes run by the Ministry of Health and Social Security (Avşar, 1983). The last eight years have however seen a marked increase in the number of homes opened by the Ministry, such that in 1983, of the 4,500 places in residential homes in Turkey, 36 per cent were controlled by the Ministry of Health and Social Security, 30 per cent by local authorities and 30 per cent by voluntary and private organisations. From 1.5 beds/ 1000 aged 65 and over in 1975, provision has increased to an estimated 3.2 beds/1000 for 1985, reflecting a doubling of the residential homes level of provision.

The contrast between local authority and Ministry of Health and Social Security residential homes is evident in the capital, Ankara. The residential home for the elderly belonging to the Ministry of Health and Social Security was opened in 1975. It has a bed capacity of just over 200, and a 90 per cent occupancy rate. Staffing includes a physician, four social workers, three dieticians, 17 nurses, psychologist, 13 technicians, 63 care assistants and domestic workers and 15 administrative staff. Admission criteria include independence in self-care activities, age over 60 years, no infectious disease or major chronic disability. The rooms vary from single bedrooms to 4-bedded rooms, and in the single rooms residents may bring in their own furniture if they wish. Payment varies according to the size of room. Approximately 25 per cent of the residents pay no charges, being supported through the social services. The waiting list, in 1984, was approximately two years. In the local authority home for the elderly, with a capacity of 110 beds, and over 90 per cent occupancy rates, most of the rooms are 6-bedded. Staffing includes one physician, five nurses, one dietician, and seven domestic/ancillary staff. Admission criteria are similar to those for the Ministry of Health and Social Security's home, but an added requirement is that the elderly person lives alone, and within the municipality. Geriatric and psychogeriatric hospitals do not exist, but plans are advanced to create a geriatric hospital unit in Istanbul. The lack of places for the elderly infirm is noteworthy, and again plans are in hand to create a large residential complex outside Ankara to serve this population. Personal social services and community health services for the elderly are virtually non-existent, although some pilot schemes to help maintain the elderly at home have been initiated on a small scale.

Summary

The demographic pattern of ageing within Turkish society illustrates a marked provincial diversity, with some areas now demonstrating an 'aged' population structure, and many more a 'young' population structure. The history of the republic has provided the present elderly generation in Turkey with a framework that has enhanced individualism and autonomy while reducing the influence of the local neighbourhood. This impact has probably had a trickle down effect across the whole of the country, influencing individuals at different points in their own development, whether as schoolchildren, workers, parents or as grand-parents. The consequences of increasing state provision for the elderly have been realised most obviously only in the last decade. How far the fruits of Ataturk's revolution are benefiting the children of that revolution in their old age remains an empirical question still to be answered, hopefully by a future generation of Turkish social gerontologists.

References

Avsar, A. (1983) 'Care in residential homes for the elderly' in D. Karsli (ed.) Symposium on Care of the Elderly at Home (in Turkish) T.C. S.S.Y.B., Refik Saydam Merkez Hifzissihha Muessesesi, Ankara pp. 39-48

Beller, S. and Palmore, E. (1974) 'Longevity in Turkey', The Gerontologist, 14, 373-376

Curuk, C. (1983) 'The provision and application of law no. 2022' in D. Karsli (ed.) Symposium on Care of the Elderly at home (in Turkish) T.C. S.S.Y.B., Refik Saydam Hifzissihha Muessesesi, Ankara, pp. 49-54

Eren, N. (1963) Turkey Today and Tomorrow, Pall Mall Press, London

Frey, F.W. (1965) The Turkish Political Elite, M.I.T. Press, Cambridge, Mass.

Lerner, D. (1958) The Passing of Traditional Society The Free Press, Glencoe, Ill.

Mardin, S. (1981) 'Religion and Secularism in Turkey' in A. Kazancigil and E. Ozbudun (eds.) Ataturk: Founder of a Modern State, C. Hurst and Co., London, pp. 191-220

Pamir, E. (1963) 'Social insurance and welfare for the elderly', in D. Karsli (ed.) Symposium on Care of the Elderly at Home (in Turkish), T.C. S.S.Y.B. Refik Saydam Merkez Hifzissihha Muessesesi, Ankara pp. 30-34

Shorter, F.C. and Macara, M. (1982) Trends in Fertility and Mortality in Turkey, 1935-1975, Committee on Population and Demography, Report No. 8, National Academy Press, Washington

United Nations (1956) The Aging of Populations and its Economic and Social Implications, Population Studies No. 26, United Nations, New York

United Nations (1984) 1982 Demographic Yearbook, United Nations, New York

PART FOUR: DEVELOPMENTS IN PSYCHOLOGY

Chapter Eighteen

PROGRESS TOWARDS THE ELUCIDATION OF EARLY DEMENTIA:
A COMMUNITY STUDY

N. Wood, J.R.M. Copeland, R.T. Searle, C. McWilliam,
M.E. Dewey, D.M. Forshaw, V.K. Sharma, P. Saunders,
J. Collins and C. Clulow

Introduction

A longitudinal prospective investigation of
early syndrome cases of dementia was started in
1982. The aims of this study, which has
concentrated on a random sample of the community
dwelling elderly in Liverpool, are essentially
threefold. Primarily, we wish to assist the
validity and reliability of early diagnosis of
dementia by charting the progress of individuals who
are being subject to extensive psychiatric and
psychological follow up over a number of years. It
is also hoped that identifiable aetiological
influences may be isolated by this method. A
further aim of the study centres on the systematic
exploration of the predictive value of technological
investigations such as computed tomography and blood
biochemical determinations.

Early or mild dementia as a diagnostic entity
has only comparatively recently become the subject
of systematic inquiry (Henderson and Huppert 1984).
This is partly a result of the more widespread
recognition that the absolute numbers of dementing
individuals is predicted to substantially increase
over the next decade and beyond (Health Advisory
Service 1983) as a direct result of increasing
average life spans. It is sometimes assumed as a
corollory that if these people can be reliably
identified at a prodromal phase of development that
suitable antecedent measures may stave off some of
the worst consequences.

For the individuals so identified, there is
little reassurance which may at present be given
concerning features of the condition which might
indicate a favourable prognosis - although Kral
(1978) had identified the presence alone of

occasional dysnomia and certain difficulties in recall as indicative of benign senescent forgetfulness with a considerably better ultimate outcome than true senile dementia. It is clearly also important at the individual level that the symptoms of pseudodementia or of drug induced cognitive clouding should be reliably set apart from those indicating features of organic deterioration.

In most western societies, the recognition that increasing numbers of elderly are surviving to extreme old age bringing an attendant multiplication of associated medical problems, including dementing illness, has prompted research effort. In this country, the phenomenon has been solicitously dubbed the "rising tide" (Health Advisory Service 1983) and has stimulated initiatives from the DHSS (Crosby et al 1984; Age Concern England 1985). It is clearly of importance that accurate estimates of the prevalence of early and established dementia within the community and of prognosis of individuals currently suffering from mild dementia be established.

The present paper reports some results to date from a study undertaken by members of the Institute of Human Ageing and which addresses some of these issues.

Methods

At the first stage of the investigation, the lists of 55 General Practitioners in the Liverpool Area Health Authority district were random sampled from information held by the local Family Practitioner Committee and 2294 subjects aged over 65 were selected. 1294 of these subjects were interviewed in their own homes over a period of approximately one year by a team of 6 psychologists and research assistants (stage 2). When the deceased and those who had moved away from the area were excluded as out of the sample, the successful interview percentage was some 66. Some 24 per cent of this sample refused interview and we were not able to contact a further 10 per cent for a variety of reasons.

The screening interview (stage 3) consisted of the short version "A" of the Geriatric Mental State Examination Schedule (Copeland et al 1984; McWilliam et al 1985), National Adult Reading Test (NART) (Nelson 1982), Mill Hill Vocabulary Synonyms

Test (MHVS) (Raven 1962), Set Test (Isaacs and Kennie 1972; Gregory et al 1983) and unpublished demographic and social information questionnaires. Blood pressure was measured 3 times at this stage. Stage 4 subjects were selected from this group by an objective method based on a calculated dementia score obtained from GMS(A) items as described previously (Searle 1984; McWilliam et al 1985). To date, 88 subjects comprised of as many as possible of those scoring 4 and over on the dementia scale (as suspected cases) together with randomly selected group of normal controls, have received computerised axial tomography (CAT) scans. 8 pictures were routinely taken at 1cm intervals using an EMI CT1010 pluridirectional head scanner. Images were stored on magnetic tape and analysed using a computer program devised by Professor Lishman's unit at the Institute of Psychiatry.

A standard physical examination, paying particular attention to the CNS, was arranged for these subjects. 45ml of blood was withdrawn from a vein in the cubital fossa for determination of full blood count, true serum B12, serum folate, total and acetyl cholinesterases, S.M.A.C. analysis, thyroid functin (serum thyroxine and if appropriate TSH) tests and serology for syphylis. Analysis of these samples was undertaken by the Departments of Chemical Pathology and Haematology at the Royal Liverpool Hospital and the Public Health Laboratory at Fazakerly Hospital in Liverpool, using standard automated procedures.

123 subjects selected on the basis of their dementia scores (63 = dementia score of 4 and above, 60 = normal controls) were reinterviewed at home by a research psychologist within 6 months of initial screening and then again 6 weeks and one year later (stage 5). The instruments used consisted of Kendrick's Battery (Gibson and Kendrick 1979), Misplaced Objects Test (Crook et al 1979), Numbers Test (D. Kendrick unpublished), Raven's coloured Progressive Matrices (Raven 1965), Activity Levels Questionnaire (R.T. Searle unpublished) and Everyday Memory Questionnaire (R.T. Searle unpublished). Descriptions of these instruments have been published in a previous paper (R.T. Searle 1984).

A number of subjects have therefore received both further medical and psychological investigations and these procedures are being repeated at annual intervals. A further small proportion of refusals (see Fig. 1) have been encountered at these stages and a number of people had become ill or had died between initial interview and follow up.

A further aspect of stage 5 follow up involves reinterview "blind" by a psychiatric registrar or senior registrar (usually with M.R.C.Psych) using the GMS(A), psychogeriatric history schedule (J.R.M. Copeland and D.M. Forshaw unpublished) and behavioural change schedule (J.R.M. Copeland unpublished) for the purposes of arriving at a diagnosis and history of mental illness (where present). These 225 subjects (to date) consist of the CAT scanned group and the psychological follow up group together with a randomly selected group of subjects from stage 3 not being followed up elsewhere.

An Automated Geriatric Examination for Computer Assisted Taxonomy (AGECAT) (see Copeland et al 1984) provides standardised computed diagnoses and is being applied to the GMS(A) data from the 1241 subjects initially screened. These will be compared with diagnoses by psychiatrist and with results from the dementia score classification.

All data was entered onto an IBM4341 mainframe and analysed using the SPSSX statistical package.

Results

Demography and general characteristics

A preliminary analysis of demographic variables has been previously reported (Wood et al 1984) and the present data, based on an analysis on 1071 individuals, extends this. 93.3 per cent of all initial interviews were conducted in subjects' own homes, and some 2.7 per cent in the homes of their relatives. The remainder were interviewed in aged persons homes, nursing homes and the like.

The age structure of the sample conforms to the pattern of the tail end of a normal distribution as anticipated. The mean age of the females was 73.9 years (S.D. = 6.4) and the mean age of the male group was 73.1 years (S.D. = 6.3) but these are not significantly different. 61.7 per cent of the sample were female. 82.1 per cent of the sample were born on Merseyside. 11.7 per cent had remained single all their lives, 44.4 per cent were currently married and 40.5 per cent had lost their marriage partner. Some 3 per cent admitted divorce or separation.

A breakdown of socio-economic groupings according to the Registrar General's classification reveals that some 45.4 per cent had been employed in a manual capacity, 16.8 per cent in a junior non-manual position, and 6.0 per cent in a personal service post. 4.2 per cent had been non-manual supervisors and 3.2 per cent ancillary workers. 14.8 per cent had been employers or managers, and the smallest group were ex-professional workers (1.5 per cent). 16 per cent did not state an occupation and the remaining small number had been self employed or employed in the Armed Services or agricultural work.

15.2 per cent of the sample claimed they had been under unusual stress in the past month and a quarter of this group attributed this to the death of a near relative. 24 per cent of the sample kept a pet of some sort.

69.2 per cent of the sample were taking at least one prescribed drug. Commonly prescribed substances included diuretics (164 instances), vasodilators (89 instances), hypnotics (84 instances) and anxiolytics (52 instances).

Psychological investigation

The distribution of the scores obtained with the three cognitive tests used at initial screening (where these schedules were attempted) are illustrated in Fig. 2. Note that scores for the Set Test indicate numbers of responses made, whereas scores for the NART and MHVS represent errors made.

In addition to obtaining dementia scores from initial interview, depression scores were similarly computed by adding together scores obtained from GMS(A) items which had been previously shown to discriminate highly for depressive symptoms (McWilliam et al 1985). Table 1 indicates the correlations (Pearson r) obtained between the depression and dementia scores and the cognitive tests used in this subject at stage 3.

Our interpretation extends the conclusions reached at an earlier stage based on an analysis of a smaller sample (Wood et al 1984). Set test performance suffers with the presence of either dementia or depression (at least as measured by these scores) although a poor performance is more highly correlated with the presence of symptoms of dementia. Significant correlations pertain also

231

between the performance on the other two cognitive tests and increasing dementia and depression scores. Increasing age and dementia scores are, as one might expect significantly correlated, although from these results increasing age alone is not a particularly good predictor for dementia. There was no relationship between age and the presence of depression as indexed by the calculated score. It may also be noted that the dementia and depression scores are correlated indicating some overlap.

TABLE 1

Pearson correlations between cognitive test performance at initial interview, age and dementia and depression scores. Number of subjects = 870 - 943. All correlations significant (p < 0.001).

	NART	MHVS	AGE	DEMENTIA SCORE	DEPRESSION SCORE
SET SCORE	-0.42	-0.47	-0.34	-0.52	-0.26
NART ERRORS	-	0.60	0.10	0.24	0.12
MHVS ERRORS	-	-	0.16	0.30	0.17
AGE	-	-	-	0.25	n.s.
DEMENTIA SCORE	-	-	-	-	0.35

Detailed results from the psychological part of the stage 5 follow up have been presented elsewhere (Searle 1984) and will not be repeated here. In brief, a comparison of three groups (DS<4, DS=4 - 7,DS>7) indicates significant differences using one way ANOVA on all the tests studied with the exception of the NART. In each case there was a decline in performance from the lowest dementia scoring group to the highest, indicating sensitivity of all these instruments to the presence of dementia even in its early stages (as defined by a dementia score in the middle range 4 - 7). These results cannot be accounted for by differences in mean age, social class or occupational levels achieved (assessed by the Goldthorpe and Hope 1974 scale) between the groups, but await comparison with psychiatric diagnoses and eventual outcome.

Psychiatric investigation

To date 225 subjects have received psychiatric diagnoses although analyses of these data are not at present complete. Analysis of the diagnoses attached to the first 76 subjects receiving CAT scans reveals that 20 have had a diagnosis of borderline ("early") or definite dementia, 17 of depression, 2 mixed pathology and 2 a diagnosis of other caseness. 35 subjects have had a diagnosis of mental normality and serve as non-case controls. We are confident that selecting a dementia score of 4 and above as a basis for follow up is missing virtually none of the cases rated early or definite dementia by psychiatrist from the psychiatric follow up study of subjects randomly selected from stage 3 (see Fig. 1).

Development of the GMS(A) as a community screening and diagnostic instrument is continuing. From data collected so far, the overall agreement between psychiatrists and screening interviewers used at stage 3 is about 80 per cent for caseness – the screeners making the judgement rather more often.

Data collected from GMS(A) interview at stage 3 is being used to provide input for the computerised diagnostic system, AGECAT, which has been developed for this purpose. Table 2 indicates the results from application of AGECAT to data collected from a randomly selected 500 subjects at stage 3. It indicates the mean dementia scores together with their standard deviations calculated from the screening interview, associated with four diagnostic categories.

TABLE 2

AGECAT computed diagnoses and dementia scores associated with 500 subjects selected from the community. S.D.= standard deviation

AGECAT DIAGNOSIS	DEMENTIA SCORE	S.D.
OTHER	2.64	2.66
DEMENTIA	9.28	4.55
DEPRESSION	3.33	2.87
NON-CASES	1.46	2.41

The table indicates that the mean dementia score associated with individuals receiving a diagnosis of dementia by AGECAT is some 6 fold greater than the non-cases, although a wide range was encountered, and provides further evidence of the utility of this measure as a basis for selected subjects for follow up. AGECAT itself has been shown to have high agreement with diagnoses made by psychiatrist (Copeland et al 1984).

Computed Axial Tomography

A tracker ball system was used to trace the outline of whole brain and of lateral ventricles from each of the 8 pictures obtained from each subject. Total area traced, in pixels, was determined as was mean density, in Houndsfield units, of each area studied. Analysis is currently proceeding and these results will be published at a later date. Preliminary indications to date reveal that cases diagnosed borderline by psychiatrists exhibit a mean whole brain/ventricle area ratio between the values obtained from normal subjects and the significantly lower values obtained from definite cases associated with brain shrinkage and ventricular dilation. It appears then that even at an early stage measurable changes can occur in brain morphology.

Blood Biochemistry

To date the results of the laboratory analyses of blood samples from the stage 5 hospital follow up group reveal some interesting findings. Table 3 presents a summary of significant findings in subjects psychiatrically diagnosed dementing compared with non-dementing controls.

TABLE 3

Summary of statistically significant results from analysis of blood samples taken from subjects receiving a diagnosis of dementia (cases) compared to non-case controls. Results are presented as means of each group together with standard deviations and represent data from 11-13 subjects (demented group) and 48-55 subjects (non-dementing group).

VARIABLE	NON-CASE	S.D.	CASE	S.D.	$p <$
Sodium (mmol/l)	136.8	5.72	131.8	7.33	0.03
Alkaline Phosphatase (U/l)	101.4	25.02	126.1	51.1	0.04
Albumin (g/l)	43.0	2.47	41.5	2.59	0.04
Iron (umol/l)	19.9	6.02	15.8	4.72	0.05

It may also be mentioned that there is a trend to a decrease in blood cholinesterase levels in dementing subjects as has been reported by other authors (Chipperfield et al 1981). So far however our results do not achieve statistical significance.

Discussion

The final success of the study measures to detect and describe the features of early dementia can only ultimately be assessed against eventual outcome of individuals being followed up. Certain indications of promising research directions can however be discerned at this stage. We have confirmed that some cognitive impairment is measurable at an early stage of dementia, at least as far as this is deemed present from dementia score classification. Verbal fluency, as measured by Set test score, appears to be a particularly sensitive index of impairment associated with senile dementia.

It is of course well known that cognitive impairment can arise from taking sedative or psychotropic drugs, and indeed be present as a result of depressive illness (Reifler et al 1982) to the extent of being termed pseudodementia. For these reasons, we have been concerned to confirm initial categorization of follow up subjects on the basis of dementia scores, by psychiatric examination. When used by itself, a schedule like the GMS(A) cannot record all items of information essential to the diagnostic process. One of us (J.R.M.C.) has therefore been developing two further schedules, the psychogeriatric history schedule to clarify diagnosis and the behavioural change schedule to record changes in behaviour over the past 5 years as assessed by information obtained from an informant. Further refinement of schedules may involve inclusion of items relating to parietal lobe function. This additional data will it is hoped in the future be incorporated into the AGECAT diagnostic procedure.

The demographic characteristics of this elderly sample are very similar to those reported in comparable studies (Gurland et al 1981) and we are confident it is representative of the elderly community population. A major problem with any longitudinal prospective research centres on the attrition rate. For this reason we are currently attempting to increase the number of individuals being followed up with CAT and blood investigations.

The preliminary results presented here from our investigation of the CAT tapes are suggestive of possible further detectable morphological changes associated with diagnoses of early dementia. Naguib and Levy (1983) report an association between cognitive deterioration and changes in brain-ventricle ratio at two year follow up and put forward changes in radiological attenuation density in the right parietal region as a prognostic indicator. Our study will offer an opportunity to pursue these findings.

The results from the blood examinations to date are also suggestive. These changes are not large in relation to the variability and as such could never be clinically useful markers. It is possible that the reduced protein and mineral levels may be related to dietary factors although this would require further investigation to establish with any certainty.

In conclusion, it is hoped that the various strands of this investigation will draw together to form a coherent picture of the pattern of early dementia as a result of repeated follow up of our subjects at regular intervals.

Acknowledgements

This research was supported by an award from the Wellcome Trust to Professor J.R.M. Copeland which is gratefully acknowledged.

The authors would also like to acknowledge the advice and assistance given by Professor Lishman and Mr Robert Baldy from the Institute of Psychiatry in connection with the analysis of the CAT tapes.

We also wish to thank the following individuals who have assisted with aspects of this study: Dr R. Abed, Mr M. Binks, Dr R. Bloor, Mr B. Carr, Dr A. Davies, Miss H. Gordon, Miss M. Heery, Miss M. Hensey, Dr M.S. Muthu, Mrs J. Silcock, Dr W.H. Taylor, Mrs J. Wood.

Finally we are indebted to the general practitioners who allowed us to interview their patients and especially to the subjects themselves who participated so willingly.

References

Age Concern England (1985) Mental Health in Old Age: A Collection of Projects 3rd Edition, Age Concern England, Surrey

Chipperfield, A., Newman, P.M. and Moyes, I.C.A.

(1981) 'Erythrocyte Cholinesterase and Dementia',
Lancet, 25(7), 199

Copeland, J.R.M., Forshaw, D.M. and Dewey, M.E.
(1984) 'A Review of the Standardised Mental State
Examination and Computer Assisted Psychiatric
Diagnoses for use in Research with the Community
Elderly' in D. Bromley (ed) Gerontology: Social
and Behavioural Perspectives, Croom Helm, London

Crook, T., Ferris, E.C. and McCarthy, M. (1979) 'The
Misplaced Objects Test: A Brief Test for Memory
Dysfunction in the Aged', Journal of the American
Geriatrics Society, 27, 284-287

Crosby, C., Stevenson, R.C. and Copeland, J.R.M.
(1984) 'The Evaluation of Instensive Domicillary
Care for the Elderly Mentally Ill' in D. Bromley
(ed) Gerontology: Social and Behavioural
Perspectives, Croom Helm, London

Gibson, A.J. and Kendrick, D.C. (1979) The Kendrick
Battery for the Detection of Dementia in the
Elderly, NFER Nelson Publishing Co., Windsor

Goldthorpe, J. and Hope, K. (1974) The Social
Grading of Occupations, Oxford University Press,
London

Gregory, S.J., Davies, A.D.M. and Binks, M.G. (1983)
'The Improvement of Verbal Fluency in the Elderly.
The Effects of Practice on the Set Test and an
Alternative Form', Educational Gerontology, 9,
139-146

Gurland, B.J., Copeland, J.R.M., Kuriansky, J.,
Kelleher, M.J., Sharpe, L. and Dean L. (1983)
The Mind and Mood of Ageing: The Mental Health
Problems of the Community Elderly in New York and
London, Hayworth Press, New York

Health Advisory Service (1983) The Rising Tide:
Developing Services for Mental Illness in Old Age,
NHS Advisory Service, Surrey

Henderson, A.S. and Huppert, F.A. (1984) 'The
Problem of Mild Dementia', Psychological Medicine,
in press

Issacs, B. and Kennie, A.T. (1972) 'The Set Test as
an Aid to the Detection of Dementia in Old People'
Age and Ageing, 1, 222-296

Kral, V.A. (1978) 'Benign Senescent Forgetfulness'
in R. Katzman, R.D. Terry and K.L. Bick (eds)
Senile Dementia and Related Disorders, Raven, New
York

McWilliam, C., Wood, N., Copeland, J.R.M. and Dewey,
M.E. (1985) 'Early Stages in the Development of a
Screening Interview for Dementia in the Community'

in press

Naguib, M. and Levy, R. (1982) 'Prediction of Outcome in Senile Dementia - A Computed Tomography Study', British Journal of Psychiatry, 140, 263-267

Nelson, H.E. (1982) National Adult Reading Test (NART) for the Assessment of Premorbid Intelligence in Patients with Dementia, Test Manual, NFER Nelson Publishing Co., Windsor

Raven, J.C. (1962) Manual for the Mill Hill Vocabulary Test, H.K. Lewis, London

Raven, J.C. (1965) Guide to Using the Coloured Progressive Matrices, Sets A, Ab and C, William Grieve and Sons, Dumfries

Reifler, B.V., Larson, E. and Hanlet, R. (1982) 'Co-existence of Cognitive Impairment and Depression in Geriatric Outpatients', American Journal of Psychiatry, 139, 623-626

Searle, R.T. (1984) 'A Community Based Follow Up of Some Suspected Cases of Early Dementia. An Interim Report', in D. Bromley (ed) Gerontology: Social and Behavioural Perspectives, Croom Helm, London

Wood, N., Copeland, J.R.M., Forshaw, D.M., Muthu, M.S., Abed, R., Sharma, V.K. and Dewey, M.E. (1984) 'The Early Detection of Dementia: Initial Findings from a Longitudinal Study' in D. Bromley (ed) Gerontology: Social and Behavioural Perspectives, Croom Helm, London

Figure 1

This diagram illustrates the overall structure of
the Liverpool community study and indicates the
numbers of subjects followed up at each stage.

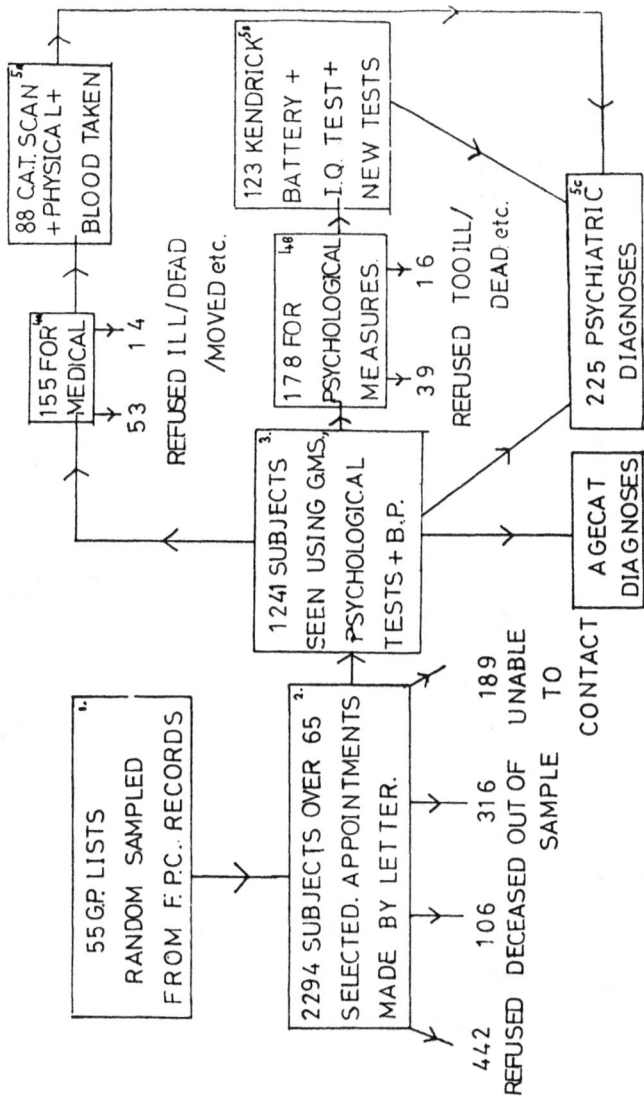

Figure 2

The frequency distributions of the scores obtained in the three cognitive tests administered at initial interview are indicated here.

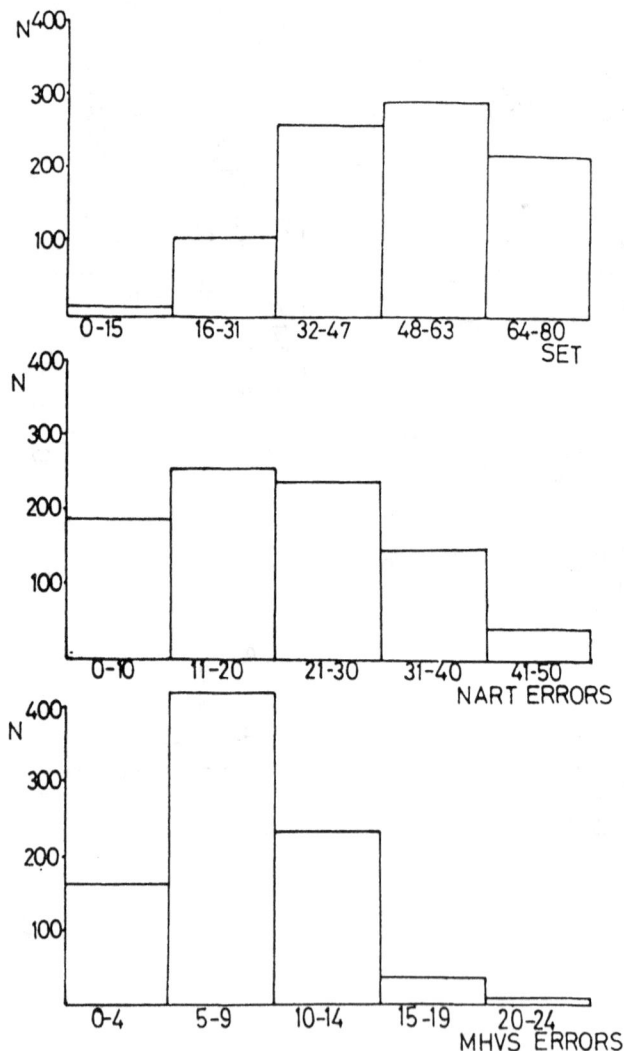

Chapter Nineteen

THE CONTRIBUTION OF THE NATIONAL ADULT READING TEST
TO THE DETECTION OF DEMENTIA AMONGST COMMUNITY
DWELLING OLD PEOPLE

M. G. Binks and A. D. M. Davies

This contribution is in three sections.

1. It describes a strategy for screening for
   early dementia using language tests that
   differ in sensitivity to dementia.

2. It discusses practical problems of using
   printed psychological tests with the
   elderly.

3. It continues the empirical evaluation of
   the assumptions made when proposing the
   National Adult Reading Test (NART) as an
   indicator of premorbid levels of
   intelligence in the demented elderly (Binks
   and Davies 1984).

SCREENING FOR EARLY DEMENTIA

   Although the pattern of cognitive impairment in
moderate and severe dementia has been described
frequently, less is known about early cognitive
change. The development of effective screening
procedures for early senile dementia hinges on the
validation of measures of such change. In the
individual case early changes may be subtle and
there is unlikely to be an accurate description of
how the person functioned with respect to language,
memory and attention before the changes occurred.
One strategy that has been developed argues that the
best one can do is to develop measures using groups
of subjects studying both dementing and non-
dementing subjects to identify two aspects of
cognition: those that in general remain relatively
stable, and those that alter as the disease
progresses. This strategy allows one to construct a

profile of cognitive abilities for an individual. Inferences are then made about the person's premorbid intellectual level on the basis of the profile. The subject's performance on tests that 'hold up' relatively well is used to estimate what the person was like intellectually before disease onset. Performance on tests that show marked changes with dementia give an indication of current level and hence the degree of change can be assessed.

For this strategy to be workable a number of conditions have to be met.

1. It has to be demonstrated that there are in fact two such classes of intellectual functioning - the dementia resistant and the dementia sensitive.

2. The dementia resistant measures must be shown to be related to intellectual level in normal non-demented people.

3. There should be no significant differences between the performance of groups of demented and groups of non-demented people on the dementia resistant tests.

4. Finally and most stringently, longitudinal studies should show that dementia resistant functioning does not change as the disease progresses through its early stages.

Nelson and her co-workers suggest that the ability to read words may be dementia resistant. She developed an ingenious reading test as a quick and easy measure of premorbid vocabulary and used it with presenile dementia and non-demented patient groups (Nelson, 1982). The test, the NART, consists of 50 words which are phonetically irregular, e.g. the word "ACHE". If a person pronounces this word correctly when presented with it visually, it demonstrates that the word was in the person's vocabulary premorbidly. Vocabulary level is known to be a good indicant of verbal intelligence e.g. the vocabulary subtests of intelligence tests such as the WAIS correlate highly with verbal I.Q. and Full Scale I.Q. (for the 45-54 age group r = 0.85 WAIS vocabulary versus Verbal I.Q. and r = 0.83 WAIS vocabulary versus Full Scale I.Q.). Nelson reported

that the reading error score so obtained correlated
highly with WAIS I.Q. in the non-demented (r =
- 0.75, Nelson and McKenna, 1975) and showed no
differences between patients with and without
presenile dementia (Nelson and O'Connell 1978).
Thus NART error score is resistant to presenile
dementia. No data have been presented by her for
elderly people, nor has the stringent longitudinal
study yet been carried out.

The present study extends investigation of the
NART to an elderly group - though this study too is
cross-sectional. In particular it examines:

1. The relation between NART error score and a
    measure of vocabulary, a half length
    version of the Mill Hill Vocabulary Synonym
    TEST (MHV), in non-dementing subjects over
    65 years of age.

2. Whether NART error score distinguishes
    those who are judged 'demented' from non-
    dementing subjects over 65 years of age.

If Nelson's strategy is to be useful in screening
for senile dementia we require a strong relationship
between NART score and MHV and no difference in
average score of the dementing and non-dementing
groups.

SUBJECTS

In twelve months of screening, 1241 elderly
people living in the community were interviewed.
From this sample two subsamples were selected. The
first was in better physical and mental health than
the parent sample since in this first subsample
illnesses and handicaps were absent or insufficient
to hinder mental functioning. Thus, none were
taking drugs prescribed by a doctor, none were
described in the summary at the end of the interview
as depressed, demented or suffering from any other
mental handicap such as a stroke. This gave a
sample of 243 men and women aged 65 - 84. Older
subjects were excluded due to small numbers. The
present results are based on 124 randomly selected
relatively healthy subjects. The rest are retained
for cross validation. The second subsample was made
up of subjects with such severe cognitive deficits
that they scored three or more errors on a seven

item mental status questionnaire (MSQ) - see Table
1. These were items selected from a modified
version of the Geriatric Mental State interview
(GMS, Wood et al. 1984) which was administered in
all screening interviews.

TABLE 1

Mental Status Questionnaire Items

a)	What year were you born?	Does not know	= 1
b)	What is the date today?	Error in day	= 1
		Error in month	= 1
		Error in year	= 1
c)	Do you remember my name?		
	What is it?	Error	= 1
d)	What is the name of the		
	Prime Minister?	Error	= 1
e)	Who was the last Prime		
	Minister?	Error	= 1

MSQ score is total errors

The seven items were chosen because they were
not only typical of a wide range of mental status
questionnaires but were also the items most amenable
to objective recording during the interview and
objective coding for analysis. The cut-off was
chosen because a score of three errors was the
maximum found in the first, relatively fit,
subsample and was rare, occurring in only three
subjects. Two of them were of low intelligence
since childhood. The remaining occurrence gives a
false alarm rate of 0.4 per cent. The validity of
the cut-off of three or more errors was assessed
using psychiatrists' diagnoses arising from the same
version of the GMS used to follow-up blind a random
20 per cent of screening interviews. 159 follow-up
interviews have been coded so far and the diagnoses
have been confirmed by an independent psychiatric
review which also used a psychiatric history
schedule and a behaviour schedule.
There are screening interviews, MSQ scores and
follow-up psychiatric diagnoses for four types of
subject. Firstly of those who were not depressed or
demented (n = 104), there were 3 per cent false
alarms who exceeded the MSQ criterion. Secondly of
those who were demented (n = 23), there were 39 per
cent misses who did not meet the MSQ criteria. All

of these were confirmed as borderline cases of dementia. Thirdly, both subjects who were both depressed and demented met the MSQ criterion. Fourthly of those who were depressed (n = 20), there were 20 per cent false alarms who exceeded the MSQ criterion. The remaining 10 subjects were excluded (diagnoses of alcoholism or schizophrenia or anxiety state). Thus the MSQ criterion of 3 or more errors rarely misclassified normal old people as cognitively impaired and was more likely to miss the cognitive impairment of demented old people than to suggest false cognitive impairment in depressed old people.

The second subsample of cognitively impaired subjects was found by examining the parent sample of screening interviews to identify subjects scoring three or more on the MSQ scale, of these 34 men and women were aged 65-84. However, there were a further 28 subjects above the MSQ criterion but lacking either or both of NART and MHV scores. Although 18 per cent of these were too confused to test, the commonest explanation was poor eye sight for 46 per cent of incomplete cases. Amongst the first sample of cognitively unimpaired old people there were fewer missing NART and MHV scores but the proportion due to poor eye sight was similar at 36 per cent. Thus the visual nature of the proposed screening procedure was a major limitation in this community screening study. To what extent can it be overcome?

PROBLEMS WITH PRINTED PSYCHOLOGICAL TESTS

Since the NART is a visual test, there will be old people who are genuinely unable to read the 0.25 cm high letters on the card. A large print, high contrast version reduces this problem since Downes (1984) in his post-graduate research with elderly normal, demented and depressed day-centre and in-patient subjects found no refusals when testing 35 subjects in a version with letters 0.9 cm high. Nevertheless any visual test introduces readily available excuses to evade the effort, strangeness and perhaps threat of psychological testing: "I haven't got my glasses with me" and "I can't read that". While some old people have a real visual handicap, the prevalence of evasions can be reduced by enquiring about the use of glasses early in the interview when collecting a brief outline of health and handicaps. Visual tests can then be deferred until glasses are available. If excuses continue, then some may be identified as evasions by asking the subject to name simple shapes or single letters that are so large and bold that only those with officially notifiable partial sight would have difficulty.

CASE STUDY

A recent patient was a 61 year old man, W.R. with chronic cognitive and behavioural disorders. These were probably partly learnt to gain attention during several years of contact with psychiatric settings and partly due to evasions and exaggerations. Psychological testing excluded the possibility of dementia. After denying that he could read the standard NART card he was willing to read letters 8.5 cm high. The subsequent series of letters were of gradually reducing size until even the longest NART items could be fitted onto a sheet of A4 paper with letters 4 cm high. After this introduction to the test material, he attempted 38 out of the 49 items presented (ie 78 per cent), with the rest being "don't know" responses. Since he made 14 correct responses and his age lay at the top of the published NART standardisation sample, a conservative estimate of his premorbid IQ score was 100. This and his O.N.C. qualification were well above his observed current IQ of 81, which also suffered from many "don't know" responses and fluctuating co-operation. Consequently he was referred to a rehabilitation ward to try to modify his disruptive and stereotyped behaviour and to try to restore his cognitive performance to that predicted by the NART and his previous educational level. This case shows that preliminary tasks may be able to funnel a wider range of subjects into the standardised NART test, converting evasions into assessments, leaving objective visual handicaps as the main source of refusals. The same approach is worth trying with other visual tests.

EVALUATION OF ASSUMPTIONS

Binks and Davies (1984) reported the first stage of an empirical evaluation of the NART as an indicator of premorbid intelligence in the elderly. The sample of mentally unimpaired old people has been enlarged to form the first sample in the present paper. In this larger sample the linear correlation between MHV and NART errors is confirmed as -0.65 with the linear regression

$$MHV = -0.18 \text{ NART} + 18.1$$

In the second, mentally impaired sample the correlation is -0.70 with the linear regression

$$MHV = -0.24 \text{ NART} + 17.4$$

Since both are significant beyond the .001 level, the strong linear relationship between reading ability and vocabulary, which is assumed by the dementia screening strategy, is confirmed for both mentally impaired and unimpaired old people.

When the two samples were compared, the mentally impaired sample was older by 4.2 years and significantly so ($t = 4.4$, 156 df, $p = .001$). Also 81 per cent of the mentally impaired sample had been manual workers compared with 62 per cent of the unimpaired sample, which was just significant (chi squared $= 3.9$, 1 df, $p = .05$). Since these differences existed before the screening interviews and may have influenced the performance on psychological tests, they were entered as the first variables in the following multiple regression tests of the assumptions of the dementia screening strategy - see Table 2. This ensured that the influence of subsequent variables were adjusted statistically to reduce the influence of the significant difference between samples in age and occupation.

TABLE 2

Multiple Regression Prediction of MHV scores

Order of adding variables	Multiple R squared Change	F	Significance
1. Age, occupation	.20	18.2	0.001
2. Mental impairment	.11	22.5	0.001
3. NART	.27	91.7	0.001
4. Interaction between mental impairment and NART	.01	2.4	0.127

Total .59

The first assumption to be tested by multiple regression was that MHV was dementia sensitive after adjusting for age and occupation. The prediction of MHV was improved slightly, but significantly beyond the .001 level, by the addition of the effects of mental impairment to the multiple regression. The prediction of MHV was improved greatly by the further addition of the effects of the NART scores, an improvement that was significant beyond the .001 level. The prediction of MHV was not significantly improved by the addition of the interaction between NART and mental impairment. These steps in the multiple regression analysis showed that after adjustment for age and occupation effects, the mentally impaired sample had significantly lower MHV scores, that NART scores made a major contribution to the prediction of MHV scores, that the slope for the mentally impaired group was not significantly greater than the slope for the unimpaired group. Thus a further assumption of the dementia screening strategy is confirmed for the elderly: that MHV scores can be predicted from NART scores by parallel multiple regression equations for the mentally impaired and unimpaired.

The final assumption to be tested is crucial: that NART score is insensitive to mental impairment in old age. Unfortunately the mentally impaired sample made 9.6 more errors, which was significant ($t = 4.2$, 153 df, $p = .001$). After statistical adjustment for age and occupation (multiple R squared change $= 0.14$, $F = 11.9$, $p = .001$) the mentally impaired sample still made 7.4 more errors (multiple R squared change $= 0.05$, $F = 9.2$, $p = .003$). So it is likely that the NART is dementia sensitive, although to a lesser extent than other tests such as MHV. The effect of mental impairment has been to move the group mean down the regression line away from the mentally unimpaired group mean. This is in contrast to Nelson and O'Connell's results (1978) with presenile dementia where the NART was insensitive to dementia. Their impaired group mean was vertically below their unimpaired group.

CONCLUSION

These violations of the assumptions of the strategy for detecting early dementia require either a revision of the NART test material or a different interpretive procedure adapted to the characteristics of dementia in old age.

References

Binks, M.G. and Davies, A.D.M. (1984) 'The Early Detection of Dementia. A Baseline from Healthy Community Dwelling Old People', in Bromley, D.B. (ed), Gerontology: Social and Behavioural Perspectives, Croom Helm, London

Downes, J.J. (1984) Personal Communication

Nelson, H.E. (1982) National Adult Reading Test (NART) for the Assessment of Premorbid Intelligence in Patients with Dementia: Test Manual, NFER Publishing Co., Windsor

Nelson, H.E. and McKenna, P. (1975) 'The Use of Current Reading Ability in the Assessment of Dementia', British Journal of Social and Clinical Psychology, 14, 259-267

Nelson, H.E. and O'Connell, A. (1978) 'Dementia: the Estimate of Premorbid Intelligence Levels using the New Adult Reading Test', Cortex, 14, 234-244

Wood, N., Copeland, J.R.M., Forshaw, D.M., Muthu, M.S., Abed, R., Sharmva, V.K. and Dewey, M.E. (1974) 'The Early Detection of Dementia. Initial Findings from a Longitudinal Study', in Bromley, D.B. (ed) op.cit.

Acknowledgements

We are grateful for the support of the Wellcome Trust which funded the data collection.

Chapter Twenty

LIFE STRESS AND DEPRESSION IN THE ELDERLY:
EXPERIENCES FROM A COMMUNITY STUDY

Susan J. Wilkinson, Owen James and Ann D. M. Davies

This paper is a first report on a community
study of elderly people living in rural areas. Some
preliminary results will be presented, within the
context of a more general discussion of the
collaborative research context in which they were
obtained; the background to the results must be
understood to interpret them with any validity.
The study, which was funded by The Mental
Health Foundation, was concerned with the mental
health of elderly people living in the community and
its relationship to the circumstances of their
everyday lives. It had a particular focus on the
role of life stress in depression, considering two
kinds of life stress:
  i) life events, which are discrete events
     occuring at one point in time (e.g. deaths,
     hospital admissions, residence changes);
 ii) long-term difficulties, which are problems
     continuing for more than one month (e.g.
     health, marital or financial difficulties).
     Although there has been extensive research
interest in recent years in relating life stress to
mental disorder (c.f. Cochrane & Sobol, 1980, for
a review), very little work has been done with the
elderly. With regard to depression, there has been
one piece of research on elderly people in an urban
context (Murphy, 1982, 1983a), while the rural
elderly have not been studied at all. Our research
was based on a random sample of elderly people
living in rural communities in South Cheshire and
North Wales.
     In this research field, the early, rather
simple, stimulus-response model of life event -
symptom connection has now given way to attempts to
identify variables that moderate or mediate the
connections. Two sets of variables of potential
importance are the social and psychological

resources of the individual. There have, however, been few empirical examinations of the coping responses used by elderly people in response to life stress (e.g. Salzman and Shader, 1980). Further, those studies which have been conducted have neglected to investigate the individual's social relationships, which are an important coping resource (e.g. Cobb, 1976). Our study considered the role of both types of variable: we have collected data both on individuals' social networks (formal and informal) and on their methods of coping with severe life events and difficulties - although most of this data has yet to be analysed.

The assessment of life stress and depression:

We have been using the investigator-based method of Brown and Harris (1978), adapted for use with the elderly, as our procedure for assessing life stress. An interviewer elicits data about the occurrence of life events and difficulties in the respondent's life over the past year, by means of a semi-structured interview. These events and difficulties are then presented by the interviewer to a trained panel of 2-4 people for 'contextual rating'. Panel members make independent judgments of the degree of threat an event would involve for most people in biographical circumstances like those of the respondent (Brown and Harris, op.cit. p.91). Raters are only provided with information about respondents' social context and circumstances, not their psychiatric status or emotional responses. Disagreements are discussed until a consensus is reached. Events are rated on 4-point scales of 'short-term threat' and long-term threat', difficulties on a 6-point scale of 'severity'. The rating procedure is aided by the use of extensive 'dictionaries' of precedents, but these are based primarily on Brown's studies of younger women and thus are of limited use in studying the elderly.

The contextual rating procedure rests on the assumption that the concept of threat is generalisable - a notion which received some support in a study by Tennant et al (1976) - but we do not know if this is the case across the life span.

In any investigation, it is essential that the disorder being studied be clearly specified and then reliably and validly identified. The Geriatric Mental State (Copeland et al, 1976), adapted from the Present State Examination (Wing et al, 1974), is a standardized psychiatric interview specifically formulated for use with the elderly. The version we used - the C.A.R.E. schedule - allows information to be elicited on symptoms of depression and a decision to be made on cases of clinical depression according to the Diagnostic and Statistical Manual of the American Psychiatric Association (3rd edition, 1980).

Research design and interviewing procedure:

Two random samples of elderly people living in rural communities were interviewed twice in their own homes: the second interview generally taking place within a month of the first. The life stress interviews were conducted by two research psychologists based in the University Department of Psychiatry in Liverpool (now in the University Department of Psychology). They were trained in Brown's contextual rating procedure and themselves trained the other two members of the rating team. The psychiatric interviews were conducted by medically qualified practitioners in N.H.S. posts at local hospitals, as part of their research interests. This collaboration was an important feature of the project for two particular reasons:

i) it allowed potentially costly research to be conducted relatively economically;

ii) it permitted the complete separation of psychiatric and life stress interviews, which is, we believe, an improvement on previous methodology. In fact, the life stress interviewers were completely 'blind' as to respondents' psychiatric status until after contextual rating had taken place.

The sampling procedure was as follows. A random sample of 1 in 6 of the over-65s was drawn from the age-sex registers (or medical records) of the 6 general practices serving the South Cheshire Study area, while a sample of 1 in 5 of the over-65s was drawn from the 3 practices in the North Wales study area. Those living in institutions were excluded. For the purpose of conducting interviews, a series of small random samples (N=50) were drawn from the larger pool of potential respondents, so that problems arising at any one stage would not reverberate on the sample as a whole.

In South Cheshire subjects were contacted by means of a letter signed by their G.P., endorsing the study and introducing the research team. This letter asked for a positive indication of willingness to take part in the study. Non-responders were followed up by means of a reminder letter one month later. All refusals were accepted as final.

The medical interview was conducted first and consisted of the C.A.R.E. Schedule, together with the SET test (Isaacs and Kennie, 1973) as an additional screening device for detecting dementia. This interview lasted about 2 hours. The life stress interview lasted about 2½ hours, and was tape recorded. The interviewer collected demographic and social data, and determined the occurrence of life events within the last year and the presence of ongoing difficulties. This information was then presented to a panel of raters, following the procedure previously described.

A small reliability study is being conducted on the two life stress interviewers' identification of events and difficulties from the tapes; together with a more extensive examination of inter-rater reliability between panel members. One further reliability check involves one of the psychologists interviewing a close relative of a small sample of the respondents, to determine their accuracy in reporting events and difficulties.

A slow rate of interviewing and low response rate led to some changes in this procedure in North Wales. Here, the life stress interview was conducted first, with the interviewer calling on respondents within a fortnight of receipt of the G.P. letter. Up to four calls were made at any one address and, again, refusals were accepted as final. In addition, the length of the medical interview was reduced by utilising the short form of the G.M.S. (Copeland et al, op.cit), together with some additional questions, instead of the full C.A.R.E. schedule.

Response rates:

In South Cheshire, a total of 221 potential respondents were contacted; of this number 189 were actually eligible for interview and 90 completed both interviews. This represents an overall response rate of 48 per cent. Table 1 gives details of the response rate for each of the sub-samples in South Cheshire.

TABLE 1 : RESPONSE RATE IN SOUTH CHESHIRE

	SUBSAMPLES				
	1	2	3	4	5
No. of subjects mailed	50	50	50	50	21
Dead	0	0	4	0	0
Moved	5	3	0	0	0
Untraceable	6	6	4	0	4
ACUTAL SIZE OF SUBSAMPLE	39	41	42	50	17
Aphasic	0	2	0	0	0
Confused/senile	3	1	1	3	1
Illness prevented interview	1	0	0	0	0
Completed psychiatric interview	21	21	22	27	9
Refused life stress interview	2	3	0	3	2
Completed life stress interview	19	18	22	24	7
REFUSED TO PARTICIPATE	14	17	19	20	7
Response rate first interview	54%	51%	52%	54%	53%
REPONSE RATE BOTH INTERVIEWS	49%	44%	52%	48%	41%

N.B. Interviewing in final subsample not completed due to lack of time

In view of the low response rate in South Cheshire the available demographic data was compared for 'refusers' and those who agreed to be interviewed. No significant differences were found between the two groups in terms of age or sex.

In North Wales, a total of 223 potential respondents were contacted; of these 190 were eligible to take part and 147 completed both interviews. This represents an overall response rate of 77 per cent. Table 2 presents details of the response rate for the North Wales sub-samples.

Preliminary data analysis:

The data presented below represent the first stage of our analysis. Table 3 indicates the number of cases of depression found in the two samples. (These figures are based solely on the DSM III criteria for clinical depression.) The rate of depression in South Cheshire was 5.5 per cent with 1.1 per cent of this representing onset cases. The rate in North Wales was 10.2 per cent, with 2.7 per cent onset cases.

TABLE 2 : RESPONSE RATE IN NORTH WALES

	SUBSAMPLES				
	1	2	3	4	5
No. of subjects mailed	50	50	50	50	33
Dead	3	3	2	2	1
Moved	5	5	1	5	4
Untraceable	1	3	2	5	1
ACUTAL SIZE OF SUBSAMPLE	41	39	45	38	27
Aphasic	0	1	0	0	0
Confused/senile	0	1	0	3	1
Illness prevented interview	1	0	0	1	0
Completed life stress interview	31	30	35	29	22
Refused psychiatric interview	0	2	3	1	2
Completed psychiatric interview	31	28	32	28	20
REFUSED TO PARTICIPATE	9	5	7	4	2
Response rate first interview	76%	77%	78%	76%	82%
REPONSE RATE BOTH INTERVIEWS	76%	72%	71%	74%	74%

N.B. Interviewing in final subsample not completed
due to lack of time

TABLE 3 : CASES OF DEPRESSION IN THE TWO SAMPLES

	SOUTH CHESHIRE		NORTH WALES	
	No.	%	No.	%
Onset case	1	1.1	4	2.7
Chronic case	4	4.4	11	7.5
Not depressed	85	94.5	132	89.8
TOTAL	90	100.0	147	100.0

A retrospective check was made on the psychiatric caseness of the 'refusers' in both areas by examining their medical records for evidence of any psychiatric illness in the preceding four years. No onset cases of depression were identified in either area. In South Cheshire there were five chronic cases of depression (6.5 per cent of the refusers) and in North Wales there were four chronic cases of depression (14.9 per cent of the refusers). These levels are not significantly different from the levels of depression found amongst those who were interviewed.

Table 4 presents the levels of life stress found in the two samples. Both the mean number of events per person and the mean number of difficulties per person is significantly higher in South Cheshire than North Wales. In both samples a lower rate of both events and difficulties is experienced by the sub-group of non-depressed subjects than by the full sample.

TABLE 4 : LEVELS OF LIFE STRESS IN THE TWO SAMPLES

	SOUTH CHESHIRE (N = 90)	NORTH WALES (N = 147)
LIFE EVENTS		
No. of life events reported	134	149
Mean no. of events per person	1.49*	1.01
Rate of events per 100 Ss	149	101
Rate of events per 100 non-depressed Ss	136	98
ONGOING DIFFICULTIES		
No. of difficulties reported	292	334
Mean no. of difficulties per person	3.24**	2.27
Rate of difficulties per 100 Ss	324	227
Rate of difficulties per 100 non-depressed Ss	314	223

     * p $<$ 0.05, Mann Whitney U-test
   ** p $<$ 0.001, Mann Whitney U-test

Discussion of results within the research context:

i) Depression:

It is difficult to comment on the levels of depression in South Cheshire and North Wales, for a number of reasons. First, there are several interpretative problems with our own data. There are residual problems regarding the low response rate in South Cheshire. While the retrospective check on the medical records of 'refusers' ruled out the possibility that it was primarily depressed people who had refused interview, this can hardly be regarded as conclusive. Individuals with psychiatric illness may vary in their willingness to consult a doctor (Kay et al, 1964) and G.P.s may vary in their reliability in diagnosing clinical depression in the elderly. There may also be a lack of comparability between our two samples regarding who is diagnosed as depressed, in that the psychiatric interviewers in South Cheshire and North

Wales used two different schedules; in addition the clinicians may differ in their exercise of clinical judgement (no reliability checks have been possible here). It is widely recognised that it is difficult to diagnose depression in the elderly, both because it may be 'masked' and because it may include somatic complaints or even cognitive impairment (Blazer & Williams, 1980). Further work is in progress to standardise the diagnosis of depression in a more satisfactory way. Meanwhile, the figures presented here (which are based strictly on the DSM III criteria for major depressive disorder) must be regarded as 'provisional' estimates of the levels of depression in the two samples. A group of respondents who did not meet the DSM III criteria, but who may be clinically regarded as 'borderline' cases, has been included in the 'not depressed' category here; this group will be analysed separately at a later date.

A second problem is the more general lack of comparability between published studies in this field. There appear to be at least four major sources of variation:

  i)   the method of sample selection (e.g. G.P. lists or electoral roll), and hence sample composition;

  ii)   the time period studied (e.g. 12 months or 15 months);

 iii)   the interview schedule used (e.g. G.M.S. or P.S.E.);

  iv)   the criteria utilised for identifying cases of depression (e.g. DSM III, op.cit., or Feighner, 1972).

In view of this it is perhaps not surprising to find that estimates of the rate of depression amongst the community elderly vary widely. For example the US/UK diagnostic study (Gurland et al, 1981) found 17 per cent depression (with 8 per cent onset cases) - however this figure comes down to about 12 per cent when strict DSM III criteria are used (Copeland, 1984). However, using the same criteria (although a different assessment schedule), Blazer (1980) reports a prevalence figure of only 1.8 per cent Murphy (op.cit.) reports figures of 14.5 per cent prevalence, with 9.5 per cent onset cases (using Feighner op.cit., criteria). Our figures would appear to be in this general range, and perhaps - tentatively - slightly lower than for the urban elderly.

ii) Life Stress:
Regarding levels of life stress a higher rate of both events and difficulties was found in South Cheshire than in North Wales. This can perhaps most easily be attributed to interviewer effects (as one interviewer conducted all the North Wales interviews, while two were involved in South Cheshire). However, it may also be due to sample characteristics (in particular, a preliminary analysis of these, to be reported, shows that there are some social class differences between the samples, with the South Cheshire sample containing more manual workers). Unfortunately, social class data is not available for the South Cheshire 'refusers', so again the effects of the low response rate in this area are not clear. We may have interviewed those leading the most stressful lives.

Only a limited amount of comparison is possible between our life stress data and the existing literature, particularly the work of Murphy (op.cit.). For example, it is not possible to compare rates or events for depressed subjects, both because our numbers in this group are so small (N=5 in South Cheshire; N=15 in North Wales) and because Murphy does not report the rate of events for depressed community subjects alone: these are combined with a group of hospital patients to form a larger group of depressed subjects. (As a research note, we are also interviewing a small sample of depressed outpatients, separately from the community study, to increase the size of our depressed sample.) Nor can our results be compared with Murphy's for the prevalence of ongoing difficulties, because she does not report results for all difficulties in any sub-group. Her analysis is based only on 'major' difficulties (i.e. those on the top three points of the six-point scale of severity, and lasting at least two years): these difficulties were found by Brown and Harris (op.cit.) to be associated with an increased risk of depression. We have not yet analysed difficulties by rated severity or duration. In addition, comparisons must again be made with extreme caution because of the procedural differences between our study and Murphy's (Murphy 1983b); the possible effect of the South Cheshire response rate; and the early stage of our own data analysis.

Our reported rate of 98 events per 100 non-depressed subjects in North Wales may be regarded as broadly comparable to Murphy's rate of 81 events per 100 non-depressed subjects in London; however, the comparable rate in South Cheshire is much higher. The possible explanations of this are similar to those suggested above for the differences between the two samples in overall levels of life stress: interviewer effects; social class differences; or other factors associated with the South Cheshire response rate. (It may also, of course, be related to the problem of reliable identification of cases of depression.) An early examination of the distribution of events and difficulties also suggests that this global comparison may mask some interesting contributory factors. A full analysis of events and difficulties will, of course, be reported in due course.

iii) Response rate and other problems:
The difference in response rate between South Cheshire and North Wales was obviously a major finding of the study - and the problems it presents for the interpretation of the substantive results have already been indicated. It remains to try and explain the difference. The South Cheshire rate was evidently based on a problem of initial access, since the interviewers reported that subjects seemed to enjoy the interviews, and the take-up rate for the second interview was high. We told some of the respondents about the response rate: several expressed a lack of surprise, but were at a loss to explain it. One suggestion was the likely suspiciousness of the rural elderly of strangers and/or various forms of officialdom. We also heard of a few cases where the spread of misinformation (e.g. about 'hidden tape recorders') had led to a refusal to see us. However in view of the much higher response rate in North Wales, it is more plausible to attribute the difference to procedural factors: a letter followed up by a personal call is obviously a much more appropriate method for work with the elderly than contact by mail alone. In general of course, it may be anticipated that it will prove more difficult to refuse interview in face to face contact with a research worker. This, indeed, was the case in North Wales. (The apparent social class difference, and other possible differences between the two samples must also be borne in mind, however.)
It will be recalled that method of contact was

only one of the procedural differences between the North Wales and South Cheshire samples (order of interviews and psychiatric schedule used being the other substantive ones). It may be noted that such modifications arose, for the most part, from the organisational problems of conducting an extensive community survey on a very economic basis, and from the collaboration of staff with different professional orientations and different available time commitments to the project. It is hoped that our experience of such problems may be of interest to others working in the field, both as potential difficulties that may be encountered, and for the perspective that they provide on our research findings.

Acknowledgements

The financial support of a Mental Health Foundation Grant to Professor John Copeland is gratefully acknowledged. Additional financial assistance from the Mersey Regional Health Authority is also acknowledged.
The director of the project was Professor John Copeland. Major collaborative support was received from: Dr David Neal, Dr Mary Harrison, Dr S. Anathakopan, John Downes and Gill Roberts.
Advice on sampling was provided by Mike Dewey and computing assistance by Peter Knoop.
The authors would also like to thank Professor George Brown and Tirril Harris for their support and advice; and the G.P.s in South Cheshire and North Wales for their assistance.

References

American Psychiatric Association (1980) Diagnostic and Statistical Manual of Mental Disorders. 3rd Edition, A.P.A., Washington, D.C.
Blazer D. (1980) 'The diagnosis of depression in the elderly', Journal of the American Geriatrics Society, 28, (2), 52-58
Blazer, D. and Williams, C.D. (1980) 'Epidemiology of dysphoria and depression in an elderly population', American Journal of Psychiatry, 137, (4), 439-444
Brown, G.W. and Harris, T. (1978) Social Origins of Depression, Tavistock, London

Cobb, S. (1976) 'Social support as a moderator of life stress', Psychosomatic Medicine, 38, (5), 300-313

Cochrane, R. and Sobol, M. (1980) ' Life stresses and psychological consequences', In: P. Feldman and J. Orford (eds.) Psychological Problems: The Social Context, Wiley, Chichester

Copeland, J.R.M., Kelleher, M.S., Kellett, J.M., Gourlay, A.J. with Gurland, B.J., Fleiss, J.L., and Sharpe, L. (1976) 'A semi-structured clinical interview for the assessment and diagnosis of mental state in the elderly: The Geriatric Mental State Schedule', Psychological Medicine, 6, 439-449

Copeland, J.R.M. (1984) Personal Communication

Feighner, J.P., Robins, E., Guze, S.B., Woodruff, R.A. Winoker, G. and Munoz, R. (1972) 'Diagnostic criteria for use in psychiatric research', Archives of General Psychiatry, 26, 57-73

Gurland, B.J., Copeland, J.R.M., Kelleher, M.J. and Dean, L. (1981) The Mind and Mood of Ageing, Howarth Press, New York

Isaacs, B. and Kennie, A.T. (1973) 'The SET Test as an aid for the detection of dementia in old people', British Journal of Psychiatry, 123, 467-470

Kay, D.W.K., Beamish, P. and Roth, M. (1964) 'Old Age and mental disorders in Newcastle Upon Tyne', British Journal of Psychiatry, 110, 146-158

Murphy, E. (1982) 'Social origins of depression in old age', British Journal of Psychiatry, 141, 135-142

Murphy, E. (1983a) 'The prognosis of depression in old age, British Journal of Psychiatry, 142, 111-119

Murphy, E. (1983b) Personal Communication

Salzman, C. and Shader, R.I. (1980) 'Active coping processes and coping dispositions', Psychosomatic Medicine, 35, 375-386

Tennant, C., Smith, A., Bebbinton, P. and Hurry, J. (1979) 'The contextual threat of life events: the concept and its reliability', Psychological Medicine, 9, 525-528

Wing, J.K., Cooper, J.E. and Sartorius, N. (1974) The Measurement and Classification of Psychiatric Symptoms: An Instruction Manual for the Present State Examination and CATEGO Programme, Cambridge University Press, Cambridge

Murphy, E. (1982) 'Social origins of depression in

old age', British Journal of Psychiatry, 141, 135-142

Murphy, E. (1983a) 'The prognosis of depression in old age, British Journal of Psychiatry, 142, 111-119

Murphy, E. (1983b) Personal Communication

Salzman, C. and Shader, R.I. (1980) 'Active coping processes and coping dispositions', Psychosomatic Medicine, 35, 375-386

Tennant, C., Smith, A., Bebbinton, P. and Hurry, J. (1979) 'The contextual threat of life events: the concept and its reliability', Psychological Medicine, 9, 525-528

Wing, J.K., Cooper, J.E. and Sartorius, N. (1974) The Measurement and Classification of Psychiatric Symptoms: An Instruction Manual for the Present State Examination and CATEGO Programme, Cambridge University Press, Cambridge

Chapter Twenty-one

SLEEP AND THE ELDERLY: SOME PSYCHOLOGICAL
DIMENSIONS AND THEIR IMPLICATIONS FOR
TREATMENT

K. J. Gledhill

Introduction

Research shows that there is a consensus
between elderly and younger adults in respect of the
high value that they attach to rest and sleep for
their day to day well-being (Canada Fitness Survey,
1982). Yet in the case of the elderly, there are
likely to be a greater diversity of factors which
impinge upon sleep, due to their increased
susceptibility to physical and mental infirmity and,
in addition, to the adverse effects of possible
endogenous alterations in circadian rhythms (Borbély
and Valatx, 1984). Sleep laboratory
(psychophysiological) and survey (self-report)
evidence confirms that the elderly experience
proportionately greater disturbances in their sleep-
wake functioning than younger adults, and, as a
consequence, have a commensurately higher level of
hypnotic drug usage (see review by Miles and Dement,
1980). However, while there would appear to be no
paucity of knowledge about the adverse effects of
hypnotic (and other) drugs taken by the elderly
(e.g., Castledon et al, 1978; Williamson and Chopin,
1980; and Morgan, 1983) there seems to be little
evidence regarding their actual efficacy amongst
older people (Miles and Dement, 1980).
Given the limitations of the predominantly
medical conceptualisation and treatment of insomnia
in old age (Gilleard et al, 1984; Gledhill, 1984),
there is a need for greater attention to be directed
to the adequacy of alternative psychological
formulations of insomnia and to the relevance of
treatment programmes arising from these. The two
principal treatment methods predicated upon
psychological theory are stimulus control and
relaxation. These are briefly described below.

Psychological treatment of sleep disturbance

The rationale of stimulus control suggests a mechanism by which environmental and behavioural factors may exert control over sleep. It is thought that the maintenance if not the onset of insomnia is due to stimuli which become a cue for wakefulness (Bootzin and Nicassio, 1978). This is considered to be the result of engaging in sleep incompatible activities at bedtime (e.g., reading, smoking, and eating in bed, as well as concomitant worries associated with not sleeping). Treatment involves both a temporal component (altering the sleep pattern), and improving discrimination cues (e.g., only carrying out sleep related activities in the bedroom).

The efficacy of stimulus control procedures for reducing sleep onset latency has been reported in many studies (Bootzin and Nicassio, 1976; Haynes et al, 1975; Lacks et al, 1983. Stimulus control methods have invariably been found to be superior to no treatment and are often regarded as having the most powerful effect upon sleep onset latency, with mean reductions of between 50 per cent and 70 per cent reported (Borkovec, 1980). However, until recently no EEG study of the effectiveness of stimulus control had been carried out, leaving open the question of convergent validity (Borkovec, 1980; Thoresen et al, 1981).

The psychological literature is replete with techniques for inducing feelings of mental calmness and ameliorating the somatic symptoms of anxiety. These can broadly be regarded as variants of applied relaxation training.

The beneficial effects of relaxation to insomnia have been linked to the hypothesis that poor sleep was associated with significantly elevated levels of autonomic arousal (e.g. raised heart rate, muscle tension, etc.) (Monroe, 1967). However, since the subsequent evidence for physiological activation was inconsistent, revised formulations of the mechanism by which relaxation appears to induce sleep have attached greater importance to the sleep antagonistic role of cognitive hyperactivity or worry (Borkovec, 1979; Borkovec, 1980).

Several investigations have shown that on both self report and EEG measures, all the forms of relaxation training are consistently more effective than placebo and no treatment (see Borkovec, 1979, for a fuller discussion). While claims have been made for the superiority of progressive muscular relaxation, with its focus on alternate tensing and relaxing (Borkovec, 1975), studies have suggested that, on the one hand, relaxation with or without muscle tension release is equally effective (Nicassio and Bootzin, 1974), or, on the other, that the presence of muscle tension release is unrelated to outcome (Woolfolk and McNulty, 1983). Most studies agree that there is a need for relaxation to be properly taught as opposed to just scheduling time for it (Borkovec, 1979).

The applicability of psychological approaches to the sleep problems of the elderly

In spite of the large psychological literature dealing with insomnia, very few studies have examined whether the rationale and treatment procedures of stimulus control and relaxation can be extrapolated to the sleep difficulties affecting the elderly. Perhaps the foremost reason for this, is, because of the belief that the insomnias of old age result largely from deteriorations in physiological functioning or age related pathologies such as, for example, myoclonus, arthritis, nocturia, and sleep apnea (that is to say, they are not primary), it is thought there is little that can can be done at the psychological level to ameliorate them. Such a view overlooks the possibility that one of the most likely routes for physical illness to affect sleep is through the experience of pain and physical discomfort, and that there is evidence of a beneficial role for psychological treatments even when insomnia is secondary to painful physical illness (see: Varni, 1980; Cannici et al, 1983). In addition to the problems of physical illness, other, non-health related worries may equally well adversely affect the sleep of the elderly.

Where studies have made a comparison between the response to treatment of young and aged adults (Nicassio and Bootzin, 1974; Alperson and Biglan, 1979), the results do not seem to have favoured the elderly. However, there is evidence from recent work (Puder et al, 1983) that stimulus control and relaxation techniques can be beneficial to some sleep disturbed elderly. A particular difficulty in addressing this whole area has been that almost the entire psychological literature deals with sleep onset insomnia when, in fact, the most prominent aspect of sleep disturbance observed in the elderly concerns difficulties in the maintenance of sleep throughout the night. In this context it is interesting to note that two recent studies (Thoreson et al, 1981; Lacks et al, 1983) have shown psychological based treatments to have an ameliorative effect upon sleep maintenance problems. In addition, the author (Gledhill, 1984) has recently completed a within subjects study that indicated a package of stimulus control and relaxation treatment to be of some benefit to elderly subjects and that such benefit was achieved partly through the improvement of sleep maintenance.

In addition to further attempts at evaluating the benefits of psychological based treatments to the sleep problems experienced by the elderly, there would seem to be a need to obtain more information about the characteristics of elderly people's sleep so that we may further adumbrate the components and rationales of treatment that might be especially appropriate for use with this age group. The remainder of this chapter is concerned with describing the findings from a survey study which was designed to gain such information.

Method

An 18 item questionnaire about the last night's sleep was distributed to all elderly people resident in two sheltered housing schemes and to people who attended a city day centre for the elderly on one or other of two consecutive days. In all, 109 completed questionnaires were returned. There was a small number of refusals: 3 and 7, and 8 and 6, from the two sheltered housing and day centre populations respectively. A further number (2 and 3, and 4 and 1) of questionnaires were discounted owing to the large number of uncompleted items. Every emphasis was placed upon the elderly person giving the information themselves as they recalled it, with assistance being offered only in respect of reading the questionnaire or recording answers. The reasons for non-participation were uncertain but given the deliberately innocuous nature of the questions, it is likely that a significant number of the non-responders and faulty responders found the questionnaire too difficult and may, therefore, have been less able in their mental functioning than those people who could respond to the questionnaire instructions.

The questionnaire differed from previous sleep surveys which have invariably utilised a generalised response format relying upon a person's recall of their sleep habits over a period of one or more months (e.g., McGhie and Russell, 1962; Gerard et al, 1978). Here, subjects were asked to recall in detail chronological characteristics about their last night's sleep as they would in a sleep diary.

Despite their sources of bias, sleep diary estimates appear to have high test-retest reliability and correlate substantially with other sleep measures (Coates et al, 1983; Carskadon et al, 1976). Given the heterogenous nature of the present questionnaire items, reliability was assessed by getting a sub-sample of 15 elderly people to complete questionnaires in the morning and afternoon of the same day. For questions relating to chronological sleep or wake times (questions 1 to 8), it was found that 79% of repeated items were either the same or within one quarter of an hour of the time given in the first questionnaire. The remaining questions were all categorical and were found to give a weighted Kappa value greater than 0.7. While these findings indicate reasonably high reliability, it nevertheless remains uncertain if what is being demonstrated is reliable recall of sleep or of answers to the questionnaire from one time to the next.

Results

(a) Patterns of sleep

Table 1 presents means, sample size, standard deviations and median values for all reported and additonal computed chronological sleep variables. In general there was close agreement between mean and median values with approximately normal distributions for all variables except time awake in the night, sleep onset latency, and duration of naps.

Mean values of sleep onset latency, total sleep time and period of wakening after sleep onset were 31 minutes, 6.8 hours and 46 minutes respectively. When these results were compared with the survey findings obtained in a study by Gerard et al (1978)

267

with a similar population of community elderly, it is apparent that total sleep time in the present study was 1 hour shorter, with people on average going to bed and getting up 1 hour later and being awake during the night for almost twice as long.

TABLE 1:   Data for reported and computed chronological sleep variables

Variable Name	Reported values			
	Mean	(n)	(S.D)	Median
Age	75.4	(109)	(6.1)	75
Time of going to bed	22:51	(108)	(48m)	23:00
Time of first trying to sleep	23:22	(106)	(53m)	23:15
Time of falling asleep	23:54	(102)	(34m)	24:00
Sleep onset latency	31m	(105)	(32m)	15m
Wake period after sleep onset	46m	(103)	(52m)	30m
Time of final waking	07:24	(108)	(60m)	07:30
Time of rising	08:12	(106)	(44m)	08:00
Time in bed during night	9.2h	(105)	(1h)	9.25h
Total sleep time	6.8h	(100)	(1.7h)	7.0h
Sleep efficiency	73.3%	(97)	(18%)	75%
Duration of naps previous day	18m	(108)	(28m)	0m
Number of times awake in night	1.8	(107)	(1.2)	2

Sleep efficiency (the ratio of sleep time to time spent in bed) is normally found to be reduced in the eldery, however, the value of 73.3% derived in the present study is lower than that generally reported by EEG studies. This arguably reflects the artificial nature of the sleep laboratory environment.

Men were under-represented in the present sample (24 per cent) which may have been due to them numbering fewer in the populations from which the samples were obtained. There was a sex difference in total sleep time and sleep efficiency, with men reporting higher values. Twenty seven per cent of the sample were married, 9 per cent single and the remaining 64 per cent widowed. Significantly more of the men were married but there was no difference in any of the sleep variables corresponding to marital status. Perhaps a more surprising negative finding was the absence of any relationship between age and sleep variables. Total sleep time and sleep efficiency values were significantly higher among the two sheltered housing populations, possibly reflecting a better underlying health status amongst sheltered housing tenants (see Butler et al, 1983, for a discussion of the health of elderly people in sheltered housing).

(b) Problem sleep

Even though the reliability of elderly persons' reporting of drug use may be in doubt, it can give some indication of the extent to which sleeplessness is a problem to the elderly. Twenty two per cent of the sample reported having taken sleeping tablets the night before while 21 per cent indicated that they had taken something for "pain or nerves" which was intended to help them sleep. As a measure of the feelings of dependence on these drugs, of the 42 per cent in total who had used one drug or another, 55 per cent felt that their last night's sleep would have been worse if they had not taken any drug the night before.

Common sense judgement would suggest that poor sleep can precipitate feelings of discomfort, tiredness and anxiety, all of which might be expected to give rise to complaint. It was hypothesised, therefore, that elderly people who reported sleep as being a problem would also report a correspondingly poorer pattern of sleep. It could, of course, be argued that amongst the elderly, ostensibly poor sleepers do not experience any concomitant discomfort due perhaps to sleep loss being well adjusted to as a result of its chronicity. A further possibility is that sleep complainers do not have a sleep disturbance so much as a proclivity to complain which generalises to the sleep.

In all 53 per cent of the sample described themselves as having a moderate or severe problem with their sleep. Table 2 shows the initial hypothesis to be confirmed in that problem sleepers have a significantly poorer total sleep time and sleep efficiency. Although a similar difference was also observed for the variables sleep onset latency and total wake period, there was some suggestion of a curvilinear relationship between these variables and sleep complaints.

While elderly people may be reluctant to identify sleep as being problematic, they may more easily be inclined to report not having had enough sleep or still feeling tired during the daytime (these are not necessarily synonymous). A subsidiary hypothesis predicted that these other modes of sleep complaint would also reflect an underlying disturbance of sleep pattern. As shown in Table 2, total sleep time, total wake period and sleep efficiency were all significantly poorer in the low sleep satisfaction group. As for the contrast between those who did or did not report daytime tiredness (where the split was nearly half and half), only sleep onset latency showed a significant difference. It is not clear through what mechanisms sleep onset latency and tiredness should be related but the lack of any association between daytime tiredness and total sleep time would suggest that feelings of tiredness are largely a function of other non-sleep factors.

(c) Type of sleep problem

While sleep maintenance problems are thought to constitute the greatest part of the sleep disturbance of the elderly, it is not always clear if by this what is being referred to is night-time wakening, or early morning wakening. When asked to identify what (if they had a problem) their main sleep problem was, the obtained frequencies for

TABLE 2

Effects of reported levels of sleep complaint (problem, satisfaction and daytime tiredness) on computed chronological sleep variables

Variable Name	Sleep as a problem				Satisfaction with sleep duration			Daytime tiredness		
	Not a problem Mean (n)	A small problem Mean (n)	Quite a problem Mean (n)	F value	Quite enough Mean (n)	Not enough Mean (n)	t value	No Mean (n)	Yes Mean (n)	t value
Sleep onset latency	0.4 (50)	0.7 (37)	0.4 (17)	3.8*	0.5 (71)	0.6 (34)	1.1 n.s	0.7 (47)	0.4 (58)	3.3***
Total sleep time	7.6 (48)	6.2 (36)	5.4 (15)	16.3***	7.2 (70)	5.7 (30)	4.7***	7.0 (45)	6.6 (55)	1.3 n.s
Total night-time wake period	0.8 (49)	1.8 (36)	1.6 (15)	9.5**	1.1 (70)	1.7 (31)	2.5*	1.4 (45)	1.2 (56)	1.1 n.s
Total time in bed	9.2 (50)	9.4 (36)	8.9 (18)	1.7 n.s	9.3 (70)	9.0 (34)	1.5 n.s	9.4 (47)	9.1 (57)	1.5 n.s
Sleep efficiency	0.8 (47)	0.7 (34)	0.6 (15)	19.9***	0.8 (68)	0.6 (29)	4.4***	0.8 (44)	0.7 (53)	0.7 n.s

* p = $<$.05;   ** p = $<$.01;   *** p = $<$.001

sleep onset, sleep maintenance, and early morning wakening were 25, 31 and 7 respectively and thus significantly different than expected by chance (ch:sq = 14.7, p $>$ .01). It would appear, therefore, that early morning wakening was not a particularly prevalent complaint amongst the elderly in the present sample.

(d) Attribution of cause

Although there appears to be little data relating to the causal attributions made by the elderly in respect of their disturbed sleep, the attributions that they do make may be relevant to the question of choice of treatment. For example, the perception of pain or discomfort at night-time due to skeletal muscular disorders such as arthritis might indicate that mental focusing relaxation techniques be preferred to relaxation involving muscular tensing.

In the present study, given five categories of possible cause, the following attributions were obtained: lack of physical exercise 13, physical discomfort 10, pain 13, worry 28, and other non-specified causes 13. This distribution was significantly different than expected by chance (chi sq = 13.3, p $<$ .01) suggesting that a considerably higher proportion of those elderly who experienced difficulties with sleep (even if only occasionally) felt that their sleeplessness was due to worry. However, if the categories of pain and disomfort are merged, it is evident that somatic complaint is also a fairly ubiquitously attributed cause.

(e) Cognitions and poor sleep

It is increasingly felt that a major cause of insomnia is the inability to turn off affectively laden intrusive thoughts or images. Research suggests that a reduction in these thoughts among insomniacs parallels both objective and subjective improvements in sleep (Borkovec, 1980). Given this possibly important role of cognitions in insomnia, there has been surprisingly little discussion of whether sleep inhibiting pre-sleep mentation is present during periods of night-time wakefulness as well as during the initial onset period. Data from a joint study by the author (Davies and Gledhill, 1983) indicated that as many as 43 per cent of an elderly sample described themselves as worrying a lot. This was a particularly vulnerable group, and it can only be assumed that worrying went on at night-time as well. A question in the present study addressed itself to the presence and type of mentation during night-time non-sleep periods.

The results indicated that the most frequently reported categories of night-time mentation were worry related to non-sleep problems and sleep related worries, while thoughts about pain or discomfort were surprisingly infrequent. Although these four categories were not mutually exclusive (i.e. a person could identify one or more), the distribution of responses obtained was significantly different than expected by chance (Cochrane's Q = 19.7; d.f.= 3; p $<$.001).

The results of this and the earlier analysis of causal attributions suggest, perhaps contrary to expectation, that preoccupation with pain and discomfort is not as salient a part of night-time non-sleep mentation of the elderly as "worry" like thoughts associated with sleep or other problems.

(f) Stimulus factors

The stimulus control paradigm would lead us to predict that chronologically poor sleepers engage in more sleep incompatible behaviours than their better sleeping counterparts (although, this has been shown in at least one research study - Haynes et al, 1982 - not to be the case). It was predicted that there would be a significant correlation between an index of sleep incompatible behaviours and the duration of sleep and/or period of non-sleep. Reported frequencies for five specified sleep incompatible behaviours (i.e. behaviours carried out in the bed or bedroom during the day or night) were as follows: reading 26; sewing, knitting, etc., 0; watching T.V. or listening to the radio 4; eating 5; smoking 1. The sparsity of these behaviours suggests that the elderly are hardly at all engaged in behaviours that could be construed as establishing a conditioning of non-sleep. It might have been expected that within the confines of a small house (such as in the sheltered housing units) the elderly would have colonised the space of their own bedrooms for daytime activities. However, the impression gained from those elderly people who were personally interviewed, suggested that in fact they enforced quite a strict discipline with regard to the times and places they allowed for specific activities.

TABLE 3: Correlations between an index of sleep incompatible behaviours and variables relating to quality of sleep (n = 97 ± 4)

	Index of sleep incompatible behaviours
1. Problem rating	.31***
2. Total sleep time	-.31***
3. Sleep onset latency	.17
4. Total night-time wake period	.27***
5. Sleep efficiency	-.33***

Kendall correlation coefficients
** p = .01;   *** p = .001

Table 3 shows the correlations between the index score and other sleep variables. These were significant on a number of counts. It might be presumed that this reflected the obvious fact that many of the people who couldn't sleep did something else such as read in bed. This, indeed, is often the advice which many well-intentioned G.P.'s seem to give to those elderly who complain that they can't sleep. It is interesting, however, that the variable showing the highest correlation with sleep incompatible behaviours was not the time spent awake at night but sleep efficiency ($r = -.33$). Sleep efficiency was also noted to be the best predictor of problem status, implying that what is most disturbing to the sleepless person is not simply the time spent awake but the amount of time spent awake relative to the time spent asleep. Since those people who get up at night or in the morning rather than read or lie awake worrying, effectively increase their sleep efficiency, it may be that, as suggested by stimulus control theory, this in turn leads to reduced anxiety, and consequently to improved sleep.

Summary

Given that in the present study elderly people were only asked to report on the characteristics of their sleep for the preceding night, it is difficult to generalise about the stability of reported patterns. However, it can be argued that not only does this focus on a recent and specific experience of sleep avoid the problems of overgeneralisation present in other studies and place fewer demands upon memory, but that it also gives a fairly accurate cross-sectional picture of the sleep patterns of this sample.

Just as global reports of health in the elderly appear to have an obvious health referent (Tissue, 1979), the results of this study would suggest that complaints of dissatisfaction with sleep usually have associated with them an underlying impoverishment of chronological sleep pattern. Such a finding lends support to the view that sleep complaints of the elderly should be taken seriously as prima facie evidence of sleep disturbance, and suggests that treatment goals might justifiably include the aim to improve sleep patterns as opposed to simply counselling tolerance of them.

In conclusion, it might be said that there is clearly a need for further research to clarify the directionality of the observed relationships between insomnia in the elderly and the presence of discomfort, worry and allegedly sleep incompatible behaviours. This would, in turn, provide a sounder basis for deciding on the type of advice that we might give to elderly people who can't sleep. In particular, since insomnia is thought to be enhanced and maintained by exacerbation cycles in which worries about not falling asleep interfere even further with one's sleep, we ought to know more about whether relaxation can improve sleep through the elimination of worry or somatic discomfort, and whether reading in bed serves to reduce sleep related anxieties or else has an incipient adverse effect on sleep due to its stimulus properties.

References

Alperson, J. and Biglan, A. (1979) 'Self-administered treatment of sleep onset insomnia

and the importance of age', Behaviour Therapy, 10
Bootzin, R.R. and Nicassio, P. (1978) 'Behavioural
   treatments of insomnia', Progress in Behaviour
   Modification, 6, Eds. M. Hersen, R. Eisler and
   P. Miller
Borbély, A. and Valatx, J.L. (1984) 'Sleep
   Mechanisms', Experimental Brain Supplementum 8,
   Springer Verlag, Berlin
Borkovec, T.D., Kaloupek, D.G. and Slama, K.M.
   (1975) 'The facilitative effect of muscle tension-
   release in the relaxation treatment of sleep
   disturbance' Behaviour Therapy, 6, 301-309
Borkovec, T.D. (1979) 'Pseudo and idiopathic
   insomnia; theoretical and therapeutic issues',
   Adv. Behav. Res. and Therapy, 2
Borkovec, T.D. (1980) 'Insomnia', Journal of
   Consulting and Clinical Psychology, 50
Butler, A., Oldman, C and Greve, J. (1984)
   Sheltered Housing for the Elderly: Policy,
   Practice and the Consumer, Allen and Unwin
Canada Fitness Survey (1982) Fitness and Aging,
   Report by Canada Fitness Survey, Ottawa
Cannici, J., Malcolm, R., and Peek, L. (1983)
   'Treatment of insomnia in cancer patients using
   muscle relaxation training', J. Behav. Ther. and
   Exp. Psychiat., 14, Part 3
Castledon, C.M., George, C.F., Marcer, D. and
   Hallet, C. (1977) 'Increased sensitivity to
   nitrazepam in old age', British Medical Journal, 1
Coates, T.J., Killen, J.D., Silverman, S., George,
   J., Marchinie, E., Hamilton, S., Thoreson, C.
   (1983) 'Cognitive activity sleep disturbance and
   stage specific differences between recorded and
   reported sleep', Psychophysiology, 20(3), 243-251
Davies, A.D.M. and Gledhill, K.J. (1983)
   'Engagement and depressive symptoms in a community
   sample of elderly people', British Journal of
   Clinical Psychology, 22
Gerard, P., Collins, K.J., Dore, E. and Exton-Smith,
   (1978) 'Subjective characteristics of sleep in the
   elderly', Age and Ageing, supplement 7
Gilleard, C.J. and Smits, C. (1984) Hypnotic
   sedative prescribing in local authority homes for
   the elderly, Final Report to Social Work Services
   Group, Scottish Education Dept.
Gledhill, K.J. (1984) Psychological perspectives of
   sleep and sleep problems in the elderly
   population: A survey and treatment study,
   Unpublished M.Sc. Thesis, Dept. of Psychiatry,

University of Leeds

Haynes, S.N., Adams, A.E., West, S., Kamens, L. and Safranck, R. (1982) 'The stimulus control paradigm in sleep onset insomnia', Journal of Psychosomatic Research, 26

Lacks, P., Bertelson, A., Sugarman, J. and Kunkel, J. (1983) 'The treatment of sleep maintenance insomnia with stimulus control techniques', Behaviour Research and Therapy, 21

McGhie and Russell (1962) 'The subjective assessment of normal sleep patterns', Journal of Mental Science, 108

Miles, L.E. and Dement, W.C. (1980) Sleep and Aging, Raven Press, New York

Monroe, L.J. (1967) 'Psychological and physiological differences between good and poor sleepers', Journal of Abnormal Psychology, 72

Morgan, K. (1983) 'Sedative-hypnotic drug use and ageing', Arch. Geront. Geriatr., 2

Nicassio, P. and Bootzin, R.A. (1974) 'A comparison of progressive relaxation and autogenic training as treatments for insomnia', Journal of Abnormal Psychology, 83

Puder, R., Bertelson, A.D., Storandt, M., and Lacks, P. (1983) 'Short-term stimulus control treatment of insomnia in older adults', Behaviour Therapy, 14

Thoreson, C.E., Coates, T.J., Kirmil-Gray, K. and Rosekind, R. (1981) 'Behavioural self-management in treating sleep maintenance insomnia', Journal of Behavioural Medicine, 4

Tissue, T. (1972) 'Another look at self-rated health among the elderly', Journal of Gerontology, 27

Varni, J. (1980) 'Behavioural treatment of disease-related chronic insomnia in a hemophiliac', Journal of Behaviour Therapy and Experimental Psychiatry, 11

Williamson, J. and Chopin, J.M. (1980) 'Adverse reactions to prescribed drugs in the elderly: A multi-centre investigation', Age and Ageing, 9

Woolfolk, R.L. and McNulty, T.F. (1983) 'Relaxation treatment: A component analysis', Journal of Consulting and Clinical Psychology, 51(4), 495-503

Chapter Twenty-two

ATTRIBUTIONS OF STAFF WORKING WITH THE ELDERLY:
A PILOT STUDY

Carol Martin

Introduction

With current conditions in the psychogeriatric
and geriatric services being stretched and with the
increasing numbers of elderly people using whatever
services are available, staff under pressure will
learn to cope with short-comings in whatever way
they can. Training must be an important part of
this process. Thus while the author instituted a
course on understanding and dealing with behavioural
problems of elderly patients, it seemed an
opportunity to investigate staff attitudes.

Several influences have left their mark on this
work. The first is attribution theory, which
developed as a model to explain the ways individuals
construe cause and effect and how this affects their
behaviour, c.f. Brewin and Antaki (1982). A
specific instance of the links between attribution
and behaviour can be termed 'helplessness' in which
an individual sees his behaviour as having no
effect on the events he experiences (Seligman 1975).
This phenomemon has been fruitfully linked with
depression. Other workers such as Beck (Beck et al
1979) have encouraged the development of specific
techniques to combat aspects of depression, such as
helplessness.

This project attempted to explore these
theories, and relate them to staff attitudes and
behaviour as it affected their work with the
elderly. As a starting point, if attributions
affect behaviour, it seemed appropriate to elicit
and examine attributional statements made by staff
working with the elderly. In order to help classify
them in some way, the author adopted the dimensions
developed by Stratton and his colleagues and defined
in Stratton and Higinbotham (1984). (See Figure 1).

Of particular interest in this study are the dimensions of positive and negative outcome, internal vs. external cause and finally controllable vs. uncontrollable outcome. These are related to 'helplessness'. It may be supposed that these dimensions will affect the amount and type of success any helping strategy may have.

Figure 1:   Dimension used for the coding of atrributions

1. stable-unstable	An attribution is held to be stable if the outcome follows the causal factor consistently.
2. global-specific	This reflects the power of an event to affect a few outcomes (specific) or many (global).
3. personal-universal	A universal attribution is one commonly held. A personal one would be considered idiosyncratic.
4. internal-external	This dimension rates the outcome as having been caused by events external to the individual, or alternatively by the characteristics or the behaviour of the individual making the statement.
5. controllable - uncontrollable	This dimension rates the speaker's evaluation of his/her ability to affect an outcome.

This may be illustrated using the following hypothetical, but commom example.

An elderly lady, Mrs Smith, is admitted to hospital, having been found wandering the streets late at night. Several factors may be noted which will affect our understanding of her behaviour. These might lead us to draw the following conclusions, each of which is an attributional statement.

a) Mrs Smith wandered because she is dementing
b) Mrs Smith wandered because she was suffering from an acute chest infection
c) Mrs Smith wandered because she moved house

recently and is unfamiliar with her new surroundings

In this example, these three attributions are not mutually exclusive - it is quite possible that all three coexist, along with many more. However, the models and hypotheses that the information-gatherer is most attuned to will influence both which attributions are rated as most important and which of several possible therapeutic interventions might be implemented. For example, if attribution a) is rated as most important, a possible remedy might be removal to a home, or supervision. If b) is diagnosed, antibiotics might be prescribed with a view to early discharge. Finally if c) is considered important, staff and family might be enlisted to help structure the opportunities for Mrs Smith to learn her way about. While this example is an extremely simplistic one in that just as the attributional statements may coexist, so might more than one intervention be implemented at once and a range of outcomes is possible.

Importantly, the staff members' actions and outcome will be linked. Attributions b) and c) offer clear and attainable goals that can be achieved and that are contingent on staff behaviour such as prescription of penicillin or walking around the neighbourhood with Mrs Smith. Attribution a) has no such likelihood of success to date; we have no way of "curing" dementia. To persist with this attribution may possibly, I would suggest, lead to a helpless view of one's situation.

A behavioural analysis of a scenario such as this may serve to widen the number and variety of attributions possible. It may also enable the analyst to focus on goals which may be achieved contingent on his or her behaviour. The second area of interest therefore was the author's prediction that a significant proportion of attributional statements with negative outcome made by staff would be external (due either to ageing or the instituton rather than because of the subject's own actions) and uncontrollable (because ageing, dementia and institutions are difficult to affect).

This prediction was not made arbitrarily. Rather, it was developed through observation of staff working in hospitals over some time, who were trained in a more or less strict medical model of diagnosis/treatment/cure. Over time, it became clear that this process was less than ideally helpful when dealing with a patients' behaviour and problems day to day. Further, there is a commonly held view that working with the elderly is depressing and frustrating. Certainly generally high levels of absenteeism, sickness and difficulty filling vacancies for posts with the elderly can be considered supporting evidence.

The Course

The Course took place over six weeks and lasted for a morning each week. A seventh, review session, took place some weeks after the course was completed. The content included a 'refresher' section on basic behavioural principles and terms, and exercises in applying these to everyday situations and episodes within institutions. The participants were required to examine influences on and consequences of their own behaviour as well as that of their patients.

The eleven Staff who participated were all employed in the psychogeriatric services. Eight of the eleven were nurse trained, the other three came from paramedical professions. They all joined the course of their own volition, which meant that they were interested in the course content, dissatisfied with their level of knowledge and highly motivated to learn. Each was asked to complete six attributional statements in the light of their own experience and to create six more. Of these twelve statements, four were required to have a negative outcome. These statements were then rated by the author and by a member of the team which developed the ratings. In Figure 2 are some examples of statements and their ratings. In addition, each statement was rated as to the strength with which that statement was held to be true. This latter exercise was repeated at the end of the course.

Figure 2: Excerpts from some typical elicited attributional statements

1. Helping the elderly is tiresome because they require so much physical input
   (external, uncontrollable, negative)

2. Jobs with old people can be difficult because you cannot plan a long way ahead
   (external, uncontrollable, negative)

3. A job with elderly people is satisfying if you understand them well
(internal, controllable, positive)

4. Elderly people need to be handled with tact as they can misinterpret actions and verbal instructions
(external, uncontrollable, positive)

The results

Of 132 statements, 13 could not be classified as attributional statements, leaving a total of 119 statements. Of these 119, 41 should have had negative outcomes. In fact, 47 were so rated. The frequency of each combination of categories is shown in Table 1.

Table 1: Coding of statements with negative outcome on two dimensions

Dimension	External	Internal	Total
Controllable	1	5	6
Uncontrollable	38	3	41
Total	39	8	47

Of interest here are the large number of statements with a negative outcome that are rated as external (due to reasons external to the writer) and uncontrollable (not amenable to change). Thus we may hypothesise that this group of staff see the frustrations and problems they come across as environmental ones that they cannot change. These statements are the 'helpless' statements. Only six of the 47 statements were rated as controllable and furthermore only one of these was rated as external, inplying that where as outcome can be influenced, it is more likely to be when it involves changing oneself in some way rather than the environment.

Discussion

For this particular group of staff, who would by no means have been regarded as depressed, the majority of statements with a negative outcome are seen as due to factors over which they as individuals feel they have no influence. Most of these factors are in the environment, in their patients or the institution. Thus the statements suggest that while they rarely blame themselves for lack of satisfaction or success, they would tend to feel unable to gain it consistently or influence the outcome of their activities. These statements are fairly resistant to change. There was little difference in the strength with which the statements were adhered to after the course.

The nature of the problems giving rise to negative outcomes for the staff were interesting. Of the 47 attributions, 37 were attributed to qualities of the elderly patient, 11 of these 37 referring to physical disability, the other encompassing behaviour and attitudes of elderly people. Nine of the attributions were located in staff, not necessarily always seen to include the writer of the statement. Only five referred to social or environmental difficulties, such as family, or provision of adequate resources. This fits in well with a medical model of illness, which is after all, what staff have been trained to. However, one is led to point out that ageing itself is not of itself an illness in spite of the higher prevalence of illnesses in this group. Further placement in institutions has not always been shown to correlate closely with the patients' degree of disability alone. A further factor seems to be the need for or lack of a supportive environment. (Townsend 1962).

These attitudes incidentally were elaborated further during the course. Behavioural problems involving elderly patients were frequently discussed and it became apparent that many of the difficulties experienced by staff were influenced by causes other than problem patients. For example, the ward environment and hospital routine preempted changes in patient management that might have been appropriate. Analysis of the problem was very easily limited to the contribution of the patient and the first choice intervention condsidered was in the majority of cases, one to inhibit or constrain the behaviour of the difficult patient. It also became clear that while the problems chosen for discussion were selected for the reason that they were unsolved, an analysis of the environmental influences in addition allowed a variety of interventions to be explored and designed. In other words, the difficulties were then seen to lie in the interactions between the institutions and the individuals within it.

The assumptions underlying the elicited statements seem pessimistic, i.e. improvement in patients is uncontrollable or even impossible because of physical disability and personality problems within this patient group. These staff see their contribution as unlikely to effect change given these limits. The attribution of failure to solve a problem of their patients may be accurate, but one wonders how much is determined, for example, by the view that old age is an illness or problem in itself. Certainly it is impossible to make people young again or give them the lifestyle youth allows. If success is defined in those terms, however, failure will almost certainly follow. Further, while training and education may lead to greater competence and success, a successful analysis of one's own gaps and strengths is perhaps only possible when a realistic appraisal of success can be worked out. Neither in terms of an 'illness' model nor a 'quality of life' model can staff working with the eldery currently expect to succeed - ageing itself and economic pressures will not allow it. Given these points, it is not so surprising that morale is often low, absenteeism and illness frequent and turnover of staff high.

This is a pilot study, a first attempt to examine the attitudes of staff in this way, and it is therefore too early to do much more than speculate from the results. The sample size (too small), the sampling (enthusiastic volunteers) and the assessment itself all leave room for improvement. However, the implications are important. Given the conditions under which staff working with the elderly currently exist, and projections for the future indicating a widening of the gap between the demand for and supply of services for this age group, it seems important not only to press for more resources, but also to look afresh at our existing models of care.

In this way, goals could be chosen which were achievable and controllable, reducing the helplessness and hence improving the morale of the staff involved - a move that in its turn can only benefit our elderly (and ourselves, in our old age). Comparisons can be drawn from the areas of work with the mentally handicapped and with the terminally ill, where in spite of similar limitations, morale can be high.

This may be difficult to achieve in practice. It is not perhaps too surprising that these well learned attributions did not alter following a course, which however relevant, was short and limited in its aims, and where follow up was obtained only shortly after the course was completed. What seemed to be important in the examples given above is the development of a model that allows for the definition of a problem, of appropriate achievable goals and that specifies some of the skills needed to reach these.

Summary

This pilot study set out to explore some of the attributions made by staff working with the elderly relating to their job satisfaction. Negative outcomes were most likely to be coded as 'helpless' statements, the outcome being perceived as uncontrollable by, and external to, the writer. Often negative outcomes were blamed on the age or personality of elderly people. A discussion of the implications of this view suggest that a change in models used by staff to allow for clearer and more attainable goals would be helpful to morale in conditions that are already stressful.

References

Antaki, C. and Brewin, C. (1982) Attributions and Psychological Change, Academic Press, London

Beck, A.T., Rush, J., Shaw, B., Emery, G. (1979) Cognitive Therapy of Depression, Wiley

Seligman, M.E.P. (1975) Helplessness: on Depression, Development and Death, Freeman, San Francisco

Stratton, P. and Higinbotham, P. (1984) Instructions for Coding of Attributions, (personal communication)

Townsend, P., (1962) The Last Refuge, Routlege & Kegan Paul

Chapter Twenty-three

SOCIAL SITUATIONS AND SELF-IMAGES OF OLDER WOMEN

Ora Cibulski

The purpose of this paper is to examine the
relationship between social situations and self-
images of ageing women in a developing country. In
Israel, elderly women have been faced with both
normal as well as extraordinary stressful life
situations: immigration and cultural adaptation,
wars and widowhood, retirement and lowered income,
poor health and physical disability. The paper
explores the hypothesis that the self-image of older
women is socially constructed and is influenced by
stressful social situations: immigrant status,
widowhood, social isolation and socio-economic
status. It is suggested that the personal resources
of women (human, economic, physical and mental)
shape and limit the qualities an individual may
attribute to the self. The question is posed
whether society's negative stereotypes of ageing
effect the self-images of older women.
   The social problems of older women stem from
the disparity between the growing number of older
women and the socially valued roles available,
institutional supports and society's invidious
stereotypes of women.
   In Israel, women's life expectancy at birth is
longer (75.0 years) than men's (71.5 years). Among
persons over 65, 96 per cent are immigrants of whom
half immigrated as older adults. In this age group,
57 per cent are widows compared to 13 per cent
widowers. More old women are illiterate than old
men (Israel, CBS, 1981). Among widows over 55
years, over half have no formal schooling, 60 per
cent are in the lowest income percentile and their
only source of income is National Insurance. Older
widows are major beneficiaries of social assistance
according to Gordon (1981).
   The social situation of older women raises the

issue of their self-image. Are older women's self-images shaped by their perception of ageing, roles or socioeconomic status or are the stigmatizing labels attributed to older females incorporated into older women's self-image?

Social psychological theory hypothesizes the construct of the "self-concept" and poses the question of the stability and consistency of the self (Rose, 1962). Cooley (1962) viewed the self as formed through the actions and reactions of others, that is the looking-glass self. Mead (1934) argued that individuals have selves because they can take the attitudes of others and see themselves as objects. The individual experiences him/herself indirectly through the interaction with particular "significant others" (persons who are important to the individual) and with the "generalized other" (society).

Goffman (1959) claims that situations shape the self. Persons take on the characteristics required by the situation in which they participate. When situations and roles change, the person's former commitments and behaviour patterns unravel. Matthews (1979) argues that the self identity of old widows are in conflict with their social identity. She suggests some of the major situations that may stigmatize older women's self-images and would require older women to develop protective strategies in order to avoid negative definitions of the self. These situations are when women require social assistance because of poverty, incapacity or widowhood. She argues that in a society that values independence, dependency may diminish a woman's evaluation of self-worth and influence the kinds of social interactions in which she is prepared to participate.

Cibulski (1981) suggests that personal resources are the means by which individuals mediate the structural conditions of their social situations. Personal resources refer to:

1. Human resources, the persons who play partners to role performance such as spouse, child, friend, neighbour or professional helpers.
2. Economic resources with which the individual maintains a style of life such as income, house, car, etc.
3. Physical resources which refer to levels of function and health.
4. Mental resources which refer to intelligence,

knowledge and skills.

The self-concept may be broadly defined as "That organization of qualities that the individual attributes to himself/herself" (Kinch, 1963). The self-image is constructed from all the subjective and objective information ego has about mind and body, roles and social links and socioeconomic position. These attributes have evaluative connotations, derived from the individual's cultural experience, which shape behaviour and self-esteem.

The social image of elderly women is pervaded by negative stereotypes and stigmatizing labels. Old women are believed to be victims of socialization to dependency and passivity and parasites on men, according to Sontag (1974). Old women are depicted as poor, isolated and unhealthy (Payne and Whittengton, 1976). In Israel, Shinar and Biber (1978) examined the images of ageing among theatre audiances who attended the play "Whatever are we going to do with Jenny?". A major character, Aunt Andora, represents many of the stereotypes mentioned in the literature. She is ill, dependent, boring, complaining and lives in the past. Jenny represents the opposite characteristics of young, interesting, independent and competent. The majority of respondents of all ages reported that most of the old people they were acquainted with were like Aunt Andora and considered Andora's behaviour undesirable.

Research has identified distinct life styles and behaviour patterns of older women (Maas and Kuyper, 1974) (Jacobs, 1976). In Israel, Weihl (1970) has found that the life styles of old women who immigrated from Asia and Africa are different from old women who immigrated from western countries.

The Study

An exploratory study to examine the relationship between social situations and self-image of older women was developed by students in a seminar on ageing in the School of Social Work, University of Tel-Aviv. The major question examined was: Are there significant differences in self-images of older women? If society's stereotypes of older women had a strong impact on respondents, most self-images scores would be in the lower range and there would be no systematic differences among items in the self-image index. On the other hand, if there were significant differences in self-image scores which varied systematically with situational factors and/or personal resources of older women, they would indicate that stereotypes have weak or differential effects on self-image.

Thus the question was posed: Are there significant differences in self-image of:

1. young-old compared with old-old women?
2. women with lesser and greater physical incapacity?
3. widows compared to married women?
4. childless women compared to women with children?
5. working women compared to women at home?
6. women in different social situations: Social Welfare clients, pensioner club members and community women who use neither service.

The theoretical rationale behind these tentative hypotheses is that the self-image is socially constructed and is influenced by the personal resources and social situations in older women's lives.

Procedures

The research instrument chosen was a structured interview schedule of which the majority of questions were closed. The index measuring self-image, in a sense, represents Israeli society's "informed stereotypes" concerning the attributes of older women, since it was constructed by young and middle aged women students (one man) of social work. The Self-Image Index consists of nine statements that reflect traits and social characteristics frequently attributed to older women.

The Self-Image Index is applied in the following manner. First each statement is read referring to the present time. "How would you describe yourself?" Then the statements are repeated, referring to the past time as perceived by the respondent. (The "past" is used here in order to indicate whether the respondent perceives continuity or discontinuity in self image.) "In the past, how would you describe yourself?" The index score sums the number of agreements with the statements: a friendly woman, a woman whose company is pleasant, a healthy woman, an optimistic woman, a woman who is satisfied with herself, a woman who is satisfied with others; and the number of disagreements with the statements: a dependent woman, a sad woman, a woman lacking roles. Scores range from 1 to 9. For the cross-tabulations, the Self-Image Index scores were collapsed into four categories: Very Low - 1 to 3, Low - 4 or 5, Medium - 6 or 7, High - 8 or 9.

Other major indices used were the ADL (activities of daily living, Shanas, 1968), the Family Help Index, Social Activity Index, Home Activity Index and Mobility Scale.

A purposive quota sample was constructed to explore the hypotheses and control for age, marital status and social situation. The students drew equal proportions of married/widowed, under 70/over 70 years old, women from social welfare agencies, pensioner clubs and the community at large in nine urban and small town communities. The 112 respondents' ages are distributed quite evenly from 58 to 82, the median age is 70. Married women are 46 per cent of the sample and widows are 54 per cent. There are 34 per cent clients of social welfare agencies, 39 per cent attend pensioner clubs and 37 per cent are community women who do not use either of these services. All of the women understood spoken Hebrew well enough to be interviewed.

The Self-Images of Older Women

There is a wide distribution of present time Self-Image Index scores: Low - 33.4%, Medium - 36.2% and High - 30.4%. Although present self-images are lower than past self-images, two thirds of the women report positive medium and high self-images. The distribution of self-images suggests that negative stereotypes about old women have weak effects or differential effects on self-image and that other factors may be operating.

A comparison of the responses to the individual statements in the Self-Image Index and the per cent difference between present and past time in Table 1 shows that three statements have very high agreement in the present and past time. Most of the women consider themselves friendly and pleasant company. Most women do not consider themselves dependent, contrary to the stereotype of women in general and the older woman in particular. At the other extreme, the women perceive a great deal of change for the worse in their health. A number of women have become sadder, less optimistic and less satisfied with themselves. Satisfaction with others is middling and few women report changes in this area. The per cent of women who perceive lack of roles has increased to a subtantial 45 per cent of the sample. Thus for close to half of the women poor health, lack of roles and sadness are perceived as components to their self-image in the present. With which variables are positive and negative self-images associated?

TABLE 1
Percentage difference between
present and past time self-image

Self -image components	Present	Past	Difference
Would you describe yourself as:			
1. a friendly woman?	88	94	6
2. a dependent woman?	18	12	6
3. a sad woman?	44	24	20
4. a woman who is pleasant company?	87	91	4
5. a healthy woman?	50	91	41
6. an optimistic woman?	69	89	2
7. a woman lacking roles?	45	29	16
8. a woman who is satisfied with herself?	68	89	21
9. a woman who is satisfied with others?	69	78	9

N = 112   Gamma = .676   P $<$ .000

Personal Resources

A number of personal resources have significant and strong correlations with the Self-Image Index. Table 2 summarizes the relationship between personal resources and self-image. Widows are significantly different from married women in self-image. Also half of the widows always feel lonely compared to 16 per cent of the married woman who always feel lonely. There is not a strong association between the frequency a woman meets friends and self-image. However, women who have a close neighbour and participate in a number of social activities outside of the home have positive self-images. Human resources appear to support a positive self-image among older women.

Among economic resources, adequate income and occupational prestige have a low correlation at an insignificant level with self-image. On the other hand, work at time of the interview appears to be related to self-image. Among the 16 women who were employed at the time of the interview, 15 women had a medium or high self-image score and they were employed in white collar and professional occupations.

TABLE 2

Summary of correlates of personal resources and the present time self-image of older women. N = 112

Personal resources	Gamma	P
Human resources		
Married/widowed	.395	.043
Frequency meets friend	.275	.075
Close neighbour	.543	.001
Social activity participation	.549	.000
Economic resources		
Source of interview: social welfare, club, community	.491	.000
Adequate income	.286	.200
Work at time of interview	.487	.115
Occupational prestige	.141	.075
Physical resources		
Incapacity to perform ADL	-.442	.010
Mobility	-.536	.000
Self-evaluation of health	-.667	.000
Mental resources		
Years of schooling	-.228	.206
Knowledge of Hebrew	-.425	.007
Young/old age comparison	.309	.000
Loneliness	-.520	.002

Among personal resources, physical resources have the strongest correlations with the Self-Image Index. Women who have many difficulties in performing the ADL activities of daily living and are not mobile tend to have low and very low self-image scores. Self-evaluation of health is the variable with the strongest association with negative self-image.

Among the indicators of mental resources in this study, feeling lonely, feeling old for one's age and not being able to read Hebrew are strongly correlated with negative self-image. Years of schooling does not appear to have a relationship with self-image. Feeling lonely may be the result of physical isolation because of poor health or social isolation because of the loss of a spouse or the inability to communicate with the persons around or understand the language and culture of neighbours and the media. We would expect that women who have a combination of few personal resources in a number of areas would be very vulnerable, persons at high risk, and this situation would be reflected in negative self-images.

The Social Situation of Older Women

The sample was purposively selected to represent older women who have had different social and economic experiences and life-styles: clients of social welfare agencies, women who attend pensioner clubs and women in the community who do not use either of these services. Indeed these three categories of women have very different human, economic, physical and mental resources as well as attitudes which are statistically significant. The source of the interview (social-welfare, pensioner club, community women) has a strong and significant association with the Self-Image Index with gamma of .497 at p $<$.000.

Table 3 compares the stressful aspects of the social situation of older women who are welfare clients, attend pensioner clubs and who use neither service. There are no significant differences among the three groups by age nor does age have a direct impact on self-image.

Almost two-thirds of the welfare clients have low and very low self-images. These women most frequently report they have no living child, no friends, do not participate in activities outside of the home, an inadequate income, incapacity in ADL, confined to the home, poor health, few years or no schooling, do not read Hebrew, feels old for her age and always feels lonely. One discerns a syndrome of poor physical and social functioning. The findings suggest a congruence between social welfare clients' personal experience and society's stereotypes. These women have few resources with which to develop protective strategies in order to avoid negative definitions of the self.

In contrast, most club women (91 per cent) and community women (80 per cent) have positive self-images, club women more frequently than community women. They usually have children, friends, an adequate income, are competent in ADL, mobile, good health and feel young for their age. They tend to have attended high school and college although a third have few years of schooling. About a fourth of the women do not read Hebrew and feel lonely. The women who worked at the time of the interview were community women and they are the most likely to see their children daily and to reside closest to their children of the three groups of women. On the other hand, club women see their friends the most frequently of the three groups.

TABLE 3
Stressful aspects of the social situation of older women by source of interview
(Percentages and significant differences)

Stressful variables	Welfare clients	Club members	Community	P
Above 70 years old	62.2	49.5	51.2	N.S.
Widowed	59.5	45.5	58.5	N.S.
No living children	24.3	3.0	9.8	.000
No friends	32.4	12.5	17.1	.004
No close neighbour	38.9	21.2	22.0	N.S.
Doesn't participate in social activities	37.1	3.0	12.2	.000
Inadequate income	43.2	9.1	17.1	.000
Incapacity in ADL	30.3	3.7	8.6	.040
Confined to home	29.7	3.1	12.2	.015
Poor health	21.6	3.0	0.0	.000
0 - 8 years of school	63.9	36.4	37.8	N.S.
Does not read Hebrew	51.4	21.2	24.4	.010
Feels old for age	42.9	0.0	7.5	.000
Always feels lonely	54.1	22.2	26.8	.008
Low self-image	62.1	9.1	19.5	.000

Social Situations and Self-Images of Older Women

Among the three categories of women, 20 social welfare clients, eight community women and three club women perceive a substantial change in their self-image from the past. The discontinuities in perception of the self may be related to losses in personal resources or changes in social situations which demand changes in perceptions of the self. Immigration, widowhood, retirement and physical incapacity are certainly situations that imply discontinuity, possible loss of control, a readjustment of relationships with others and a re-evaluation of one's values and goals in life.

Hilgard and Atkinson (1967) claim that the "phenomenal self" that is the self of which the person is aware, is perceived as an agent, as continuous, as reflected in relations with other people, and as the embodiment of goals and values. The findings of this study suggest that when women have control of social relations, physical functioning, income and knowledge of Hebrew (e.g. the symbolic environment), their self-images are likely to be positive. However, women who have little control over social relations, are incapacitated, are dependent upon social services and have experienced discontinuities over the life span are likely to have negative self-images.

Summary and Conclusions

Structured interviews with 112 older women residing in nine different communities in Israel show that there are significant differences among the respondents' self-images. An examination of the questions posed show that:
1. Chronological age from 58 to 82 is not correlated with self-image;
2. Women with much incapacity as measured by ADL and mobility, frequently have negative self-image;
3. Widows more frequently than married women have negative self-image;
4. Having a child or frequency of meeting a child is not associated with self-image;
5. Women who are employed tend to have positive self-image;
6. The social situations of women are strongly associated with self-image.

Three tentative explanations of the distribution of self-images are suggested:

labelling, personal resources and social situation.
Two-thirds of the women have positive self-images
and do not seem to be affected by labelling, at
least not directly. The third of the women who have
negative self-images also have few personal
resources, particularly human and physical
resources. A very disadvantaged configuration
appears among social welfare clients. In contrast,
club women and community women report many personal
resources as well as positive self-images. The
findings suggest that personal resources are the
means by which women mediate their social situation,
construct and interpret reality. A woman's
interpretation of the configuration of her social
situation reflects upon her definition of self and
self-image. This exploratory inquiry suggests that
when women have had early life opportunities, stable
life arenas and have late life alternative
resources, the likelihood of maintaining a positive
self-image increases. Longitudinal studies of women
throughout the life cycle are required in order to
learn whether the self-image of women develop and
change in the expected direction.

References

Cibulski, O. (1981) Social Support Networks of the
Elderly, unpublished doctoral dissertation,
University of Tel-Aviv, Tel-Aviv
Cooley, C.H. (1962) Social Organization, Schocken,
New York
Goffman, E. (1959) The Presentation of Self in Every
Day Life, Double Anchor Books, New York
Gordon, D. (1981) Widows and their Rehabilitation by
the National Insurance Institute, Survey No. 30,
National Insurance Institute, Jerusalem (Hebrew)
Hilgard, E.R. and Atkinson, R.C. (1967) Introduction
to Psychology, 4th Edition, Harcourt, Brace &
World Inc., New York
Israel, Central Bureau of Statistics (1981) Old
People in Israel: Statistical Data, Office for
Pensioners and Elderly, and Central Bureau of
Statistics, Jerusalem (Hebrew)
Jacobs, R.H. (1976) 'A Typology of Older American
Women', Social Policy, November-December
Kinch, J.W. (1963) 'A Formalized Theory of the Self-
Concept', American Journal of Sociology, 68: 481-
486

Maas, H.S. and Kuypers, J.A. (1974) From Thirty to Seventy, Jossey-Bass, San Francisco

Matthews, S.H. (1979) The Social World of Old Women: Management of Self-Identity, Sage Publications, London

Mead, G.H. (1934) Mind, Self and Society, University of Chicago Press, Chicago

Payne, B.P. and Whittington, F. (1976), 'Older Women - An Examination of Popular Stereotypes and Research Evidence', Social Problems, 23, 4

Rose, A.M. (1962) Human Behaviour and Social Process, Routledge & Kegan Paul, London

Shanas, E. (1968) Old People in Three Industrial Countries, Atherton Press, New York

Shinar, D. & Biber, A. (1978) Images of Ageing among Specific Groups: The Theatre as a Research Framework, Discussion Paper D-32-78 Joint Israel and Brookdale Institute, Jerusalem (Hebrew)

Sontag, S. 'The Double Standard of Aging', Saturday Review, 55, September

Weihl, H. 'Jewish Aged of Different Cultural Origin in Israel', The Gerontologist, 10, 2

Chapter Twenty-four

A BRIEF SELF-REPORT SCALE FOR ASSESSING PERSONAL
ENGAGEMENT IN THE ELDERLY: RELIABILITY AND VALIDITY

Kevin Morgan, Helen M. Dallosso and Shah B.J.
Ebrahim

Introduction

The constructs of wellbeing and engagement
have, in the past 20 years received considerable
gerontological attention. The quantification of
these phenomena has subserved theory testing, theory
construction, and, more recently, clinical
assessment. Such measurement has been greatly
facilitated by the use of brief assessment scales
completed either by the individual alone, or in the
context of a structured interview. However, efforts
to develop such scales have not been divided
symetrically between the two constructs. Thus,
while there are now several validated scales which
reliably measure semantic relatives of wellbeing in
elderly populations, e.g. Morale (Kutner et al,
1956; Lawton, 1975); Life Satisfaction (Neugarten et
al, 1961); Affect Balance (Bradburn, 1969), there
exists no standardised instrument for assessing the
degree to which an elderly individual is personally
engaged in (or, by inference, disengaged from) the
social milieu. Indeed, it is now common practice in
social gerontology to utilise an existing
questionnaire to assess wellbeing, and to generate
ad hoc a collection of items to assess engagement.
While information concerning the validity and
reliability of the former may be found in the
appropriate literature, these data are frequently
not reported for the latter. As regards engagement,
this omission can only reduce the quality of
reported survey findings and frustrate effective
cross-study comparisons.

In the absence of standardised procedures,
terms used to nominate, and techniques used to
assess engagement have proliferated. Nevertheless,
it is evident from the literature that there is some
overlap in the types of behaviour considered

indicative of personal or social involvement. In particular, frequency of association with others, current membership of groups, personal mobility, and contact with the media appear, singly or in combination, as components of "Activity Participation" (Desroches and Kaiman, 1964), "Formal and Informal Activities" (Lemon et al, 1972), "Leisure Behaviour" (Schmitz-Scherzer, 1976), and "Primary and Secondary Disengagement" (Abrams, 1977). While terminology may differ, then, the behaviours of interest show many common features, and may be subsumed within the definition of personal engagement adopted here, viz: social participation (actual and symbolic) beyond that necessary for personal or physical maintenance. The present study examines the reliability and validity of a brief 13 item questionnaire designed to assess personal engagement by focussing upon these particular aspects of behaviour.

This research derives from a project which aims to evaluate the role of Customary Physical Activity (CPA) in promoting and maintaining psychological wellbeing in the elderly. It is recognized that covariation between CPA and wellbeing may be mediated by several factors. While the relationship between physical and psychological wellbeing in the elderly has received little direct attention, indirect evidence supports the assumption that personal engagement represents one such factor. Jeffers and Nichols (1961), for example, found positive correlations between physican-rated functional capacity on the one hand, and levels of social activity on the other. Positive correlations have also been reported between certain forms of social activity, and life satisfaction scores (Lemon et al 1972). When satisfactorily developed, the personal engagement assessment scale will be included in a structured interview which, together with selected antrhopometric measurements, will be used to assess random samples of the community-based elderly. The resultant information will address specific gerontological issues now, and also serve as a database for future longitudinal studies.

The Assessment Scale

Items included in the scale were required to be brief, suitable for both self-report and professionally administered questionnaires, and free from any obvious sex or class bias. To facilitate the first two of these requirements, the scale utilised a dichotomous (YES/NO) response format, and dealt only with objective circumstances of life (i.e. not attitudinal ratings). Items were equally weighted, a YES response scoring 1, and a NO, zero. The following 13 items were included:

1: Have you access to a telephone in your household?
2: Have you made a personal call in the last week?
3: Have you written a personal letter in the last week?
4: Do you usually read a national or local newspaper?*
5: Do you take a weekly or monthly magazine or journal (including TV journals)?
6: Do you attend religious services, or religious gatherings or meetings?
7: Did you vote in the last general, local, or European elections?
8: Have you been on holiday in the last year?
9: Are you planning to go on holiday in the next year?
10: Do you use the public library?
11: In the past month, have you attended a meeting, or gathering of any club, organisation, society, or group?
12: Do you have a senior citizens rail-card?*
13: Do you have a senior citizens bus pass?*
   * omitted from 10 item scale (see below).

Items 6 (attendance at religious services .....) and 10 (use of public library) were rated NO if attendance was "rare".

The survey sample was drawn from 4 groups differentiated by the level of customary physical activity or functional ability judged to be associated with each. From the most to the least active, these were: i. Swimmers (regular attendants at local authority swimming pools during concessionary periods for pensioners); ii. Workers (active participants in the quasi-industrial workroom of a day centre for the elderly); iii. Independent (elderly individuals living independently in the community, but not typical of Swimmers or Workers); and iv. Outpatients (consecutive patients attending a medical geriatric outpatient department).

Members of the four groups were asked to complete a questionnaire containing the 13 item engagement scale together with Wood et al's (1966) modification of Neugarten et al's (1961) Life Satisfaction Index (the LSIZ). Respondents also provided their date of birth, and their sex. Questionnaires were completed anonymously, and returned by post.

From this single presentation of the engagement items, internal consistency reliability was assessed using Guttman's split-half and Cronbach's reliability (alpha) coefficient. The construct validity of the scale was assessed by inter-group comparisons of scale scores, higher engagement scores being anticipated for the groups judged as being more active.

Results

Completed questionnaires were returned from 33 swimmers, 20 workers, 19 independent individuals and 39 outpatients. This total of 111 respondents included 79 females (mean age 71.7y) and 32 males (mean age 69.9y). There was no significant association between sex and group membership. However, a significant association between age structure and group membership was present (X^2 = 48.44, $p < 0.001$). While 12.1 per cent of Swimmers were aged 75y and over, these proportions were 15 per cent, 21.1 per cent and 61.2 per cent for the Workers, Independent and Outpatients respectively. For the 13 item scale, the split half coefficient was 0.53, and alpha = 0.6. Item to scale correlations were also computed. Item 4 (read national/local newspaper), 12 (Do you have a ... rail-card?) and 13 (Do you have a ..... bus pass?) showed particularly low, i.e. < 0.2, item-scale correlations and were therefore removed. Both reliability coefficients re-calculated for the resulting 10 item scale showed improvement: Guttman Split Half coefficient = 0.61; alpha = 0.67.

Analysis of variance (Kruskal-Wallis) of the scale scores for Swimmers, Workers, Independent and Outpatients indicated significant inter-group difference (X^2 = 26.52; $p < 0.001$). Subsequent paired comparisons using the Mann-Whitney U test showed that the swimmers differed significantly from all other groups ($p < 0.005$). No other significant inter-group differences were present. In all cases, swimmers had higher engagement scores.

Finally, a Spearman rank order correlation coefficient computed between each subject's score on the 10 item engagement scale, and the LSIZ, showed a highly significant positive correlation (rho = 0.59; n = 101; p < 0.001). (As some subjects refused or omitted items, pairs of LSIZ and engagement scale scores were available for only 101 respondents).

Conclusions

The 10 item engagement scale shows a level of internal consistency reliability compatible with its use as a survey tool. Indeed, the alpha coefficient for the 10 item version is superior to that reported by Abrams (1983) for a considerably more homogeneous 10 item "Disengagement" Scale (7 items of which referred to discontinued membership of recreational, political, or trade union organisations).

It is interesting to note the response structure for the items showing least variability (i.e items 6, 12 and 13). Almost all respondents possessed concessionary bus passes (or tokens, etc), and not infrequently read a newspaper. The former item perhaps indicates the increasing efficiency with which these concessions are advertised and distributed, while the latter probably reflects current trends in the unsolicited delivery of free "trade" newspapers.

The ability of the 10 item scale significantly to distinguish between the (presumably highly active) swimmers and the other groups provides some support for the validity of the Engagement construct. The 10 item scale scores were less successful, however, in differentiating the remaining three groups. Nevertheless, examination of the 10 item scale means for each group did show a trend consistent with the original judgements of intra-group activity/engagement levels: Swimmers = 8.5 (SD = 1.2); Workers = 6.7 (SD = 1.7); Independent = 6.8 (SD = 1.8); and Outpatients = 5.6 (SD = 2.6). While it is probably that differences in the age structure of the groups influenced mean engagements scale scores, this influence should not be over emphasised. The magnitude of age structure differences is not reflected in the magnitude of scale score differences.

The high positive correlation between LSIZ scores and the 10 item engagement scale scores is particularly interesting, indicating that levels of psychological wellbeing are closely related to, and predictable from levels of personal engagement. This finding also shows that <u>attitudes</u> to age and the ageing process are predictable from a brief inventory concerning <u>objective</u> circumstances of life.

In the future development of the 10 item scale, further items which meet the criteria provided above will be added. Probable future items include ownership of/access to transport, excursions from home in the previous 24 hours, and pet ownership. In its present form, the scale is considered suitable for cautious use in further surveys.

References

Abrams, M. (1983) <u>People In Their Late sixties: a longitudinal study of ageing</u>, Part 1: Survivors and non-Survivors. Age Concern Research Unit, Mitcham, Surrey

Bradburn, N.M. (1969) <u>The Structure of Psychological Well-being</u>, Aldine, Chicago

Desroches, H.F. and Kaiman, B.D. (1964) 'Stability of Activity Participation in an Aged Population', <u>Journal of Gerontology</u>, 19, 211-214

Jeffers, F.C. and Nichols, C.R. (1961) 'The Relationship of Activities and Attitudes to Physical Well-being in Older People', <u>Journal of Gerontology</u>, 16, 67-70

Kutner, B., Fanshiel, D., Togo, A. and Langer, T. (1956) <u>Five hundred over sixty</u>, Russel Sage Foundation, New York

Lawton, M.P. (1975) 'The Philadelphia Geriatric Rating Scale: A Revision', <u>Journal of Gerontology</u> 30, 85-89

Lemon, B.W., Bengston, V.L. and Peterson, J.A. (1972) 'An Exploration of the Activity Theory of Ageing: activity types and life satisfaction among in-movers to a retirement community', <u>Journal of Gerontology</u>, 27, 511-523

Neugarten, B.L., Havighurst, R.J. and Tobin, S.S. (1961) 'The Measurement of Life Satisfaction', <u>Journal of Gerontology</u>

Schmitz-Schertzer (1976) 'Longitudinal Change in Leisure Behaviour of the Elderly', In <u>Patterns of Ageing: findings from the Bonn Longitudinal Study of Ageing</u>, H. Thomae (Ed), S. Karger, Basel

Wood, V., Wylie, M. and Sheafor, B. (1966) 'An
    Analysis of a Short Self-Report Measure of Life
    Satisfaction: correlation with rater judgement',
    The Gerontologist, 6, (2), 31

DETAILS OF CONTRIBUTORS

M. Bernard, The Beth Johnson Foundation, Stoke-on-Trent.

M. G. Binks, Department of Psychology, University of Liverpool.

D. Brown, School of Urban Planning, McGill University, Canada.

A. Butler, Lecturer in Social Work, Department of Psychiatry, University of Leeds.

D. Challis, Personal Social Services Research Unit, University of Kent.

O. Cibulski, Schools of Social Work, Universities of Tel Aviv and Haifa

C. Clulow, Department of Psychiatry, University of Liverpool.

J. Collins, Department of Psychiatry, University of Liverpool.

J. R. M. Copeland, Department of Psychiatry, University of Liverpool.

S. O. Daatland, Norwegian Institute of Gerontology, Oslo.

H. M. Dallosso, Medical School, University of Nottingham.

A. D. M. Davies, Department of Psychology, University of Liverpool.

B. Davies, Personal Social Services Research Unit, University of Kent.

M. E. Dewey, Department of Psychiatry, University of Liverpool.

R. M. Eley, Social Work Department, Royal Liverpool Hospital.

Shah B. J. Ebrahim, Medical School, University of Nottingham.

G. Fennell, School of Economic and Social Studies, University of East Anglia.

E. Ferlie, Personal Social Services Research Unit, University of Kent.

D. M. Forshaw, Department of Psychiatry, University of Liverpool.

A. Froggatt, Lecturer in Social Work, University of Bradford.

C. J. and E. Gilleard, Clinical Psychology Section, Department of Psychiatry, University of Edinburgh.

K. Gledhill, Psychology Department, St Luke's Hospital, Huddersfield.

A. A. Gurkan, Department of Economics, Middle East Technical University, Ankara.

D. Howes, Department of Geography, King's College, London.

V. Ivers, The Beth Johnson Foundation, Stoke-on-Trent.

O. James, Department of Psychology, University of Liverpool.

D. Jerrome, Lecturer in Continuing Education, University of Sussex.

M. J. MacLean, School of Social Work, McGill University, Canada.

C. McWilliam, Department of Psychiatry, University of Liverpool.

C. Martin, Psychology Department, High Royds Hospital, Menston, Ilkley.

L. M. Middleton, Social Work Department, The Spastics Society, Liverpool.

E. Midwinter, Director, Centre for Policy on Ageing.

K. Morgan, Medical School, University of Nottingham.

A. Osborn, Age Concern Scotland, Edinburgh.

C. Phillipson, Department of Adult Education, University of Keele.

P. Saunders, Department of Psychiatry, University of Liverpool.

R. T. Searle, Department of Psychiatry, University of Liverpool.

V. K. Sharma, Department of Psychiatry, University of Liverpool.

P. Sijpkes, School of Architecture, McGill University, Canada.

P. Strang, Department of Adult Education, University of Keele.

A. Tinker, Senior Research Officer, Department of the Environment.

L. Took, Department of Geography, King's College, London.

C. R. Victor, Department of Sociology, University of Surrey.

A. M. Warnes, Department of Geography, King's College, London.

S. J. Wilkinson, Department of Psychology, Liverpool Institute of Higher Education.

N. Wood, Department of Psychiatry, Manchester Royal Infirmary.

All the contributors from Liverpool are members of the Institute of Human Ageing, University of Liverpool

SUBJECT INDEX

Subject Index

Dementia: management in the community: 139; 279-280

Depression: 200; 250-262; 278

Dysnomia: 228

Education: 94-96

Engagement: 298-303

Everyday Memory Questionnaire: 229-240

Family Care: 178-180

Feminism, and old age: 45-48

Fraternity, and the elderly: 23-32; 180-186

Geriatric Mental State Examination (G.M.S.): 228-240; 243-249; 251-253

Government funding: 125-136; 137-156

Greater London Council (G.L.C.): 160-176

Growing Older, Government White Paper (1981): quoted, 125

Health education: 95-97; 192-203

Helplessness: 278

Hospitals, care in: 204-214

Housework: 69-76

Housing, poor quality of: 3, 160, 204

Income, in the Elderly: 160-176

Insomnia: 263-277

Institutionalisation: 68-69; 222-223

Israel: elderly women in, 286-297

Joint finance (funding): 137-156

Kendrick Battery: 229-240

Leisure: 81-90; 93-97; 113-122; 299-300

Lickert Scales: 163

Life Events (stress): 250-262

Life-Satisfaction indexes: 298-303

Manpower Services Commission (M.S.C.): 126-128; 130-136

Mental Health Foundation: 250, 260

Mentally infirm, Elderly: 154

Mental Status Questionnaire: 244-249

309

For Product Safety Concerns and Information please contact our EU
representative GPSR@taylorandfrancis.com
Taylor & Francis Verlag GmbH, Kaufingerstraße 24, 80331 München, Germany

www.ingramcontent.com/pod-product-compliance
Lightning Source LLC
Chambersburg PA
CBHW070716280326
41926CB00087B/2343

9 781032 710112